IRONIES of
IMPRISONMENT

To my sisters and brothers:
Margaret, Patrice, Kevin, Joe, and Greg

IRONIES of IMPRISONMENT

MICHAEL WELCH
Rutgers University

SAGE Publications
Thousand Oaks ▪ London ▪ New Delhi

For information:

Sage Publications, Inc.
2455 Teller Road
Thousand Oaks, California 91320
E-mail: order@sagepub.com

Sage Publications Ltd.
1 Oliver's Yard
55 City Road
London EC1Y 1SP
United Kingdom

Sage Publications India Pvt. Ltd.
B-42, Panchsheel Enclave
Post Box 4109
New Delhi 110 017 India

Printed in the United States of America

Library of Congress Cataloging-in-Publication Data

Welch, Michael
Ironies of imprisonment / Michael Welch.
    p. cm.
Includes bibliographical references and index.
ISBN 1-4129-0480-3 (cloth)
ISBN 0-7619-3059-0 (pbk.)
    1. Imprisonment—United States. 2. Prisons—United States. 3. Corrections—United States. 4. Criminal justice, Administration of—United States. I. Title.
HV9471.W4594 2005
364.6′0973—dc22   2004007913

This book is printed on acid-free paper.

04   05   06   07   10   9   8   7   6   5   4   3   2   1

Acquisitions Editor:	Jerry Westby
Editorial Assistant:	Vonessa Vondera
Production Editor:	Denise Santoyo
Copy Editor:	Teresa Herlinger
Typesetter:	C&M Digitals (P) Ltd.
Cover Designer:	Michelle Lee Kenny

Contents

Foreword

When it comes to the problem of imprisonment in the United States, there are indeed a host of ironies worth our contemplation. For instance:

- A nation whose self-image boasts a proud claim as the founder and defender of human freedom operates a penal system that denies freedom to a greater proportion of its citizens than any other democratic nation.
- Our incarceration rate seems to have little to do with our crime rate: Prison populations continue to grow, despite close to a decade of falling crime; indeed, since 1975, we have had almost the same number of years of declining crime rates as years of increasing crime rates—but prison populations have gone up every year regardless.
- Everyone would agree that among our most pressing social problems are disparities among the races in wealth, access to opportunity, and quality of life; yet the prison system, which locks up 8% of African American males, and will be home to almost one third of all black males sometime during their lifetimes, must surely be seen as making a major contribution to those very disparities.

When it comes to penal policy, we have a problem in language. Our penal policy seems made up of soundbites and social metaphors. We find ourselves drawn to confident-sounding phrases, such as "a thug in jail can't shoot your sister," or "don't do the crime if you can't do the time." And we seem ever to be building laws that resonate with other spheres of social activity, for instance sports ("three strikes you're out") and war (as in, "war on drugs"). This problem in the capacity of our language interferes with our ability to develop sound crime policy, since once we become enamored of the metaphor, we lose track of the meaning.

Sensible talk about crime policy requires more reflection than a soundbite and more depth than a metaphor. If we are to ever become wise in crime policy we must be willing to think about it, and to think critically about our most cherished assumptions. Let me provide an example of what I mean.

A great deal has been made recently of "truth in sentencing." The idea behind this simple phrase is that when a sentence is announced by the judge in court, the offender ought to serve it—or at least in today's version of the "truth" serve at least 85% of it—and that such "truth" will be an improvement in justice. The idea is undeniably appealing; who can argue against "the truth?" But if we look behind the soundbite, we find much that might trouble us. The most obvious question would be: Who can say that any sentence imposed by a judge is the correct sentence? Take the situation, for example, of two offenders standing before two judges, each convicted of the sale of an illegal drug. One gets a sentence of 10 years, the other a sentence of 2 years. Under "truth in sentencing," the first will serve 120 months, the second more than 20 months. Which sentence is "true," in any meaningful sense of the word "true?" If we require that justice be true, how can such disparate sentences be just? How, then, can they both be "true?"

In fact, when we think about such a sentence, what "truth" is it trying to communicate? The amount of time a person will eventually serve is such a limited and insignificant portion of the "truth" at the time of the sentence, it is as though we all want to participate in a fiction and call it the "truth" when it is only a part of the story. A judge, required to tell the *whole* truth at the time of a sentence, might need to say something like this:

> For the crime of drug selling, I sentence you to 10 years in prison. I am doing so even though we know that this sentence will not prevent any more drugs from being sold, and that it will probably even result in someone not now involved in the drug trade being recruited to take your place while you are locked up. I impose this sentence knowing that the main reason you have been caught and convicted is that we have concentrated our police presence in the community where you live, and that had you lived where I live, your drug use and sales would most probably have gone undetected. I impose this sentence knowing that it will cost taxpayers over a quarter of a million dollars to carry it out, money we desperately need for the schools and health care in the area where you live, but instead it will go into the pockets of corrections officers and prison builders who live miles away from here and have no interest in the quality of life in your neighborhood. I impose this sentence knowing that it will most likely make you a worse citizen, not a better one, leaving you embittered toward the law and damaged by your years spent behind bars. You think you have trouble making it now? Wait until after you have served a decade of your life wasting in a prison cell. And I impose this sentence knowing that it will make your children, your cousins, and your nephews have even less respect for the law, since they will come to see you as having been singled out for this special punishment, largely due to the color of your skin and the amount of money in your pocket. I impose this sentence knowing that its only purpose is

to respond to an angry public and a few rhetorically excited politicians, even though I know that this sentence will not calm either of them down in the slightest. This is the truth of my sentence.

Now, wouldn't *that* be a "truth in sentencing!"

Of course, we never hear such a sentence imposed. In that sense, regardless of the "truth in sentencing" movement that has recently swept the nation, every sentence coming under this policy contains deep and profound untruths—the lies of silence, omission, and misrepresentation. The fact that a judge who imposes a sentence is not required to say any of the above is a social manipulation, the fact that it gets called "truth" is an insult to our intelligence.

The book you hold in your hands is about these much more subtle, more profound truths in our penal policy. These truths are described as "ironies." The dictionary defines an "irony" as "the use of language with one meaning for a privileged audience and another for those addressed or concerned." Today's penal apparatus is a litany of ironies, speaking the harsh tones of crime control and public safety to those who never come close to its manifestations, and shrieking the even harsher messages of repression and arbitrary power to those grasped in its tentacles. It is simply not possible to develop an informed view of modern penal activity without cultivating an ear attuned to both messages.

Michael Welch's book is an invitation to think. It is an invitation to grow intellectually and critically, as a consumer of crime policy and an observer of the American scene. Written by a scholar who has dedicated his work to uncovering the hidden ironies of formal crime policy, this is a collection of essays of depth and significance. Those who read it will be challenged, and those who engage with the challenges contained within these pages will have their views of the realities of penal policy changed, deepened, and made more honest, more complete. More true.

—TODD R. CLEAR
Distinguished Professor,
John Jay College of Criminal Justice

Preface

As the title suggests, this book explores the ironies of imprisonment while contributing to a critical penology that strives to understand problems facing punishment. It draws heavily on leftist sociology and critical criminology by placing special emphasis on social control. The work consists of substantive changes and revision of my earlier book, *Punishment in America: Social Control and the Ironies of Imprisonment*, a volume that combined some of my previously published articles with several original chapters on punishment, corrections, and social control. In this incarnation, the entire book stands as an original body of work while retaining the previous volume's major themes and topics. The much-improved continuity adds tremendously to the overall narrative, and each chapter offers an up-to-date presentation of the subject matter, reviewing chief developments in research and theory.

Taken together, the 10 chapters in this book cover a good deal of territory. While attending to key historical, conceptual, and theoretical cornerstones of the critical tradition, the book examines some of society's most pressing problems, including drug dependency, inadequate health care, violence, capital punishment, the war on terror, and prison profiteering. Issues pertaining to race, ethnicity, and class are discussed throughout. Above all, the purpose of the book is to trace the ironies of imprisonment to their root causes manifesting in social, political, economic, and racial inequality.

While maintaining a scholarly presentation, each chapter contains review items for those who wish to adopt the book for classroom use. Indeed, the controversial nature of the ironies of imprisonment promises to stimulate spirited discussion and debate over the use of prisons.

In reading these pages, my intellectual debts become quite evident, and there are many research assistants and colleagues whom I would like to acknowledge. Several Rutgers University students in the Criminal Justice Program in New Brunswick were instrumental in retrieving literature and assembling data; they are Meredith Roberts, Patricia Cavuoto, Richard Linderman, Eric Price, Karen Kabara, Joseph Fredua-Agyman (a.k.a. Haas), Daanish Faruqi, Bindi Merchant, Frank Carle, and Todd Margiotta. I would also like to thank my colleagues at Rutgers University for their support of my work: Dean Arnold Hyndman, Freda Adler, Gerhard O. W. Mueller, Lennox Hinds, and Albert Roberts, as well as the staff at the University's libraries.

In addition, I am grateful to the following reviewers for their candid and constructive criticism:

Laura E. Bedard, Florida State University

Mary Bosworth, Wesleyan University

Michael Lynch, University of South Florida

Barbara Owen, California State University, Fresno

Lisa Rapp-Paglicci, University of Nevada, Las Vegas

Stephen C. Richards, Northern Kentucky University

James Robertson, Minnesota State University

Larry E. Sullivan, John Jay College of Criminal Justice

Rich Wallace, University of Wisconsin—River Falls

Terri A. Winnick, Ohio State University

At Sage Publications, I wish to acknowledge the strong support of my editor, Jerry Westby, and his editorial assistant, Vonessa Vondera, along with Terry Hendrix, Kassie Gavrilis, Catherine Rossbach, Denise Santoyo, Julie Ellis, Elisabeth Magnus, and Teresa Herlinger in the Thousand Oaks office, and Carolyn Porter in the London office.

Finally, I wish to express enormous gratitude to Todd R. Clear, Distinguished Professor at John Jay College of Criminal Justice, City University of New York (and former guitarist in the famously obscure surf rock band, The Retroliners) for writing the foreword to this book. Likewise, I appreciate the wit and wisdom of fellow musical bohemians Mike "Coffee Can" Beckerman and Dave "Bogart" Schreck.

—MICHAEL WELCH
Hoboken, New Jersey

1

Introduction

New York State has the most stringent and unyielding drug laws in the country—just ask Terrence Stevens. Stevens, an African American with no previous drug convictions, was busted for possessing five ounces of cocaine. Some say that he was lucky to draw the minimum allowed under the so-called Rockefeller statute. Still, that meant 15 years to life; that sentence is the same punishment for murder and kidnapping and longer than the minimum terms for armed robbery, manslaughter, and rape. Due in large part to his medical condition, there are many who question the wisdom of incarcerating Stevens, including the judge who sentenced him and the prosecutor who tried him. Stevens developed muscular dystrophy while growing up in a housing project in East Harlem. At the time of his arrest, he was confined to a wheelchair. In prison, Stevens relies on inmates to bathe, dress, and lift him onto and off the toilet. During a routine strip search, he told corrections officers that he was physically unable to remove his pants; for not complying with the order, he was disciplined by being locked in a cell for 23 hours a day for 40 days. He appealed the disciplinary charge and it was reversed, but only after Stevens had served the punishment. The man who was arrested along with Stevens was not sentenced to prison. He received probation for testifying against Stevens (Purdy, 2000).

Furthering his re-election campaign, New York Governor George E. Pataki delivered a toughly worded speech on crime, defending punitive policies he believes are necessary to ensure public safety. In many ways, his rhetoric mirrored that of other law-and-order crusaders. Pataki aimed directly at criminologists who take a deeper look at crime, and he ridiculed the idea that unlawful behavior stems from adverse societal conditions. The governor proclaimed that the "root causes of crime are the criminals who engage in it." He also stated that, "In no uncertain terms—we, as servants of the people, are not charged with carrying out a sociological study. We are charged with maintaining public order and saving lives" (Nagourney, 1998). For those who do not share that conservative view of crime, Pataki's address reeks of anti-intellectualism. Regrettably, political and public forums on crime are so rife with that way of thinking about crime that it has become difficult for criminologists to persuade policy makers and citizens to look beyond simplistic notions of crime.

Undeniably, the consequences of anti-intellectualism surrounding penal policy are real. Mass incarceration has transformed the United States into the world's leader in imprisonment, producing an expensive prison system that fails to contribute to public safety, since much of the current influx of inmates is nonviolent drug violators (Austin, Bruce, Carroll, McCall, P. L., & Richards, S. C., 2003; Garland, 2002; Irwin, Schiraldi, & Ziedenberg, 2000). Race, ethnicity, and class figure prominently in the emergence of a nation of prisons. Correctional institutions continue to lock up more and more people of color along with the poor, who have few resources to defend themselves against an over-funded, overzealous criminal justice machine that does not hesitate to fill prison cells (Wacquant, 2000, 2001, 2002).

Moving toward a critical penology, this work attends to the ironies of imprisonment that have become defining features of the American prison apparatus. In doing so, careful consideration is given to key developments, problems, and issues that fuel the system's contradictions, biases, and inconsistencies. Chapter 2 begins with a socio-historical look at the emergence of the penitentiary, a troubled institution whose problems persist today. In his analysis of early American institutionalization, David J. Rothman (1971, 1990) concludes that prisons—along with almshouses and insane asylums—represent state responses to growing concerns that crime and other social problems threatened the stability of the new republic. Rothman documents significant shifts in the conceptualization of crime and punishment that together created the belief that imprisonment was a legitimate, progressive, and humane form of crime control. Still, American penal history teaches us that the establishment of corrections has had less to do with crime control and more to do with social control (Blomberg & Cohen, 2003; Blomberg & Lucken, 2000). The chapter tracks the emergence of the term "social control" in critical criminology and the role that incarceration plays in perpetuating social, racial, and economic inequality.

The idea that prisons reproduce racism and classism is brought into sharper focus in the third chapter. There, the thrust of a critical penology exposes the linkages between the political economy and criminal justice system, creating a coercive prison apparatus serving the status quo. Situating social inequality at the center of analysis, a critical penology points to evidence of racial and socio-economic disparities in sentencing— along with a host of other injustices—that have become defining features of American penal policy.

Given its enormous impact on the soaring correctional population, Chapter 4 takes an in-depth look at the war on drugs. In this chapter, the American war on drugs is subject to the test of *just war theory*, a uniquely innovative framework. Both figuratively and literally, drug control policy in the United States has become increasingly criminalized and militarized. Left in the wake of those transformations is an array of self-defeating strategies. Most notably is the reliance on high-priced incarceration rather than cost-effective rehabilitation for a population that needs treatment more than punishment.

Similarly, in the fifth chapter, problems facing correctional health care are examined in light of the huge proportion of prisoners suffering from drug addiction, compounded by various diseases including HIV/AIDS and tuberculosis. Indeed, the war on drugs and its mandatory minimum sentences—even for first-time, nonviolent drug violators—has generated expensive tactics that do little to reduce drug dependency. Moreover, those ill-advised policies are contributing to a vast prison population growing old behind bars.

Institutional violence is the subject of Chapter 6, in which the sociological model proposed by Gary T. Marx (1981) is applied to corrections. That paradigm offers a systematic tool in discerning the ironies of social control, most notably the tendency for authorities to contribute to rule breaking. The brutal truth is that violence behind bars is reproduced by interdependent behaviors between keepers and the kept. Those dynamics manifest in escalation, nonenforcement, and covert facilitation, all of which feed the cycle of violence in prisons. Likewise, Marx's theory of irony serves as the conceptual architecture for Chapter 7 on capital punishment. Relying on an expanding body of research, it is revealed that the death penalty paradoxically serves to promote lethal violence rather than deter it. Moreover, capital punishment widens a deadly net of social control laced with racial and socioeconomic biases; as a result, juveniles and the mentally handicapped as well as innocent people become trapped in the machinery of death.

The war on terror promises to remain at the forefront of criminal justice policies for the foreseeable future. While the events of September 11th, 2001, have given rise to new anxieties over national security, civil liberties and human rights groups are worried that recent counterterrorism legislation is endangering democracy. Furthermore, there is mounting evidence that government agents, in their quest to identify and prosecute those involved in terror-related crimes, have overreached their authority. Critics of the way the war on terror is being conducted point to well-substantiated reports that detainees swept up in post-September 11th campaigns were subjected to physical and psychological abuse at the hands of their keepers. Chapter 8 examines the controversy over ethnic profiling, along with detention practices shrouded in government secrecy.

Given the symmetry between economics and punishment, a critical penology does well to explore the inner workings of the corrections-industrial complex. By taking a hard look at punitive profit, the ironies of imprisonment become all the more apparent. Chapter 9 dispels the myth that a greater use of imprisonment deters street crime, turning to evidence that the prison population is being driven up by economic and market forces. The corrections enterprise is a phenomenon created dialectically by several interlocking machinations of the political economy. Under the conditions of postindustrial capitalism, there are fewer legitimate financial opportunities for members of the lower classes; therefore, some of them stray into illegitimate enterprises (e.g., drug trafficking) where they risk being apprehended, prosecuted, and sentenced to prison.

Once incarcerated, prisoners' value in the commercial market increases as they are commodified into raw materials for the corrections industry. Privatization also contributes to the acceleration of prison construction because it operates on free-market principles that generate a high-volume, high-dividend system of punishment. Whereas the economic-punishment nexus is good news for financial players in the corrections enterprise, it is bad news for those ensnared in its net of coercive social control. The chapter finds that punishment for profit imperils communities, society, and American democracy.

The concluding chapter features a final glimpse at "prisonomics" and its influence on government spending on corrections. Critical thought also is given to the role of culture in shaping a society that embraces mass incarceration despite its blatant biases against the poor and people of color (Garland, 2001). The discussion hinges on key social constructions that produce both overreactions to crime in the form of moral panic, and underreactions to unfair and unjust punishments (Cohen, 2001). In its unwillingness to overtly condemn racist and classist penal policies, mainstream American society has attached itself to a culture of denial and disbelief.

This work views punishment through the critical perspectives of intellectualism and radicalism, thereby illuminating dominant aspects of social control and the ironies they produce. It is argued that the state's increased reliance on penal sanctions marks an even greater commitment to coercive social control. Higher rates of incarceration, complemented by a growing roster of penalties (e.g., "three strikes" legislation, mandatory minimum sentences, the abolition of parole and prison amenities), indicate a degree of retribution rarely found in comparable democracies. There is disturbing evidence that political leaders, rather than simply treating lawbreakers firmly but fairly, are becoming increasingly intolerant and vindictive. In a sense, the state appears to have crossed the line from "getting tough" to "getting rough" by encouraging institutions and authorities to bully individuals lacking the power to defend themselves adequately against an ambitious and overzealous criminal justice system (see Bottoms, 1995). Those most vulnerable to the prevailing spirit of meanness are the impoverished and racial and ethnic minorities.

Regrettably, the state seems to have transformed the criminal justice system from a shield designed to protect all citizens to a sword used to intimidate and control the less powerful. Those unfortunate trends in American punishment suggest chilling prospects for social and economic justice. To quote a high-ranking corrections official who wishes to remain anonymous for fear of reprisals from conservatives who dominate his agency, "zero tolerance means zero thinking." Indeed, the culture of control undermines critical analysis by resorting to various forms of criminal justice propaganda, including signs, slogans, and sound bites that are publicized in order to justify increases in penalties, police, and prisons.

End-of-Chapter Questions

1. What is meant by an anti-intellectual approach to crime?

2. What are the key features of mass incarceration in the United States?

3. What is meant by "getting rough" in the realm of criminal justice?

4. What are some of the components of criminal justice propaganda?

2

Discovery of the Penitentiary

At Auburn, we have a more beautiful example still, of what may be done by proper discipline, in a prison well constructed. The whole establishment from the gate to the sewer, is a specimen of neatness. The unremitted industry, the entire subordination and subdued feeling of the convicts, has probably no parallel among an equal number of criminals. In their solitary cells they spend the night, with no other book than the Bible, and at sunrise they proceed in military order, under the eye of the turnkeys, in solid columns, with the lock march, to their workshops; then, in the same order, at the hour of breakfast, to the common hall, where they partake of their wholesome and frugal meal in silence. At the close of the day, a little before sunset, the work is all laid aside at once, and the convicts return in military order to the solitary cells; where they partake of the frugal meal, which they are permitted to take from the kitchen, where it is furnished for them, as they returned from the shops. After supper they can, if they choose, read the scriptures undisturbed, and then reflect in silence on the errors of their lives.

—The Reverend Louis Dwight,
secretary of the Boston Prison
Discipline Society (1826, pp. 36–37)

Offering a sophisticated look into a complicated past, socio-historical works contribute tremendously to the study of prisons. In *The Discovery of the Asylum: Social Order and Disorder in the New Republic,* David J. Rothman (1971) expands our understanding of key normalizing institutions, namely, penitentiaries, asylums, and workhouses. Whereas Rothman's book is not usually catalogued as a work of critical penology, advocates of the perspective find his analysis useful in sharpening our awareness of the emergence of institutionalization (Welch, 1996a). Embarking on a critical exploration of punishment, attention is turned to Rothman's work in an effort to demonstrate how conceptualizations of incarceration have changed over time. As we shall see, *The Discovery of the Asylum* segues nicely to truly critical insights into the emergence of imprisonment as a measure of social control.

Rothman's chief task in *The Discovery of the Asylum* is to examine the underlying rationale for the construction of prisons, insane asylums, and reformatories during the presidency of Andrew Jackson. Emphasizing the role of the Jacksonian vision in reconceptualizing the social order, Rothman reveals not only the immediate impact of the rise of institutionalization but also its lasting legacy, the uncritical acceptance of wide-scale incarceration. Due to its continued influence on the literature, *The Discovery of the Asylum* was reprinted in 1990. In the revised edition, Rothman issues a new introduction but leaves the book in its original form, saying, "Since the book has earned a life of its own, I have refrained from making any changes in the text" (1990, p. xii). Indeed, many penologists agree that *The Discovery of the Asylum* has earned a life of its own, having been standard scholarly reading for more than 25 years. This is not to suggest that Rothman offers the last word on the history of institutionalization, as shall be discussed later; his contribution is only one of several historical interpretations.

The Discovery of the Asylum has helped shape contemporary reflections on the history of corrections. Rothman notes that before 1970, there were only a handful of studies in the area; by the 1990s, hundreds of articles and books devoted to the social history of institutionalization had been published. Perhaps more than at any other point in time, contemporary scholars are pursuing their fascination with institutions and those confined to them. Equally important, intellectuals are attending to the significance of the larger social forces on institutionalization, including historical, political, economic, cultural, religious, and technological forces (see Welch, 2004a). The merits of Rothman's analysis of insane asylums and almshouses notwithstanding, the scope of this chapter is limited primarily to the penological segment of *The Discovery of the Asylum* and its capacity to shed light on the emergence of social control.

Punishment in Colonial America

Rothman offers repeated lessons as to the importance of viewing corrections socio-historically. *The Discovery of the Asylum* simultaneously traces the rise of a new republic and the rapid development of its penal practices; that sequence of events is most pronounced in late colonial America, continuing through the Jacksonian era. During the colonial period, notions of crime and punishment differed fundamentally from those of the Jacksonian period. Comparing those two time frames shows how the penitentiary emerged from changes in ideas about crime along with broader perceptions of social disorder. Those developments interacted with other advances in society, particularly in the realm of politics and economics. In colonial America, crime was not viewed as a critical social problem. "They [the colonists] devoted very little energy to devising and enacting programs to reform offenders and had no expectations of eradicating crime. Nor did they systematically attempt to isolate the deviant or the dependent" (Rothman, 1971, p. 3).

The colonial perspective on crime contrasted sharply with that of the Jacksonians, who like their contemporary counterparts, exerted enormous time and effort toward reducing crime. Unlike modern theories of crime, colonists refused to link lawbreaking to its social structure. Certainly colonists punished criminal offenders, but they did so without concern of reducing crime. Rather, they accepted lawbreaking as an inevitable and unfortunate part of society. Colonists' "Christian sense of crime as sin, their belief that men were born to corruption, lowered their expectations and made deviant behavior a predictable and inevitable component of society" (Rothman, 1971 p. 17). Colonial Americans embraced a simplistic understanding of lawlessness and regarded errors by parents as the primary cause of crime (e.g., the failure to give one's children adequate social and religious training). Still, their religious commitment did not lead to a humane treatment of offenders; on the contrary, they frequently resorted to brutal forms of corporal and capital punishments (Wines, 1895).

Institutionalization During the Jacksonian Era

In the 1820s and 1830s, the direction of American punishment took a new and sudden turn with the presidency of Andrew Jackson. During the Jacksonian era, notions of crime, poverty, and insanity were drastically reconceptualized as critical social problems. In response to a sense of growing social disorder, penitentiaries, insane asylums, and almshouses were constructed as institutions uniquely designed for criminals, the mentally ill, and the impoverished. Within the larger social context, institutionalization emerged at a time when the United States struggled with its newborn nationhood, a period imbued with anxieties over social disorder and economic instability. Rapid societal changes along with a booming population produced dense urban centers and geographic mobility, inviting new ideas about crime, poverty, and mental illness. Traditional forms of social control were believed to be inadequate in a complex society facing imminent social disorder, prompting state officials to plan revised measures of discipline. Whereas colonial leaders relied on institutions usually as a last resort, Jacksonians ambitiously constructed a correctional apparatus from which prisons became places of first resort. Clearly, that innovative—albeit regressive—direction in punishment has had a lasting effect on contemporary corrections (see Hirsch, 1992; Staples, 1990).

Political forces figured prominently in the transformation of penal sanctions in the early years of nationhood. A greater sense of civic pride evident in the new republic led to a sense of responsibility for dealing with crime and other social problems. Boasting more enlightened views of crime control, early Americans' realization that harsh penalties served merely to perpetuate rather than eradicate crime reduced their reliance on banishment and corporal punishment. Social reformers, reinvigorating the principles of William Penn, rejected repressive British laws while adopting humane criminal codes suitable for their vision of a new nation. But despite significant legal reform, political leaders were aware that unlawful behavior was not manageable solely by instituting rational and humane criminal codes. Moreover, in the 1820s, there was growing concern that crime could endanger the newly inspired social order, prompting officials to look deeper into the sources of lawbreaking. Citizens found cause for both deep despair and incredible optimism. The safety and security of their social order seemed to them in far greater danger than their fathers' had been, yet they hoped to eradicate crime from the new world. The old structure was crumbling, but perhaps they could draw the blueprints for building a far better one (Rothman, 1971, p. 62).

Jacksonians began to sense that crime was symptomatic of a failing social order; consequently, two aspects of social life were scrutinized closely, the family and the community. Because the corrupting forces were believed then to exist within society, policies to deal with the criminality faced crucial reconceptualization. A movement aimed at controlling the corrupting influences in the community earned some popular support, such as closing taverns and houses of prostitution. Still, those measures by themselves proved insufficient to control lawlessness.

Another alternative then became not only feasible but essential: to construct a special setting for the deviant. Remove him from the family and community and place him in an artificially created and therefore corruption-free environment. Here he could learn all the vital lessons for law-abiding behavior, while protected from the temptations of vice. A model and small-scale society could solve the immediate problem and point the way to broader reform. (Rothman, 1971, p. 71).

Significant developments in criminological theory also occurred during the Jacksonian period, most notably, an emerging environmental theory linking crime to adverse societal conditions. Rather than protecting society from the offender, the original rationale for imprisonment was to isolate the lawbreaker from the corrupting temptations inherent in the environment.

The Pennsylvania and Auburn Systems of Prison Discipline

Simultaneously, Jacksonians formulated theories of crime and corresponding interventions, producing two notable correctional innovations. The Pennsylvania and Auburn models of prison discipline became cornerstones of a disciplinary system committed to enforced silence. The practice stemmed from an emerging environmental criminology proposing that compulsory silence prevented criminal contamination. Moreover, such silence was consistent with religious notions of spiritual reform and moral correction. While remaining connected to past penologies, the Pennsylvania and Auburn systems relied heavily on religious protocol. The experience of imprisonment was intended to incorporate the purifying practices of penitence and monastic isolation. In fact, penitentiary derives from the Latin *paenitentia*, meaning penitence, and also shares the same roots with the words for punishment, pain, and revenge (see Norris, 1985). The invention of the penitentiary during the Jacksonian era, with its emphasis on architecture, internal arrangement, and daily routine, reflected the American vision of what a well-ordered society should be (Barnes, 1968 [1972]; Barnes & Teeters, 1946).

Another prominent feature of the new penitentiary was its work programs. At Auburn, a congregate work regimen required that prisoners work side by side while observing silence. Auburn's reputation for productivity inspired other institutions to follow suit. Soon America's innovative penitentiary became the fascination of government leaders and intellectuals around the world. American and European visitors, most notably Alexis de Tocqueville and Gustave Auguste de Beaumont, traveled to Auburn to witness the remarkable correctional experiment (de Beaumont & Tocqueville, 1833). Departing from American colonists whose brand of imprisonment was essentially small scale and makeshift, Jacksonians issued a grand vision for eradicating crime and other social problems. The penitentiary became known worldwide as an ingenious American enterprise (see Dwight, 1826; Hall, 1829). Although advocates of the Pennsylvania and Auburn systems often debated which of the disciplinary systems was superior, the lasting Jacksonian contribution to corrections was evident in its uncritical acceptance. Throughout that era, few questioned imprisonment as a primary strategy for crime control (Rothman, 1971; see Klein, 1920; Powers, 1826).

Rothman and Social Control

In the introduction to the second edition of *The Discovery of the Asylum* (1990), Rothman reflects on his work, situating it within the growing literature on the social history of institutions. While contributing substantially to the discourse on penology, Rothman expresses reservations over some of the broader interpretations of his work. In particular, he disagrees with scholars who classify *The Discovery of the Asylum* into the emerging rubric of the social control school of history. Rothman devotes several passages to that concern in an attempt to separate his work from the social control thesis. Rothman contends that the social control school of history is poorly defined and too often clumsy. More to the point, "the social control label is an ill-suited one, obfuscating more than it clarifies and oversimplifying a complex historical analysis" (1990, p. xxxvi). Rothman recognizes that the concept of social control has multiple and shifting connotations. In the 1920s and 1930s, American sociologists used the term to denote instillation of the subjective values of society. Sociologists George Herbert Mead and E. A. Ross described social control as the process of transmitting shared values through primary and secondary socialization. In Meadian sociology, agents of social control were not the police or other agencies of the state apparatus, but rather families, schools, and community churches. Simply put, social control was indistinguishable from socialization. At that juncture of American sociology, symbolic interactionists were still operating within a functionalist framework enabling the concept of social control to be influenced by conservative and benevolent views of the social order (see Welch, 2003e).

After the Second World War, however, the notion of social control shifted to the political left, thus reversing its meaning. Conflict theorists and neo-Marxist scholars, along with Frances Fox Piven and Richard Cloward (1971), referred to social control as a structural mechanism that reproduced a class-based society. It was postulated that economic elites co-opted the state for the purpose of imposing measures of social control designed to regulate labor and suppress opposition to the prevailing power structure. In the end, the criminal justice system and the welfare state would become key institutions in maintaining control over workers and the poor. According to Rothman (1990), "It was with this negative connotation, not with its Progressive roots, that social control came to the attention of historians" (p. xxxvii). Eventually, social control—though still not sharply defined—was used by some historians to formulate unorthodox questions about prisons and the meaning of reform. As a concept, social control invited stimulating inquiries into the history of institutionalization: "It encouraged a group of historians to stop taking claims of benevolence at face value and start investigating the purposes, benign or not so benign, that a purported reform might fulfill" (Rothman, 1990, p. xxxvii). Rothman acknowledges that the social control perspective serves as a useful corrective to the prevailing notions of reform, but concludes that revisionist historians have failed to establish a persuasive interpretation of social control in the sphere of institutionalization. To him, it is not clear whether social control is introduced as a statement of fact ("This organization is charged to maintain social order.") or as a proposition ("This is an organization that attempts to buttress the social order by coercing or deceiving the lower classes.") (1990, p. xxxvii).

Summarizing his criticisms of the social control thesis, Rothman insists that the concept in its present usage neither advances knowledge nor clarifies subtle nuances. Still, Rothman's objections to the term social control may have had less to do with its alleged lack of precision and more to do with how it has been applied to his work. Certainly, it is unfair to directly impose the social control thesis on *The Discovery of the Asylum* because social control, however defined, falls outside the immediate scope of Rothman's investigation; he avoids examining features of the political economy that make social control comprehensible. Critics insist that Rothman neglects crucial developments such as unemployment and the emergence of monolithic industrial and financial regimes in early America (Adamson, 1984; Durham, 1989). Those aspects of capitalism contribute tremendously to a reproduction of the underclass, which is then subjected to a form of social control administered by the criminal justice apparatus. In examining the ironies of imprisonment in this work, the use of the term social control derives from leftist sociology and critical criminology aimed at detecting and confronting failed penal policies and practices (see also Blomberg & Lucken, 2000; Blomberg & Cohen, 2003; Matthews, 1999).

Critical Interpretations of the History of Prisons

Due to sustained interest in penological history, many scholars have joined a growing dialogue on the emergence of corrections. Alexis Durham (1989) sorts the various strains of penology into four major explanatory perspectives so as to classify divergent schools of thought. Whereas considerable overlap exists among the interpretations of Rothman (1971), Foucault (1979), Ignatieff (1978), and the economic determinist position, each of those historical analyses reaches a distinctly unique conclusion about the emergence of corrections. Together, however, they remind us that historical penology not only enriches the study of corrections but also advances critical criminology and the study of social control (see Garland, 2001; Ross, 1998; Welch, 1998a).

Michel Foucault's (1979) theory of the birth of the prison in the context of the French monarchy focuses on the sovereign power of the state and its struggle with its citizenry. At that point in history, the king exercised corporal punishment to reinforce his power over citizens, thus maintaining social order. Ironically, as public spectacles of punishment grew increasingly brutal, the masses began to question the legitimacy of the king's rule. Lawbreakers eventually gained sympathy from fellow citizens who also began to view themselves as victims of tyranny and repression. To offset a sense of imminent rebellion, the prison emerged as a way to remove punishment from public view. Moving penal sanctions from the public eye resulted in mystifying incarceration; citizens were left to imagine the horrors taking place behind thick prison walls. Unlike corporal punishment that was directed at the body, imprisonment evolved into a measure of social control aimed more at the mind, affecting the prisoners' consciousness. Foucault proposed that the chief purpose of the penitentiary was not to punish *less* but to punish *better*—in doing so, transforming prisoners from subjects to objects.

Like many intellectuals delving into the past, Foucault's work has drawn criticism. Historians Rothman (1990) and Adamson (1984) point out several empirical inadequacies evident in Foucault's analysis, including his unsystematic and anecdotal examination of history (also see Megill, 1979; Stone, 1983). In a parallel vein, sociologists are distracted by his nonsociological use of the concept of power (Dreyfus & Rabinow, 1983; Giddens, 1982; Hoy, 1979). Still, Foucault's perspective is similar to that of Rothman in that he links political forces and perceived threats of internal disorder to the transformation of penality (see Garland, 1990). In an effort to untangle the complexity of penality in a changing political economy, Michael Ignatieff (1978) also weighs into the debate over the emergence of institutionalization as a mechanism for social control. Ignatieff takes into account declining social solidarity and growing disorder during the Industrial Revolution, concentrating on the adverse effects of industrialization, particularly, unemployment, vagrancy, crime, public disturbances, and urban riots. According to Ignatieff, the penitentiary played a vital role in the transformation of class relations between workers and industrialists by introducing a unique style of isolation, punishment, and correction for members of the lower classes.

Attempting to sort neatly the other explanatory perspectives, Durham (1989) groups together Rusche and Kirchheimer (1939/1968), Melossi and Pavarini (1981), and Adamson (1984), referring to them as economic determinists. While each delivering unique contributions, those penologists all place economic cycles at the center of their analyses. Overall, they find that patterns of punishment remain consistent with particular forms of economic activity. For instance, during economic cycles in which labor is abundantly available, convicted criminals are more likely to be imprisoned than during periods when labor is scarce. Therefore, the historical development of the prison along with its many penal measures (e.g., retribution, reform, forced labor) is easily traced to specific economic conditions (see also Garland, 1990; Hirsch, 1992; Staples, 1990).

The first in an important line of studies aimed at examining the interactions between economic conditions and imprisonment was *Punishment and Social Structure,* by Georg Rusche and Otto Kirchheimer (1939/1968). While their pioneering work promised to transform the field of penology by revealing linkages between surplus labor and the use of prisons, its significance was overshadowed by the Second World War

(Levy & Zander, 1994). Amid political and social upheaval in the 1960s and 1970s, however, Rusche and Kirchheimer earned belated praise from a new generation of criminologists committed to critical studies of the penal apparatus, among them Ivan Jankovic (1982), David Greenberg (1977), and Dario Melossi (1976, 1977). That body of research was driven by methodologies designed to test the so-called Rusche and Kirchheimer hypothesis proposing a direct positive relationship between fluctuating incarceration rates and corresponding rates of unemployment. As these and other criminologists discovered evidence supporting the Rusche and Kirchheimer hypothesis, the nature of penological sanctions became more clearly understood (see Box & Hale, 1982; Chiricos & DeLone, 1992; D'Allessio & Stolzenberg, 2002). Whereas *Punishment and Social Structure* is associated with the works of critical criminologists, it retains respect from researchers across the theoretical spectrum (see Welch, 2004a).

Enthusiasm for *Punishment and Social Structure* persists into the new millennium. As Dario Melossi emphasizes in the introduction of the book's third edition (2003), the Rusche and Kirchheimer hypothesis captures the imagination of penologists striving to narrow the symbolic, political, and cultural connections between economic cycles and reliance on corrections as a measure of social control (Sutton, 2000; Weiss, 2001; Western & Beckett, 1999). Moreover, *Punishment and Social Structure* reaches beyond its macro-sociological significance, matching the influx of convicts into prisons to corresponding reductions in employment opportunities. Rusche and Kirchheimer turn critical attention to shifts in the conditions of confinement. During periods when the market is flooded with available labor, prison conditions decline, affirming the assertion that prison life tends to remain worse than in the free world. Conversely, conditions behind bars improve when labor becomes scarce, prompting correctional managers to institute vocational and work programs. Those policies reflect the need to prepare convicts for their return to the workforce upon release. Realizing those developments, Melossi cuts to the heart of the matter: "*Inside* the domain of the political economy is the value of labor. The value of a human being is therefore the value of his labor" (2003, p. 252).

Admittedly, the Rusche and Kirchheimer hypothesis is complicated, especially in light of the multitude of societal effects produced by long economic cycles. Researchers continue to sort an array of interactive variables manifesting in economics, politics, and culture so as to decipher precisely the ongoing interaction between imprisonment and other social forces (see Vanneste, 2001). Still, there remains a nearly axiomatic understanding of the use of imprisonment. During historical moments of prosperity, when most people looking for work can find it, incarceration becomes less of a necessity for the social system. Recognizing the impact that *Punishment and Social Structure* has had on the field, Melossi contends that it "represents the most elegant and parsimonious idea that the social sciences have produced to help us understand the social and economic context of developments in penality" (2003, p. 258).

Conclusion

Placing socio-historical perspectives in their proper context, Adamson reminds us that: "no single theory accounts for the complex historical process whereby imprisonment has become the dominant form of punishment in western societies" (1984, p. 435; see Bottoms & Tonry, 2002; Walker, 1998). That said, *The Discovery of the Asylum* is appreciated beyond a like-minded circle of historians. Even scholars who quibble over certain aspects of his treatise are indebted to Rothman for bringing his analyses to the forefront of historical penology. Among those benefiting from his work are critical criminologists who argue that historical forces figure prominently in the character and content of the criminal justice apparatus. It is through the work of Rothman, Foucault, Ignatieff, and the economic determinists that crucial lessons are learned concerning the rise of the penitentiary—in particular, lessons regarding a public and political acceptance of institutionalization as the dominant response to crime. Regrettably, that prevailing view of corrections persists today, producing an array of contradictions and self-defeating measures. Distinguishing itself from mainstream criminology that so often lacks sufficient historical references, the critical perspective tremendously values the socio-historical contributions for deepening our comprehension of punishment.

End-of-Chapter Questions

1. Describe punishment in colonial America.

2. Why was institutionalization so significant during the Jacksonian era?

3. Describe the changing definitions of the concept of social control.

4. What are some of the critical interpretations of the history of prisons?

3

Critical Penology

Martha Weatherspoon grew up farming in Alabama before moving north where she cleaned houses in the New York City suburbs, then picked fruits and vegetables on farms on the outskirts of Syracuse. While picking apples in the early 1980s, she slipped off a ladder and cracked her ribs, an injury that left her disabled and destitute. Even though two of her four daughters were consumed by a life of drug addiction, Weatherspoon began selling drugs to survive financially. She purchased furniture, clothes, and lots of food; then she got out of the drug business. But when her funds ran dry, Weatherspoon reluctantly returned to her wayward ways. At the age of 60 she sold eight ounces of cocaine to an undercover narcotics agent and wound up with a 20-year prison term. At the Bedford Hills Correctional Facility where she has been since 1989, she hobbles around with the help of a cane that takes the pressure off her replaced knee. Many people, including the prosecutor who secured her conviction, wonder about her punishment, "What's being served by her continued incarceration?" (Purdy, 2002, p. B1). With a third-grade education, Weatherspoon immersed herself in basic educational programs at the institution. In addition to mastering pottery, she says proudly, "I've learned lots of things. I never knew fractions and division" (Purdy, 2002). Weatherspoon recently had to forgo educational programs due to her back injury that makes it painful to attend class.

The prevailing conservative view of crime has dominated criminal justice policy and practice for decades. While relying on law-and-order rhetoric, conservative politicians have made significant changes in the way government spends money: most notably, the transfer of financial resources from social services to criminal justice. Critics of the conservative model of crime control question seriously the prudence of accelerating prison construction and other tough-on-crime initiatives while gutting social services, especially considering that those measures, such as job programs, often have crime control potential. Adding to complaints over the conservative agenda are critical criminologists who look deeper at the role of capitalism in the formulation of penal sanctions. Greater investment in criminal justice is consistent with a political economy devoted to accumulating wealth for the rich while subjecting the poor to coercive measures of social control (Blomberg, Thomas, & Cohen, 2003; Blomberg & Lucken, 2000; Welch, 2004a).

This chapter explores the potential of critical penology by shedding light on linkages between the criminal justice apparatus and the structural components of capitalism, which together reinforce inequality and the repressive mechanisms of social control. As we shall see, critical penology offers insights into the ironic features of incarceration, particularly those proven to be financially inefficient, biased against the poor and people of color, and woefully self-defeating since they fail to contribute to public safety. The discussion begins with a look at the emergence of critical criminology along with its contemporary vision of penology. Taking into account the inner workings of the political economy, analysis is aimed at the production of problem populations in a capitalist society and institutions designed to deal with them. Likewise, evidence is presented verifying significant socioeconomic and racial disparities in prison sentences. Demonstrating the continued development of a critical penology, other forms of intellectual radicalism are considered, namely postmodern feminism and anarchist criminology.

Emergence of Critical Criminology

As an alternative to mainstream criminology, the critical perspective issues a divergent view of the sources of crime and their corresponding remedies. Among its primary influences, critical criminology draws on the writings of Karl Marx, most notably those works examining the rise of capitalism and the complex class relations it produces (1867/1967,

1981). "Above all," according to Lynch, Michalowski, and Groves, "Marxism is a critique of capitalism" (2000, p. 19). As early capitalism generated unprecedented industrial wealth, it created a society divided sharply along lines of social class. That development is key, becoming "one of the most important organizational features of society and a construct that would have to be addressed in any study related to human society (Lynch & Stretesky, 1999, p. 18). In essence, class is a person's location in the social and economic hierarchy; moreover, that position determines the amount of monetary and material power the individual possesses (see Arrigo, 2003). Those concepts figure prominently in a critical penology that sets out to comprehend the degree of social, economic, and racial inequality evident in the criminal justice system, an apparatus that maintains a class-based society (Welch, 1998a).

Whereas Marx's analysis of capitalist society led to substantial contributions to understanding economic and political power, alienation, and social change, he wrote surprisingly little about crime. Early critical criminologists, therefore, formulated theories of crime and punishment by connecting the dots between Marxist interpretations of the political economy and the emergence of a criminal justice enterprise that perpetuates inequality. One of the first formal applications of Marxist social thought to crime is found in the work of Dutch criminologist Willem Bonger, author of *Criminality and Economic Conditions* (1916). Elaborating on Friedrich Engels' (1845/1973) observation that capitalism produces forms of competition that harm society, Bonger issued a coherent criticism of culture, in particular its drives. Capitalist culture is notable for its egoism, whereby individuals strive toward individual materialism; such greed is pervasive insofar as it drives people of all classes to engage in activities so self-serving that they become socially harmful, including crime.

In capitalist society, manifestations of greed are affected by class position. Whereas the rich enjoy legal opportunities to increase their wealth, such as exploiting workers, members of the working classes who engage in predatory behavior, such as theft of property, risk being apprehended by the criminal justice system. Under capitalism, it is the greed of the poor—not the wealthy—that becomes criminalized. That form of criminalization lends itself further to the class-based tactics of criminality. The poor who commit crime generally rely on offenses that are easily detectable, such as theft and drug peddling. Due to their privileged class position, white-collar and corporate offenders, by contrast, engage in crimes that are better concealed, including embezzlement, fraud, price fixing, and insider trading. It ought to be emphasized that Bonger did not characterize the crimes of the poor as romantic or as noble rebellion against the oppression of capitalism. Like offenses committed by members of the capitalist class, crime among the poor also harms society and fragments communities where many crime victims also are poor. In the final analysis, Bonger endorses democratic socialist reforms that would reduce inequality and crime simultaneously, giving way to a less predatory and more altruistic culture.

Contemporary Critical Criminology

Bonger's critical view of crime remained popular among European criminologists during the early part of the 20th century, however, it did not take the stage in American criminology until the turbulent 1960s and 70s. During that period, criticism was directed at political and economic systems that supported an unjust war in Vietnam while repressing poor people, racial minorities, and women. In light of the shifting social landscape, it became difficult for progressive criminologists to overlook the role of the political economy in crime causation and class-based criminal justice policies. The critical perspective benefited tremendously from the research of many influential criminologists (Chambliss, 1975; Greenberg, 1981; Michalowski & Bolander, 1976; Quinney, 1970). Likewise, many took notice of the work of those on the faculty at the School of Criminology at the University of California, Berkeley (Platt & Takagi, 1974; Schwendinger & Schwendinger, 1977, 1981). The program at Berkeley is worth noting because it produced another generation of progressive and critical criminologists (Barak, 1982, 2003a; Currie, 1985; Humphries & Greenberg, 1981; Klein & Kress, 1976). Critical criminology in America also drew from its British counterparts (Taylor, Walton, & Young, 1973, 1975; see also Lea, 2002; Taylor, 1999) and in doing so, the perspective also absorbed an array of critical concepts, including moral panic (Cohen, 2002; Hall, Critcher, Jefferson, Clarke, & Roberts, 1978).

Since then, the radical approach to crime continues to be shaped by diverse and sometimes competing points of view (see Schwartz & Friedrichs, 1994). "Contrary to some views, critical criminology is not a utopian perspective but an invitation to struggle; it is a call to recast definitions of social offense more broadly than traditional criminologists, who rarely challenge unnecessary forms of social domination" (Thomas & O'Maolchatha, 1989, p. 148; see also Danner, Michalowski, & Lynch, 1994). Critical criminology is not so much a theory as a theoretical perspective based on social critique. According to Thomas and O'Maolchatha (1989),

> Social critique, by definition, is radical. Derived from the Greek *krites* ("judge"), the Latin term *criticus* implies an evaluative judgment of meaning and method in search, policy and human activity. (Critical thinking implies *freedom* by recognizing that social existence, including our knowledge of this existence, was not simply imposed on us by powerful and mysterious forces. This recognition leads to the possibility of transcending our immediate social or ideational conditions. The act of critique implies that we can change our subjective interpretations and our objective conditions by thinking about and then acting on the world. (p. 147)

For purposes of drawing a coherent picture of critical criminology and its implications to critical penology, this treatment of the subject does not dwell on the distinctions between overlapping rubrics. Rather, it concentrates on some of the shared assumptions defining the perspective that challenge the hegemony of traditional classical and positivist criminologies (Bohm, 1982). Although critical criminologists debate the finer points of theory in greater detail, there is a degree of consensus on the following assumptions that serve as the foundation of this perspective:

1. Conflict, domination, and repression are characteristic elements of a capitalist society.

2. The majority of crime in capitalist societies is a result of the inherent contradictions of capitalist social organization.

3. Laws and the criminal justice system generally protect the interests of the powerful to the disadvantage of the powerless.

4. Criminal justice makes sense only in the larger context of social justice. (Maguire, 1988, p. 134)

Since the first assumption has already been addressed, attention is turned to the inherent contradictions of the capitalist society. Whereas the overarching aim of capitalism is to generate wealth, it is fraught with the contradiction of generating poverty; indeed, it takes a lot of poor people to make one person rich. Or as Marx put it, "One capitalist kills many" (1867/1967, p. 763). To be sure, the capitalist system is not designed to distribute the wealth fairly among all people, even though workers contribute directly to the proliferation of profits (Glyn, 1990). In a capitalist society, profit is highly concentrated among the few who, due to their immense wealth, wield enormous political power. As a result, the economy and the nation's wealth become polarized, meaning that the rich get richer, and the poor—and the middle class—become poorer (Clemetson, 2003; Kilborn & Clemetson, 2002; Reiman, 2004).

A capitalist system also rests on the contradiction that unemployment is as necessary as employment. Obviously, the employment of workers is required to manufacture goods and provide services. At the same time, however, unemployment also is required to keep wages low, thereby maintaining the system's economic stability (Glyn, 1990). If all workers were to have jobs, then it is likely that they would—perhaps collectively—demand a raise in pay, perhaps threatening instability in the form of worker strikes and stoppages. Nowadays, unemployment remains a serious social crisis in light of the realization that there are more workers than jobs. The unemployed, in Marxist terminology, are known as the surplus population. Capitalists take advantage of the surplus population, knowing its existence is functional in that the unemployed serve as examples of what happens to workers when they do not comply with the demands of employers. Consider the situation of a worker earning minimum wage in a fast food restaurant. The worker quickly discovers how difficult it is to survive on those wages. That is, if one works at minimum wage (set at $5.15 an hour) and works 40 hours per week, 52 weeks a year (no vacation), one earns $10,712 per year (before taxes are deducted). Compare those earnings to the federal poverty levels formulated by income and number of people living in a household. The 2002 guidelines show that for one person, the threshold for poverty is $8,860. In light of that predicament, the worker requests an increase in wages; not surprisingly, the worker is denied a raise. Furthermore, the employer suggests that if the worker were to vacate the job, the position could be easily filled by one of the many local residents who would gratefully embrace the opportunity to work, even at minimum wage. The worker is left with the option of either continuing to work there at minimum wage or joining the ranks of the unemployed. That scenario demonstrates that the existence of the surplus labor pool not only keeps wages down but also serves as a viable threat, making workers compliant (see Aronowitz & DeFazio, 1994; Ehrenreich, 2001; Selke, Corsaro, & Selke, 2002).

A third contradiction in a capitalist society is the tendency to treat products and services as commodities that are used for means of exchange rather than using products and services for their original purpose. "Capitalist production is guided by profit, not social need, or to put it more abstractly, by exchange value rather than use value" (Glyn, 1990,

p. 108). For example, investors purchase property and housing, not for the sole purpose of providing shelter for those who need it, but to profit from their investment. The contradiction here is that houses and apartments remain vacant until prospective tenants fulfill the investor's profit expectation—that is, to pay the landlord a certain amount of rent. Nowadays, a popular myth persists insinuating that there is a housing shortage when actually there is a shortage of *affordable* housing. That social condition contributes substantially to a growing segment of the population known as the renting poor, who are forced to cut back on food and other necessities of survival because they are spending a huge proportion of their income on housing. Similar forms of commodification also are found in health care and education, where workers have to spend an increasingly greater percentage of their earnings on services that many people believe ought to be provided by the state.

Production of Problem
Populations in Capitalist Society

Unemployed workers are the most recognizable manifestations of the internal contradictions of capitalism, a system that paradoxically requires a certain level of unemployment to function properly. Still, unemployed workers (the surplus population) do not become a problem until they threaten the social relations of production; when that occurs, they are subject to becoming labeled a problem population by the state. Specifically, problem populations become eligible for social control when they disrupt or challenge the following components of a capitalist society:

1. The capitalist modes of appropriating the product of human labor (e.g., the poor who "steal" from the rich)

2. The social conditions under which capitalist production takes place (e.g., those who refuse or are unable to perform wage labor)

3. Patterns of distribution and consumption (e.g., those who use drugs for escape and transcendence rather than for sociability and adjustment)

4. The process of socialization for productive and nonproductive roles (e.g., youth who refuse to be schooled or those who deny the validity of "family life")

5. The ideology that supports the functioning of capitalist society (e.g., proponents of alternative forms of social organization) (Spitzer, 1975, p. 642)

As the problem population swells, it is in the interests of the state and capitalism to devise mechanisms of class (social) control in an effort to maintain the social order and status quo (Russell, 2003; White & Haines, 1996). Two major groupings within the problem population are commonly identified, *social junk* and *social dynamite*. From the perspective of the state, *social junk* is viewed as costly but as relatively harmless to the social order. "The discreditability of *social junk* resides in the failure, inability, or refusal of this group to participate in the roles supportive of the capitalist society" (Spitzer, 1975, p. 645). The category of *social junk* is made up of the elderly and the physically and mentally disabled. Because *social junk* is deemed relatively harmless to the stability of the capitalist system, social control mechanisms in the form of therapeutic and welfare agencies serve to regulate rather than eliminate or suppress them. By contrast, the portion of the problem population labeled *social dynamite* is portrayed as a serious threat to the prevailing social and economic order. Due to its presumed volatility, *social dynamite* is subject to the coercive components of the social control apparatus, namely the criminal justice and correctional systems.

Despite the seemingly discrete categories within the problem population, the social control apparatus often operates equivocally in that all members of the problem population, including the impoverished, problem youth, drug addicts, and nonviolent offenders who commit minor crimes, are processed alternatively as either *social junk* or *social dynamite* or as both. More so than prisons, city and county jails tend not to distinguish between harmless *social junk* and menacing *social dynamite*, serving as unspecialized catch basins for both types of problem populations (Irwin, 1985; Welch, 1991). Accounting for that lack of uniformity in processing deviance, Spitzer (1975) notes that social control is shaped by political, economic, and ideological priorities that are subject to change. In a similar vein, Marx (1867/1967) characterized capitalism as dynamic rather than static, a political economy in constant transformation.

A key economic development in the United States during the past five decades has been the shift from industrial to corporate capitalism, resulting in the erosion of manufacturing jobs formerly occupied by workers in inner cities, many of them people of color (Wilson, 1997). That economic transformation has contributed tremendously to the surplus population, prompting the state to invest greater resources in coercive mechanisms of social control, namely the criminal justice and correctional systems (Garland, 1990, 2001; Sparks, 2003). Containment has emerged as an increasingly expansive measure of social control, evidenced by the largest incarceration rate in American history and in the world (Welch, 1996b, 2004a; Welch, Fenwick, & Roberts, 1997, 1998).

Disparities in Sentencing

With an eye on social control, a critical penology attends closely to disparities in sentencing contoured along lines of race, ethnicity, gender, and class. Criminologists have long been interested in studying problems in sentencing but until recently, various methodologies produced conflicting results. Current empirical analyses of sentencing, however, demonstrate compelling relationships among key demographic variables. Steffensmeier, Ulmer, and Kramer (1998) document the "punishment cost of being young, Black, and male" by revealing that, compared to any other group, they are sentenced to the harshest prison terms. Steffensmeier et al. interpret their findings according to a focal concerns theory of sentencing in which judges' sentencing decisions reflect their evaluation of the blameworthiness of the offender, their desire to safe-guard the community by incapacitating dangerous criminals, and the social costs of their sentencing decision. But judges rarely have sufficient information to assess accurately the offender's blameworthiness or dan-gerousness; consequently, they resort to a form of perceptual shorthand that rests on negative stereotypes of young, black males.

As a follow-up study, Spohn and Holleran (2000) replicated the research of Steffensmeier et al., finding comparable results. "Young black and Hispanic males face greater odds of incarceration than middle-aged white males, and unemployed black and Hispanic males are sub-stantially more likely to be sentenced to prison than employed white males" (p. 281). Confirming Steffensmeier et al.'s notion of perceptual shorthand, Spohn and Holleran conclude that their study provides evidence of the perception that certain types of offenders are regarded as being more problematic than others, thus requiring greater formal social control. That interpretation parallels Spitzer's (1975) work on social dynamite, a concept used to describe popular perceptions that a certain segment of the deviant population, namely young minority males, is particularly menacing. Furthermore, these studies emphasize that unem-ployment remains a key factor, since young minority males who are out of work are perceived as posing the greatest threat to public safety (see Everett & Nienstedt, 1999; Nobiling, Spohn, & DeLone, 1998; Steffensmeier & Demuth, 2001; Crawford, Chiricos, & Kleck, 1998).

Compounding matters, fear of crime is tremendously racialized in that negative stereotypes of young black and Latino males shape popular perceptions. Likewise, it is that racialized fear of crime that drives not only criminal justice policies (e.g., mandatory minimum drug sentences, three-strikes laws) but, as the aforementioned research suggests, also creates disparities in sentencing (see Covington 1995, 1997; Welch, Price, & Yankey, 2002a, 2002b).

Hispanics and Punishment

The changing ethnic landscape of America reflects the growth of the Hispanic (or Latino) population, particularly in major cities. Overall, the number of Hispanic Americans has increased 55% since 1980, currently comprising 10% of the U.S. population. By 2010, Hispanics are expected to represent the largest minority group in the United States, surpassing the number of African Americans. Much like previous shifts in America's ethnic composition, Hispanics face discrimination, most notably in criminal justice. But until recently, few criminologists focused specifically on problems facing Hispanics, opting to sort them conveniently into the minority category with African Americans (Aguirre & Baker, 2000a, 2000b; Marshall, 1997; Sampson & Lauritsen, 1997). Breaking new ground, Steffensmeier and Demuth (2001) set out to measure the degree of prejudice and hostility toward Hispanics manifested in harsh sentencing, particularly in the war on drugs. Based on Pennsylvania sentencing data, Steffensmeier and Demuth discovered that "besides the overall more lenient treatment of white defendants, our main finding is that Hispanic defendants are the defendant subgroup most at risk to receive the harshest penalty" (2001, p. 145; see also DeJesus-Torres, 2000; Diaz-Cotto, 1998, 2000; Munoz, 2000).

While addressing the significance of focal concerns theory, Steffensmeier and Demuth (2001) expand their interpretation to include problems of cultural assimilation. First, Hispanics, much like urban African Americans, struggle against effects of poverty, unemployment, poor education, and single-parent families (Healey, 1995; Tarver, Walker, & Wallace, 2002). Second, Hispanics commonly are stereotyped as lazy, irresponsible, and prone to crime and gang activity (Alvarez, 2000; Katz, 1997; Rodriguez, 2002). Third, due to such negative stereotyping, Hispanics are targets in ambitious law enforcement campaigns, namely the war on drugs (Birbeck, 1999; Meeker, Dombrink, & Mallett, 2000; Portillos, 2002). Fourth, the growing Hispanic population has been met with resistance by dominant white groups who perceive them as a social threat, including competition for jobs, threatening the primacy of the English language, and straining the welfare system (Mata & Herrerias, 2002; Welch, 2002a). Together, those factors add to an understanding of the social threat hypothesis in which relatively large increases of the Hispanic population over a relatively short period of time produce social and economic conflict with dominant (white) groups who are influential in intensifying greater social control such as tougher criminal justice sanctions (Crawford, Chiricos, & Kleck, 1998).

Postmodern Feminism

Contributing to critical penology is postmodern feminism, an emerging school of thought capturing the imagination of a new generation of criminologists. Proponents of the perspective contend that social control and social justice can be better understood by merging postmodernism with feminism. Borrowing from postmodern theorists Derrida (1976) and Baudrillard (1983), this school of criticism is aimed at the role of language in constructing realities of women. By deconstructing language, signs, symbols, and text, postmodern feminists demonstrate how narratives, or stories, are used to perpetuate gender inequality. Nancy Wonders (1996, 1999) presents the fundamentals of the paradigm by turning attention to four points of convergence linking postmodernism and feminism: a critique of objectivity, a focus on process, the centrality of identity and difference, and a new conception of power (see also Hallsworth, 2002).

Postmodernists and feminists question the notion of an objective reality or truth, insisting that social reality is subject to interpretation. For example, "the truth that some women are witches and deserving of punishment and incapacitation seems like a fact at one point in time, but it was determined to be a story at a later point in time" (Wonders, 1999, p. 116). Similarly, slavery remained an integral part of America's early experience, largely due to the so-called "truth" that slaves were not fully human, a version of reality that was inscribed in law designed to undermine their emancipation. By attending to the subjective nature of social reality, it is clear that the truth or stories or narratives are inherently political, privileging some perspectives over others.

The "truth" also serves to produce notions of identity that exclude certain people from participating in the construction of reality because they are viewed as different. Social identity is predicated on race, class, and gender, and those considerations are used as the basis of difference, thus perpetuating inequality. Postmodern feminism traces inequality to the ways in which meaning is attached to certain behaviors, reinforcing notions of difference. "If the state claims that young people who used drugs are criminal (rather than 'ill' as is done in many other industrialized countries), then the state has played an active role in shaping the identity of teenagers and others who used drugs—it has changed who they are" (Wonders, 1999, p. 118).

Attending to process also refines our understanding of the construction of social reality. Concentrating on interpretative strategies, postmodern feminists reveal the process by which social reality is created day to day. In studying the criminal system, an interpretative approach yields crucial information about how criminal identities and notions of justice are shaped. Any person who has visited a courtroom or a prison realizes that judges, prosecutors, defendants, convicts, and corrections officers conform to a shared reality about who plays the role of the controller and who plays the role of the controlled. Unquestionably, those roles are shaped by structures of power that exist in hierarchies. Postmodern feminists remind us of the importance of language—particularly sexist vocabularies—that reproduces gender inequality, since linguistic systems convey meaning, positionality, identity, and difference (see Arrigo 1995, 2003; Butler, 1990; West & Fenstermaker, 1995). The significance of exploring gender within a critical penology is discussed further in subsequent chapters.

Anarchist Criminology

Critical penology, as an emerging paradigm, continues to benefit from other strains of radical criminology. Still, some perspectives go unnoticed even though their contributions are well documented. A case in point is anarchist criminology, which like other forms of radicalism challenges the power structure and its dominance over the criminal justice system. Contemporary anarchist thought is indebted to the work of its pioneers, namely, William Godwin, Max Stirner, Michael Bakunin, and Peter Kropotkin, as well as the Industrial Workers of the World (the Wobblies). Anarchism holds that "the absence of government would not be a condition of chaos, but of harmonious order. The state, with its extensive apparatus of administration and coercion, is seen as a major source of oppression and inequality in society" (Mann, 1984, p. 10). Anarchism rejects the state, its power, its (rational) authority, and its structural hierarchies, all of which protect the privilege of the few while forcing the masses into subordination. Acts of resistance, therefore, are generally emblematic of the struggle to unchain citizens from state repression that obstructs personal and social autonomy (Kropotkin, 1975; Tracy, 1996). Anarchists envision a society "organized from the bottom upwards, with wider arrangements being agreed by negotiation between autonomous units" (Mann, 1984, p. 10; Wolff, 1998).

Ferrell (1998) reminds us that anarchism is not a general theory but rather an orientation toward social life and social relations. With its emphasis on social justice, anarchist criminology complements critical intellectualism found in an array of radical and postmodern perspectives (Arrigo, 1995, 2003; MacLean & Milovanovic, 1997; Michalowski, 1996; Ross, 1998; Welch, 1998a). From an anarchist standpoint, "if law and legality are worth preserving at all, their mission must be radically altered; instead of protecting property, privilege, and the state, as they now do, they must be made to insure tolerance and protect diversity" (Ferrell, 1996, p. 187). In that vein, anarchist criminology strives toward an anti-authoritarian vision of justice. Although its application to the study of lawlessness remains limited to a handful of works, anarchist criminology offers the field a valuable framework for deconstructing the state, its authority, and its machinery of repressive social control, as well as the resistance it evokes (Ferrell 1997; Gil, 1996; Pepinsky, 1978; Ryan & Ferrell, 1986; Sullivan, 1980; Tifft & Sullivan, 1980).

Anarchism's contribution to a critical approach to justice is its endorsement of alternative meanings, various reality systems, and tolerance for ambiguity. It demystifies the state's mythology of absolute truth, justice, certainty, and universal knowledge (Pepinsky, 1978; Tifft, 1979). Given that political mythologies reinforce hierarchies and perpetuate inequality, Guerin advocates challenging authority by engaging in a "vast operation of deconsecration" (1970, p. 13). Becker (1967) expresses a similar viewpoint in questioning the hierarchy of credibility from which authorities maintain their foothold on criminal justice policy. Anarchist criminology, according to Ferrell, ought to dismantle legal and political configurations, exposing the state's principal myth that its authority is a "reasonable and legitimate medium for making sense of the world, and in doing so conceals its abuses" (1996, p. 189). Anarchist criminology has the potential to further advance critical penology by offering a fluid approach to law and justice, inviting scholars to incorporate an array of sociological concepts into their analyses of the state, the criminal justice system, and the corrections apparatus. Moreover, anarchism promises to make penal policies more humane, since it defies the status quo and resists calcified social arrangements in which "concern for humanity [displaces] a respect for authority" (Ferrell, 1998, p. 64; see also Arrigo, 2003).

Conclusion

Beginning in the early 1970s, conservatives embarked on a regressive social campaign manifesting in a steady assault on liberal initiatives, becoming a dominant force in criminal justice and corrections. Soaring prison populations and expanded construction of prisons are evidence that the conservative approach remains exceedingly popular today. Still, conservative criminal justice policies are fraught with resounding contradictions. Prisons are grossly expensive and fail to contribute to public safety, since the current influx of prisoners consists mostly of nonviolent offenders, predominately drug violators (Irwin, Schiraldi, & Ziedenberg, 2000; see also Currie, 2003). Such self-defeating measures also raise serious questions as to whether conservatives can adequately dispense basic forms of justice, given that their policies are blatantly biased against the poor and people of color.

As a response to the conservative penal agenda, this chapter introduced the fundamental components of critical penology. Through a critical lens, we are able to view corrections in the context of the political economy and its many contradictions. Reiterating some principal themes of critical penology that will echo throughout the book, we turn to four propositions that illuminate linkages between economic structures and punishment (Lynch, Michalowski, & Groves, 2000).

Proposition 1: The nature of the basic productive activities of a given society will shape the forms of punishment appropriate to that society (Michalowski, 1985, p. 225; Rusche & Kirchheimer, 1939/1968).

Proposition 2: As the type of production carried out in society changes, so, too, will the form of punishment (Rusche & Kirchheimer, 1939/1968).

Proposition 3: Imprisonment is 'not only caught up in the economic structure of early capitalism, but is unable to be understood apart from it' (Miller, 1980, p. 100).

Proposition 4: Prisons in modern capitalist society reinforce ideological notions about criminals that justify repression of the lower classes, and thereby reaffirm the class structure of capitalism (Fine, 1980; Reiman, 2004).

As this chapter demonstrates, the ironies of imprisonment represent challenges not only for policymakers interested in making the correctional apparatus a just system, but also for criminologists committed to revealing the truths about crime and punishment (see Matthews, 1999; Matthews & Young, 1986). A critical penology offers lessons for both, especially in the realms of race, ethnicity, and class. As pointed out by various types of radicals, including postmodern feminists and anarchists, the critical project remains squarely focused on the political economy and the culture it produces. Recognizing the enduring contribution of the Marxist perspective, Stuart Russell reminds us that it "continues to be relevant to the contemporary world, given the ongoing crisis of capitalism which includes criminality and anti-social behaviour, its ability to analyse moves towards a more authoritarian state, and its overall penetrating analysis of socio-economic and political phenomena" (2003, p. 121; see also *Contemporary Justice Review,* 2003; Stetson, 1999, 2000).

End-of-Chapter Questions

1. Describe the emergence of critical criminology.

2. What are the major assumptions supporting contemporary critical criminology?

3. Describe the production of problem populations in a capitalist society.

4. How does postmodern feminism shape a critical understanding of criminal justice and punishment?

4

War on Drugs and Just War Theory

By 6:00 A.M., the 57-year-old Alberta Spruill was dressed and prepared to leave for her job at the Division of Citywide Administrative Services where she had worked for 29 years. Suddenly her apartment door blew off its hinges from the blunt force of a battering ram. A swirling concussion grenade flooded the room with a thunderous blast. Spruill was quickly tackled and handcuffed, another target of an NYC police drug raid known as a no-knock search. But since her apartment did not fit the floor plan described on the warrant, the six members of the quasi-military tactical unit realized their mistake. Information provided by a confidential informant turned out to be a bad tip. There were no drugs and no guns. Spruill remained stunned on the floor. She complained to the officers that she had a heart condition and an ambulance was dispatched. At 7:50 A.M., Spruill died of cardiac arrest while being transported to Harlem Hospital Center. Police Commissioner Raymond Kelly apologized to the family and publicly announced: "This should not have happened" (Rashbaum, 2003, p. B3).

Both figuratively and literally, the American war on drugs has emerged as an increasingly militarized social policy. While the U.S. military engages in drug control campaigns abroad, it also continues to shape law enforcement tactics at home (Husak, 2002; Inciardi, 2002). Campaigning for the presidency in 1996, Republican Bob Dole proclaimed, "As President of the United States, within my first 45 days at the White House, I will work with my Secretary of Defense and the Joint Chiefs of Staff to seek further ways to use our military power—particularly technological capabilities—to fight the war on drugs. We will come up with a plan that focuses on the appropriate military means to augment our Federal and state drug-enforcement agencies" (Seelye, 1996, p. A13). Although the G.O.P. suffered a setback with the re-election of President Clinton, militarized drug control policies surged forward. Clinton persuaded Congress to approve a 67% increase in U.S. financial support for Latin American counternarcotics programs. That $92 million increase was partly paid by transferring $53 million that had been designated to aid the world's poorest citizens through the U.N. Children's Fund and the U.N. Development Program that support child-nutrition and family-planning programs ("Election-Year Posturing on Drugs," August 19, 1996).

Despite the political popularity of militarizing drug control, such policy has caught the critical eye of scholars. Christina Johns (1991, 1996) questions the Pentagon's reasons to invade Panama in 1989, a maneuver known as Operation Just Cause—resulting in an expansion of U.S. military involvement in the war on drugs. Similarly, Peter Kraska (1993a, 1993b, 1996, 1997) points to a key motive behind increased military activity in the war on drugs, namely, the need for U.S. armed forces to become socially useful in the post–cold war era (see also Committee on Armed Services, 1988). Domestically, the appeal of militarism in drug control policy has contributed to a greater investment in hard control (e.g., law enforcement) at the expense of soft control (e.g., treatment) (Barlow, Barlow, & Chiricos, 1995a, 1995b; Welch, Wolff, & Bryan, 1998). In fact, militarized tactics in the form of law enforcement (and corrections) account for 70% of the federal drug control budget, whereas medical strategies in the form of treatment are left with 30% of the anti-drug dollars (Office of National Drug Control Policy, 2003).

In an effort to illuminate further the ironies of imprisonment caused by a militarization of drug control policy, this chapter embarks on an examination of the war on drugs from the perspective of just war theory, a paradigm that evaluates the justness of military action (see Welch, Bryan, & Wolff, 1999). Philosophical discourse on militarism and warfare is often shaped by moral considerations through the prism of just war theory (Bove & Kaplan, 1995; Cady & Werner, 1991; Walzer, 1977). Though it might be argued that the war on drugs is merely a metaphor—similar to the war on poverty—it is clear that the prevailing drug control policy has been militarized to the point where just war theory is appropriate. According to Sterba, just war theory does not pertain exclusively to warfare; in its most basic form, it is a theory of just defense that "can also apply to a wide range of defensive actions short of war" (1991, p. 36). This use of just war theory is not an endorsement of war. Rather, just war theory serves as a conceptual framework that furthers an assessment of the militarized drug control strategy; moreover, it offers an opportunity to develop alternatives that are non-invasive, non-violent, and contribute to a justly arranged society.

Just War Theory

In contrast to pacifists, just war theorists presume that certain wars can be justified (Bove & Kaplan, 1995; Cady & Werner, 1991; Walzer, 1977). While acknowledging the horrific nature of war, they painstakingly attend to key details of conflict in determining the justness of military action. Warfare can be regarded as just, provided that military action preserves the values, dignity, and rights of human beings (Sterba, 1991). The analysis of just war theory is as systematic as it is complex, resting firmly on a set of six criteria. Moreover, each and every criterion must be satisfied for a war to be considered just; therefore, if any of the criteria fail to be upheld, military action is deemed unjust, unjustly fought, or both (Kunkel & Taylor, 1995).

Just war theory is composed of two fundamental elements: justice *of* war (*jus ad bellum*) and justice *in* war (*jus in bello*). The criteria of the justice *of* war include just cause, legitimate authority, right intention, and last resort. The principles underlying the justice *of* war are necessary in determining whether a warring faction has *just reasons* for military action. In evaluating the means of military action, proportionality and discrimination serve as the criteria for justice *in* war. Briefly, proportionality weighs the relative harm caused by military strategies against those related to the medical approach. Discrimination refers to the importance of containing violence so that it does not spill—indiscriminately—into a civilian population. Taken together, both elements of just war theory—*jus ad bellum* and *jus in bello*—provide a basis for appraising the justness of a particular military action, including the justness of its means (Richards, 1995; Walzer, 1977). In applying just war theory to the war on drugs, we attend to its two basic elements—the justice *of* war and the justice *in* war.

Justice of the War on Drugs:
Evaluating the Moral Reasons

Just Cause

An overarching concern facing drug control is whether the drug problem in the United States constitutes a just cause for the war on drugs. Sociologically speaking, perceptions of the drug problem are shaped according to three stages of social constructionism. First, the drug issue is selected from among many social ills (e.g., poor education, poverty, unemployment) then elevated to the status of a problem demanding serious policy consideration. Next, the drug problem is sufficiently narrowed to include only illegal substances, while neglecting other types of harm (e.g., the potentially harmful effects of legal drugs such as alcohol and tobacco). In the final stage, the drug problem is framed as a phenomenon necessitating criminal justice intervention rather than other forms of public policy (e.g., health and human services) (Reinarman & Levine, 1997; Welch, Wolff, & Bryan, 1998). In light of social constructionism, a crucial question persists: Why is there so much fanfare—and financial expenditure—devoted to drug control while other "good causes" remain relatively neglected (e.g., homelessness, inaccessible health care, poverty, substandard education)? As shall be discussed further, there are several social, political, and economic forces shaping perceptions of the drug problem, resulting in repressive, militarized drug control strategies and a simultaneous neglect of other social ills.

From the perspective of just war theory, the issue is whether the drug problem constitutes a just cause. Whereas pacifism has been interpreted as ruling out "any use of violence in response to aggression," just war theory "permits a measured use of violence in response to aggression" (Sterba, 1991, p. 35). According to Sterba, "just cause is usually specified by three requirements: there must be substantial aggression; nonbelligerent correctives must be either hopeless or too costly; belligerent correctives must be neither hopeless nor too costly" (1991, p. 35). In that framework, substantial aggression is defined as a violation of people's most fundamental rights. Attending to those requirements, it is clear that the war on drugs in the form of a militarized drug control policy does not satisfy the criterion of just cause. First and foremost, there lacks a substantial aggression that would otherwise permit a measured use of violence. Secondly, several nonbelligerent correctives are neither hopeless nor too costly; as we shall elaborate on further, a genuine commitment to drug treatment, education, and alternative ways to modify one's moods are effective and less costly remedies. Finally, belligerent correctives via military and quasi-military organizations (i.e., law enforcement and corrections) are not only costly but due to their limited effectiveness, ultimately erode a sense of hope.

Legitimate Authority

The federal drug control policy is administered by the Director of the Office of National Drug Control Policy, a cabinet post established during the George H. Bush presidency in the late 1980s. From its inception, the agency has boasted of its militaristic features, including the unofficial title of the director popularly known as the drug czar. In formulating an effective and humane drug control policy, the just war perspective challenges the appeal of criminalization and militarization; moreover, it calls for a greater application of the medical, educational, and preventative models. Given the significance of legitimate authority, a prudent drug control policy perhaps would be better served if directed by public health and education administrators (e.g., the Department of Health and Human Services, the Department of Education) rather than criminal justice officials, including military and quasi-military personnel (see Musto, 1999). In proposing an alternative to the war on drugs, it is important to realize that much like militarization, treatment also is aimed at individuals rather than at the social conditions that promote social sedation. However, unlike the military paradigm, the medical model can be cost-effective and humane as long as participation of those selected for treatment is maximized.

America's response to drug usage will not be afforded legitimacy if it relies solely on rehabilitation as a corrective measure. Wide-scale substance abuse remains a symptom of deeper social, political, and economic contradictions. For decades, scholars have confirmed that endemic drug abuse is strongly associated with mass deprivation, economic marginality, and cultural and community breakdown (Currie, 1993; Gans, 1995; Rose & Clear, 1998; Welch, 1996a, 1997a). As life for many of those alienated people grows bleaker, the peddling and consumption of drugs as novocaines for human suffering become more tempting. For treatment to maintain long-term effectiveness, it must be coupled with realistic possibilities for an alternative way of life, including viable employment. Given the problems associated with drugs, reconceptualization is needed to confront social, political, and economic infrastructures that keep people from meeting their basic human needs, prompting them to resort to novocaines. Such recommendations intend to deal humanely with the harms of drug addiction while striving to reduce forms of inequality (e.g., racism and classism), contributing to the drug crisis. Critical perspectives remain useful because they advocate the realignment of social arrangements whereby the basic needs of all people are taken into account from the outset and are ultimately met (Gil, 1996; Sullivan, 1980; Welch, 1997a).

Another concern related to legitimate authority extends beyond domestic drug control strategies to include international campaigns that are increasingly militaristic (e.g., maritime and aerial interdiction, eradication of drug crop cultivation; refer to Office of National Drug Control Policy, 2003). In light of recent events, there remain serious diplomatic, moral, and ethical questions about the use of military personnel in expanding U.S. drug control policy. A case in point is the 1989 United States invasion of Panama, a military action operating under the guise of the war on drugs. Johns (1991, 1996) reveals crucial political and military activities by the United States in Panama, many of which clearly violated both international law and human rights. It should be noted that the Organization for American States condemned the United States for unjustifiably crossing the sovereign borders of Panama and arresting its head of state, Manuel Noriega. Among a host of atrocities and violations of just war principles (e.g., just cause, last resort, proportionality, and discrimination), the lack of legitimate authority behind military action in Panama and other Latin American nations remains a key problem in U.S. drug control policy abroad (Ehrenfeld, 1990; Riley, 1996).

Right Intention

According to *National Drug Control Strategy*, the goals and objectives of the current drug control policy include the following: (1) motivate America's youth to reject illegal drugs and substance abuse; (2) increase the safety of America's citizens by substantially reducing drug-related crime and violence; (3) reduce health, welfare, and crime costs resulting from illegal drug use; (4) shield America's air, land, and sea frontiers from the drug threat; and (5) break foreign and domestic drug sources of supply. Measures used to accomplish those objectives, however, are riddled by problems caused by a reliance on hard control (i.e., military and quasi-military tactics) (Office of National Drug Control Policy, 2003).

Compounding matters, such belligerent tactics are financed at the expense of soft control (i.e., treatment, education, and prevention) (Austin & Irwin 2001; Walker, 2001). To reiterate, the prevailing approach to drug control diverts attention from deeper structural problems in society that contribute to greater inequality. More and more people are experiencing difficulty meeting their basic needs for survival because legitimate economic opportunities continue to dwindle (Chomsky, 2003; Herivel & Wright, 2003; Lynch, Michalowski, & Groves, 2000).

American criminal justice history offers many examples in social policy that demonstrate how good intentions sometimes lead to bad policies. Prohibition in the 1920s, for example, serves as a stark reminder of the limits of banning intoxicating substances (Matza & Morgan, 2003; Nadelmann, 1989). Likewise, the rise of America's penitentiary movement beginning in the 1820s was similarly inspired by benevolent intentions but ultimately resulted in a coercive and repressive prison machinery, a failed system that persists today (Pisciotta, 1994; Rothman, 1980, 1990). Taken together, current drug control policy ignores painful lessons from both Prohibition and a historically flawed correctional apparatus. The persistent lack of success, however, has prompted critics to argue that such strategies actually are designed to fail, so as to justify greater use of repressive measures of social control (Reiman, 2004).

Within the framework of just war theory, Richards (1995) warns of hidden intentions and unspoken agendas; unquestionably, the presence of ulterior motives can invalidate claims of a just war. The drug war is driven by several hidden intentions. Many of those unspoken agendas are the result of deep structural contradictions in the nation's political economy, including the increased militarization of social policy and the emergence of a criminal justice-industrial complex (Austin & Irwin, 2001, see Chapter 9). Kraska's (1993b, 1996, 1997; Kraska & Kappeler, 1997) research offers a useful paradigm for understanding how the U.S. military has redefined itself in ways that make it appear socially useful in the post–cold war era. As a hidden agenda, the drug war offers the military another reason for existence, particularly in the face of proposals to reduce military spending and resources. Similarly, the expansive scope of the current drug control policy provides generous funding for government agencies (and private corporations), fueling the criminal justice-industrial complex. In addition to the vast resources already allocated to law enforcement and corrections, the Office of National Drug Control Policy (2003) distributes millions of dollars—pork barrel-style—to numerous agencies in the federal government.

Many critical criminologists view criminal justice as a state-protected racket, arguing that the government has a vested interest in maintaining prevailing notions of crime that, in turn, legitimize its authority (Huggins, 1998a, 1998b; Pepinsky & Jesilow, 1985; Welch, 1998a). Along those lines of reasoning, the character of the state's drug control policy reflects the prevailing dominant ideology in which the causal relationship between crime and economic conditions is disavowed (Hall, Critcher, Jefferson, Clarke, & Roberts, 1978; Welch, Fenwick, & Roberts, 1997, 1998). The dominant ideology relies heavily on hard-control mechanisms aimed not at the social structure, but at the individual level of the problem. Likewise, critical notions of domination have been examined by scholars such as David Gil (1996), who insists that violence is socially structured according to three interacting phases. First, societal violence is initiated within and among human groups involving domination for social and economic gain, thus prompting a second stage, that of reactive counterviolence by those who are dominated and exploited. In the final phase, the dominant group or groups (e.g., the state) respond with repressive societal violence in reaction to counterviolence. Together those stages illuminate the character of socially structured violence perpetuated by vicious circles of spiraling aggression. Such violence is exacerbated further by "societal conditions that inhibit the development of individuals, social groups, and entire peoples by obstructing fulfillment of inherent human needs and potentials" (Gil, 1996, p. 78; see also Barak, 2003b; Sullivan, 1980).

The militarization of drug control also invites greater capital-intensive strategies, including the procurement of expensive technology and equipment (e.g., interdiction, surveillance, drug testing) as well as the construction of more prisons. Those capital-intensive measures also are coupled with labor-intensive needs in the form of additional manpower for law enforcement and corrections. The war on drugs creates opportunities for more money, more personnel and, most importantly, greater police power (Kappeler, Blumberg, & Potter, 2000). Despite an onslaught of criticism for its failures, current drug control policy has not been met with reductions in hard-control resources; on the contrary, its shortcomings have been compensated by greater government funding and private investment.

A final hidden agenda of the war on drugs is its attack on basic social equality—a crucial consideration for public policy in a democratic society. As shall be addressed later, the militarized drug control policy undermines individual constitutional rights (e.g., privacy, protections against unreasonable search and seizure) and perpetuates inequality by disproportionately affecting the poor and people of color.

Last Resort

Even if the war on drugs had the benefit of a just cause, legitimate authority, and right intention, it is easy to see that the militarized drug control policy is not the last resort. Clearly, other options in drug control have yet to be exhausted nor even moderately implemented, including alternatives to a militarized and criminalized drug control policy such as treatment; education; prevention; and social, political, and economic reform. In sorting the diverse opinions on drug control, there are three general schools of thought on drug control policy: public-health generalism, legalism, and cost-benefit specificism (Zimring & Hawkins, 1991). Public-health generalists point out that the consumption of psychoactive substances (including alcohol) leads to such problems as greater health treatment costs, excessive time off from work, family problems, and shortened life spans. The focus of that perspective remains on the harmfulness of substances rather than on their legality, viewing substance abuse as a disease or illness. Legalists, on the other hand, concentrate not on the personal harm inflicted on the individual, but the social harm inflicted on society; therefore, they believe that the consumption of legally prohibited substances ought to be sanctioned because such illegal behaviors strain normative boundaries and erode societal cohesion. Cost-benefit specificism balances the costs of abuse and the likelihood of reducing them by legal prohibition against the overall expense of upholding prohibitive laws. Four components of drug control strategy (supply reduction, treatment, prevention/education, and decriminalization) make up the larger debate on the war on drugs; these competing schools of thought issue different views on each of the following issues.

Supply reduction. The legalistic perspective, strongly endorsed by federal officials, proposes continued expenditures on law enforcement and interdiction to reduce the supply of illegal drugs (Office of National Drug Control Policy, 2003). In turn, it is assumed that the consumption of illegal drugs will decline. Public-health generalists are less concerned with limiting the supply of illegal drugs due to the abundance of nonprohibited drugs that have been proven harmful. Alcohol and tobacco products are advertised and marketed, producing profits for private interests. In the end, government and citizens are left with the tasks of dealing with—and paying for—the harms produced by such substances. In 2001, it was estimated that more than 430,700 Americans died due to illnesses caused by tobacco and another 110,649 died from the effects of alcohol. By comparison, illicit drugs were blamed for 16,926 deaths (Common Sense for Drug Policy, 2002; see also Musto, 1999). Unlike public-health generalists, cost-benefit specifists do not view all substances as equally harmful; for example, they contend that cocaine is more harmful than alcohol. (Critics of that perspective, however, argue that since alcohol abuse is more widespread than cocaine abuse, it constitutes a greater social problem). Accordingly, efforts to limit drugs perceived as being more harmful (such as cocaine) are supported by cost-benefit specifists.

Campaigns to reduce the supply of illegal drugs ought to be addressed in the context of market forces. Simply put, prices attached to illegal drugs are contingent upon supply and demand. Therefore, reducing the supply merely drives up the price of the drug, making trafficking more profitable and attracting those willing to take such risks. According to Leslie T. Wilkins, "The cost [of illegal drugs] is a reflection of the risk, not the type or quality of the product. Thus, we might say that, for the most part, drug pushers are not selling drugs; rather, like insurance companies, they are trading in risk" (1994, p. 151). In light of prevailing market forces, Wilkins insists that if there were no risks in peddling illegal drugs, prices would drop to levels that might even fail to attract legitimate industry.

Treatment. In the confines of the criminal justice system, rehabilitation troubles some experts who contend that punishment remains at odds with effective programs since coercion impedes lasting recovery (Gray, 2001; Walker, 2001). Despite that limitation, legalists (including proponents of the *National Drug Control Strategy*) endorse treatment and recommend that participants be forced or intimidated into treatment. Upon completion of those programs, participants are similarly coerced into abstinence by threatening them with criminal sanctions if they suffer a drug relapse. In the few prisons that offer treatment, forms of intervention may include detoxification, counseling, education and/or awareness programs, urine surveillance, and treatment in special residential units within the facilities.

Government funding for drug treatment remains insufficient, even though programs for addicts have strong public support. In California, residents backed Proposition 36 with 61% of the vote. Under the new law that took effect in 2001, first-time and second-time drug violators are subject to treatment rather than imprisonment, making this law the nation's most ambitious experiment in drug rehabilitation (Butterfield, 2001). By a substantial margin, substance abuse programs are not only cheaper than idle incarceration but are also cost-effective. In a widely cited study, *Behind Bars: Substance Abuse and America's Prison Population*, the National Center on Addiction and Substance Abuse (NCASA, 1998) estimates 70 to 80% of all inmates have committed a crime while under the influence of drugs (and/or alcohol), committed a drug crime, or used a drug on a regular basis. NCASA approximates that figure to be around 1.2 million of the more than 1.7 million offenders incarcerated. By enrolling those offenders in drug treatments while behind bars, the chances of them returning to drugs and crime is reduced. Furthermore, NCASA states that drug addicts commit an average of 100 crimes per year; therefore, a state will gain $36,700 dollars in avoided criminal justice and health care expenditures for every inmate who completes a treatment program at a cost of $6,500. The cost-benefit analysis also takes into account the assumption that each successfully treated offender will likely be employed at a salary of $21,400, producing $32,100 in overall economic benefits. According to that formula, NCASA reports that only 10% of the prisoners entering drug treatment have to succeed for the intervention to be financially justified (see Austin & Irwin, 2001; Welch, 1995a).

Prevention/Education. Whereas each of the schools of thought endorses substance-abuse prevention campaigns, they differ with regard to the content of preventative and educational messages. Legalists support antidrug propaganda and oppose the dissemination of factual informative messages. "The legalist drug message to children is that illegal drugs are a bad thing and that drug takers are bad people" (Zimring & Hawkins, 1991, p. 112). In 2003, drug czar John Walters earmarked $150 million to further a propagandistic anti-marijuana campaign, including full-page advertisements from the Office of the National Drug Control Policy aimed at generating a heightened sense of parental anxiety and moral panic, suggesting that aggressive or violent behavior—and even psychoses—are among the consequences that await young people who try marijuana" (Talvi, 2003a, p. EV1). The campaign resorts to emotionally provocative and hysterical imagery—including televised images of a teen being molested and another girl ending up with an unwanted pregnancy, the implication being that they suffered these fates because they smoked marijuana. Another commercial shows a boy accidentally shooting his friend after getting high. To date, there is no evidence that any of the ONDCP tactics are effective, including the creation of websites such as TheAntiDrug.com, Freevibe.com, TeachersGuide.org, and DrugStory.org. An independent group hired by the government to evaluate the campaign last year found that there had been "no statistically significant decline in marijuana use, to date, and some evidence of an increase in use from 2000 to 2001. . . . Also there's no tendency for those reporting more exposure to Campaign messages to hold more desirable beliefs" (Talvi 2003a, p. EV3).

Gordon (1994a, 1994b) reminds us that antidrug slogans such as the now-famous "Just Say No" are banal statements that both arouse anxiety and assuage it. As an antidrug semantic, "drugspeak" serves to legitimize law enforcement as the primary solution to America's drug crisis. By contrast, public-health generalists and cost-benefit specifists claim that revealing pure information about drugs featuring both the desirable effects (e.g., euphoria and mood-altering escape) as well as the undesirable effects (e.g., withdrawals, physiological damage) promotes an honest representation of substances. It is their view that persons who are well educated about legal and illegal drugs are more likely to avoid substance abuse than those who have been subjected to inaccurate or incomplete information concerning drugs.

While progressives continue to emphasize the value of education in drug control policy, conservatives recently have enforced measures stripping college students of financial aid as a punishment for drug violations. Although the law had been in effect since 1998, it was not fully enforced until President George W. Bush took office. Specifically, students become ineligible for federal financial aid and loans for one year after a possession conviction, or for two years after a conviction for selling drugs, unless they undergo a rehabilitation program that requires two random urine tests. Repeat offenders face permanent loss of federal aid to attend college. Republican Gary Johnson, Governor of New Mexico, points out that no other law carries such a provision. Johnson, who has sponsored state legislation to decriminalize possession of small amounts of marijuana, states, "You can rob a bank, you [can] commit murder, [or] just about any other crime and not be denied student aid, but a drug charge would deny you student aid" (Schemo, 2001, p. A12).

The penalty disproportionately affects the poor who rely on financial aid, and racial minorities who make up a large percentage of those arrested for drug offenses. Indeed, students from wealthier families who are convicted on drug charges are not adversely affected since they do not rely on financial aid. Of the more than 10 million students who applied for federal financial aid in 2000, more than 9,000 were found to be ineligible due to drug convictions. Shawn Heller, who founded Students for a Sensible Drug Policy, reminds us that during the 2000 presidential campaign, Vice-President Al Gore acknowledged having smoked marijuana while in college. George W. Bush declined to answer questions about whether he had used cocaine and other drugs, saying, "When I was young and irresponsible, I was young and irresponsible." To that statement, Heller responded, "If you're president of the United States of America, you don't have to answer these questions, but if you're coming from a poor family and trying to get an education, you do" (Schemo, 2001, p. A12). Making matters worse, the Department of Education has been applying the law retroactively to any aid applicant with a drug conviction in the last couple of years.

As another mainstay in the war on drugs, drug testing of students has been criticized for its violation of privacy. Still, its supporters claim that urinalysis serves as a significant deterrent, and the U.S. Supreme Court issued its approval of such testing in 2002. Contradicting that stance, the first large-scale national study, released in 2003, found that drug testing in schools does not deter drug use any more than doing no screening at all. After studying 76,000 students, Dr. Lloyd D. Johnston at the University of Michigan, concluded, "It's the kind of intervention that doesn't win the hearts and minds of children. I don't think it brings about any constructive changes in their attitudes about drugs or their belief in the dangers associated with using them" (Winter, 2003, p. A1). Graham Boyd of the American Civil Liberties Union, who argued against drug testing before the Supreme Court, points out that the justices did not have the benefit of Johnston's research when they ruled that such tactics were necessary to combat drug use. "Now there should be no reason for a school to impose an intrusive or even insulting drug test when it's not going to do anything about student drug use," said Boyd. (Winter, 2003, p. A14).

Decriminalization. Public-health generalists favor decriminalization because it reconceptualizes substance abuse from a criminal justice problem into a public health issue. In doing so, it also invites experts to discuss more openly the harm caused by legal drugs (e.g., alcohol and prescription medication). Cost-benefit specifists similarly endorse the decriminalization of less harmful drugs and the continued prohibition of those deemed more harmful (see Nadelmann, 1991). Distinguishing between legalization and decriminalization is crucial to a sensible understanding of drug control. Legalization of drugs parallels the regulation of drugs that are currently legal, such as alcohol and tranquilizers. Decriminalization is considered less drastic, insofar as some drug offenses (e.g., marijuana possession) would not be subjected to punitive sanctions but instead processed as minor infractions similar to traffic violations. As a result, the violator would be issued a summons, required to appear in court, and made to pay a fine. Although advocates of legalization and supporters of decriminalization do not agree on all aspects of drug control policy, they do concur with three basic assumptions: under legalization, drug use and abuse would not rise beyond current rates; some illegal drugs are not as harmful as widely believed; the criminalization of drugs creates more problems than benefits (Gray, 2001; Husak, 2000, 2002).

Serving as a useful model, the Netherlands in 1976 decriminalized the use and sale of marijuana and decriminalized (de facto) the possession and sale of small amounts of other drugs. Still, marijuana and hashish are heavily regulated by the Dutch government, which restricts consumption to licensed coffee shops that are required to enforce age eligibility. By design, Dutch police serve as conduits between drug addicts and treatment services; consequently, there are fewer arrests, trials, and convictions for drug violations. Evaluation studies of the Dutch policy report that decriminalization has not led to any increase in the use of drugs. In fact, reported drug use among the 12 to 70 age group (especially among secondary school students) is higher in the United States than in the Netherlands. In addition, since decriminalization was introduced in the Netherlands, there has been a reduction in the amount of crime associated with drug use and trafficking (Chambliss, 1995; Grapendaal, Leuw, & Nelen, 1992; Gray, 2001; Vliet, 1990; Wijngaart, 1990).

Finally, the criminalization of drugs remains counterproductive in that it contributes to street crime owing to the profit motive. Legalization/decriminalization proposes to eliminate the profit motive from the drug trade, thereby reducing the form of violence common among drug dealers. Moreover, spending fewer tax dollars on expensive armaments for the war on drugs (i.e., law enforcement, courts, corrections) means that greater funding would be available for health care, education, housing, and other social services (Welch, 2004a).

Justice in the War on Drugs: Evaluating the Means

Proportionality

While assessing the means of fighting the war on drugs, proportionality requires that we weigh the overall harm caused by a militarized drug control policy against the damage sustained by non-belligerent means. Clearly, the war on drugs does not sufficiently remedy problems associated with drugs; on the contrary, it merely deepens and escalates such problems. Compounding matters, crime and drug controversies are manipulated and exploited for political purposes. Perhaps the most significant harm to a democratic society from the war on drugs is its attack on social equality. With scant recognition of the root causes of drug use, the state has accelerated the war on drugs in low-income neighborhoods. Within the framework of structured violence, drug consumption can be understood as a novocaine used to alter one's mood to escape the harsh reality of domination. By its neglect, the state contributes to adverse social conditions, and to make matters worse, it imposes a form of repressive social control that punishes poor people who resort to psychoactive escapism (see Gil, 1996; Sullivan, 1980).

Whereas the war on drugs has failed to reduce the supply or consumption of illegal drugs, it *has* succeeded in increasing the number of arrests, convictions, and incarcerations. The war on drugs is waged less often against the so-called king pins and more often against low-level drug violators who are typically minority, poor, and have few resources to defend themselves legally against ambitious law enforcement campaigns. The percentage of state prisoners incarcerated for a drug violation nearly quadrupled from 1980 (6%) to 1996 (23%). Likewise, the percentage of drug offenders among federal prisoners jumped to 60% in 1996 from 25% in 1980. The increase in drug violators accounted for nearly three-quarters of the total increase in federal inmates and one-third of the total increase in state inmates during that 16-year span (Bureau of Justice Statistics, 1998; Menhard, Mihalic, & Huizinga, 2001; Spohn & Holleran, 2002).

Drug enforcement campaigns contribute to the disproportionate numbers of African Americans in corrections facilities because police target minority communities where drug dealing is more visible and it's easier to make arrests. African Americans represent 12% of the U.S. population, 13% of drug users, 35% of arrests for drug possession, 55% of convictions for drug possession, and 74% of prison sentences for drug possession (Mauer, 1999). The increasing number of drug offenses accounted for 27% of the total growth among black inmates, 15% of the total growth among Hispanic inmates, and 14% of the growth among white inmates between 1990 and 1999. In 1999, 144,700 blacks were imprisoned for drug offenses, compared to 52,100 Hispanics and 50,700 whites (Beck & Harrison, 2001). In light of those elements of classism and racism, critics insist that the war on drugs in low-income neighborhoods targets those victimized by chronic unemployment caused by a post-industrial economy. Paradoxically, minorities who have been marginalized and excluded from trends of prosperity currently serve as the principal raw materials for an expanding prison industrial complex (Welch, 2003e, 2004a; see Chapter 9).

Among the various institutional biases in the American criminal justice system disproportionately affecting people of color and the poor, is the assignment of disparate penalties for similar drug offenses. Even though experts conclude that the pharmacological differences between crack and powdered cocaine are negligible (Hatsukami & Fischman, 1996), many legislators support tougher sanctions for crack. Proponents argue that the nature of trafficking crack invites greater violence and gang activity, but critics disagree and insist that the policy is unfair, impractical, and perhaps in the end profoundly racist (Jones, 1995, p. A1). According to the Bureau of Justice Statistics (1995), the average federal drug sentence (in 1994) for trafficking crack was 133 months in prison, whereas the trafficking of powdered cocaine drew an average of 94 months. In 1994, 90% of those convicted of federal crack offenses were African American and 3.5% were white. By contrast, 25.9% of those convicted on federal powdered cocaine violations were white, 29.7% were African American, and 42.8% were Hispanic (Bureau of Justice Statistics, 1995).

In 1996, the U.S. Supreme Court refused to address an egregious racial bias in the Los Angeles criminal justice system. Twenty-four black defendants, all charged under federal law with crack offenses, cited compelling statistical evidence confirming racial prejudice and discrimination. Between 1990 and 1992, over 200 white crack dealers were prosecuted by state authorities, while none was prosecuted by federal authorities, and federal penalties for crack offenses are far more severe than state penalties (*U.S. v. Armstrong*, 1996; see also *Edwards v. U.S.*, 1996). Adding to the growing body of evidence of racial biases in drug control, the U.S. Sentencing Commission (1995) reports that only minorities were prosecuted under federal law for crack in 17 states and many cities (see Egan, 1999).

More recently, in 2002, the U.S. Department of Justice remained steadfastly opposed to changing the law to reduce prison terms for crack offenses, arguing that the disparities were not as large as generally believed. When faced with the evidence that showed that drug sentences unfairly punish blacks, Deputy Attorney General Larry D. Thompson stated, "The current federal policy and guidelines for sentencing crack cocaine are appropriate" (Lewis, 2002, p. A24). Thompson added that if there are to be any changes, the sentences for powdered cocaine offenses should be increased. The Justice Department analyzed 46,413 cases of those convicted and sentenced under federal guidelines from 1996 and 2000. The study found that the average sentence for possession of five grams of crack cocaine with intent to distribute was 71 months, compared to 13 months for those involving five grams of powder. Thompson insisted that some disparity was justified because "higher penalties for crack offenses appropriately reflected the greater harm posed by crack cocaine" (Lewis, 2002, p. A24). Critics flatly disagree. Federal Judge Terry Hatter, Jr., a fierce opponent of the sentencing guidelines, said, "If there is any disparity, it should be the reverse. There should be higher penalties for powder. I mean, you can't make the crack form without having the powder form first, and the powder form comes from outside [the country]" (Lewis, 2002, p. A24). Hatter elaborated on his position, saying that the government was associating crack with crime because it was sold in impoverished neighborhoods where crime was already rampant. Opponents of current drug sentencing guidelines recently received support from conservative lawmakers. Republican Senators Orrin Hatch and Jeff Sessions proposed that the law be changed by raising the amount of crack that mandated a five-year sentence while reducing the amount of powdered cocaine for the same sentence (see Kautt & Spohn, 2002).

Racial disparities also are found in drug rehabilitation in that whites are more likely to be assigned to coveted treatment programs in prison than are African Americans. "Yet those who receive drug treatment are more likely to be paroled and much less likely to re-offend upon release. Because African-American addicts have less access to drug treatment, they are more likely than white addicts to stay in prison longer under harsher conditions of confinement" (Donziger, 1996b, p. 120). The existence of such programs suggests that the medical model of treatment (soft control) remains available for white, middle-income users, whereas the military and punitive models (hard control) are reserved for users among racial minorities and the impoverished.

In sum, the current drug control policy violates the principle of proportionality because its militarized tactics disproportionately target the poor and people of color (Welch, Bryan, & Wolff, 1998). Even if the racial and socioeconomic biases of the war on drugs were corrected, it is unlikely that prevailing strategies of drug control through militarization and criminalization would be considered just. Taken further, it is difficult to imagine a war on drugs that does not adversely affect the poor and minorities because drug control strategies are mechanisms of a social structure predicated on controlling—rather than liberating—oppressed people.

Discrimination

Discrimination requires that violence remain within combatant circles of war, and not reach—indiscriminately—into the innocent population. In military parlance, casualties among innocent victims are known as collateral damage. Due to the militarized drug control policy, collateral damage manifests in persons harmed by overzealous and corrupt law enforcement officers (e.g., false arrests, convictions, imprisonments) and children of drug violators sentenced to prison.

Convinced that a half-blind, 61-year-old millionaire owner was growing marijuana on his Malibu ranch, a Los Angeles County police unit embarked on an early morning raid. When the rancher appeared from his bedroom with a pistol in his hand, the detective shot him dead. In a subsequent search of the $5 million estate, no marijuana plants were found. The local District Attorney later concluded that the Los Angeles County Sheriff's Department was motivated partly by a desire to seize and forfeit the ranch for the government, thus exposing the legal excesses in the war on drugs (Baum, 1996). Once again, events such as this one are indicative of key economic forces that motivate managers of the state and its criminal justice machinery to accumulate property and wealth.

The criminalization of drugs creates opportunities for those inside as well as outside the law. The precise scope of police corruption, however, is difficult to measure because it tends to be concealed by government and law enforcement officials in an effort to minimize embarrassment. Still, some egregious violations by police are publicized. In a widely cited controversy, officers in the 30th Precinct in New York City were investigated by Internal Affairs, leading to the prosecution of dozens of officers later convicted of dealing drugs, illegally breaking into property, taking payoffs from narcotics dealers, and conspiring to violate civil rights.

In one incident, a pair of officers received $16,000 from a drug sale; those officers also stole a bag containing $115,000 from an apartment they illegally entered (Krauss, 1996). The impact of the drug scandal at the 30th Precinct promises to be felt for years. In all, 25 police officers were convicted; 125 cases were dismissed; 98 defendants were cleared (due to perjured testimony by police, a tactic known as "testilying"); at least 25 civil cases were filed against the police department; and thus far, $1.3 million has been paid in awards and settlements (Kocieniewski, 1997; Nossiter, 1996). Similarly, the City of Philadelphia paid nearly a million dollars in compensatory damages to Reverend Betty Patterson, a Baptist minister framed by the police as a cocaine mastermind and sent to jail for three years ("Wrongful jailing to cost Philadelphia $1 million," 1996b; see also Dewan & Rashbaum, 2003; Terry, 1996).

In one of the more bizarre cases stemming from the war on drugs, Thomas Coleman carried out an extensive 18-month investigation as part of the Panhandle Regional Narcotics Task Force in Texas. Coleman's work earned him praise from the law enforcement community, who named him Lawman of the Year. The media followed suit, capturing on camera the 46 people Coleman arrested during his undercover campaign against drugs. However, Coleman's unorthodox tactics began to raise doubts about the guilt of those convicted, mostly poor and black residents of Tulia, a dusty town of 5,000. No drugs, guns, or large sums of cash were ever seized. Coleman worked alone and did not record his drug purchases. His investigation notes sometimes consisted of vague information jotted down on his leg, much of which was contradicted by other, more compelling evidence. As an official inquiry into the drug sweep took form, Coleman's lies and racist motives were too clear to ignore. Eventually, the courts began releasing the 38 people wrongly incarcerated, some of whom had been sentenced to terms of up to 90 years (Davey, 2003; Herbert, 2002). As those incidents suggest, people most vulnerable to abuse from overzealous and corrupt police are those lacking social, political, and economic power. Likewise, the erosion of constitutional protections (e.g., protection from unlawful search and seizure, the right to privacy) disproportionately affects those people who truly need such protections—namely, the poor and minorities.

Incarcerating drug offenders who are also mothers produces another form of collateral damage, namely its effect on their children. As of the year 2000, drug trafficking accounts for 30% of women sentenced to local jails, 34% of those incarcerated in state prisons, and 72% of those confined in federal prisons. Approximately half of women offenders confined in state prisons had been using alcohol, drugs, or both at the time of the offense for which they were incarcerated (Greenfeld & Snell, 2000). Nearly 7 in 10 women under correctional sanction have children under the age of 18, including 72% of women on probation, 70% of women held in local jails, 65% of women in state prisons, and 59% of women in federal institutions. Those women, on average, have 2 to 3 children who are minors. In all, 1.3 million children are directly affected by their mothers' correctional sanction (Greenfeld & Snell, 2000; see also Sharp, 2003). Adding to the problem of parents behind bars, male inmates in state prisons are estimated to be fathers to about 1.1 million children under age 18, about 11 times the number of minor children attributable to female inmates (Greenfeld & Snell, 2001). One can only imagine the long-term negative effects that incarcerating mothers and fathers who commit criminal offenses will have on future generations. Compounding the tragedy is the realization that many of those offenders are nonviolent, and are not a threat to society. Common sense suggests that the vast majority of those offenders could be supervised in the community while enabling them to care for their children (Chesney-Lind, 2002; Richie, 2002).

The links between the war on drugs and public assistance became increasingly clear in 1996 when President Clinton enacted the Welfare Reform Act of 1996. That law includes a provision denying welfare bene-fits to more than 92,000 women convicted of drug violations as well as their 135,000 children (Rubinstein & Mukamal, 2002). Oddly, ex-cons who had served time for murder or other violent offenses are fully eligible for welfare benefits. The law targets primarily the poor, especially women of color, considering that more than 48% of those affected by the statute are African American or Latina (Ridgeway, 2002; Tourigny, 2001). States can opt out of the lifetime ban, but 42 still enforce it. In many instances, the person requesting welfare benefits is only a minor or first-time offender who is a single parent in need of treatment rather than punishment (Schwartz, 2002; Sentencing Project, 2002; Thompson, 2002).

Finally, since the war on drugs involves American armed forces maneuvering outside our borders, collateral damage remains an ethical issue in U.S. foreign policy, most notably in Latin America (Ehrenfeld, 1990; Riley, 1996). As mentioned, the U.S. invasion of Panama resulted in horrific atrocities, including the killing of an estimated 5,000 civilians, many of whom were buried in mass graves (Johns, 1996). Similar viola-tions of human rights have been documented in several South American nations, for instance in Peru, where the United States has forged a misguided alliance with the Peruvian military known to have undertaken a brutal campaign of torture, "disappearance," and extrajudicial execution (Huggins, 1998a, 1998b; Kirk, 1991).

Conclusion

To reiterate, just war theory rests on the premise that military action may be considered just, provided that each and every criterion is satisfied; however, if any of the criteria fail to be supported, war is then ruled unjust, unjustly fought, or both (Kunkel & Taylor, 1995). Based on this evaluation, it may be concluded that the current militarized drug war is both unjust and unjustly fought. There is compelling evidence negating each of the requirements of a just war. Beginning with the criterion of just cause, there is a lack of the substantial aggression needed to justify a measured use of violence. What is more, nonbelligerent correctives (i.e., treatment, education, prevention) are neither hopeless nor too costly; by contrast, belligerent measures are not only costly, but given their record of failure, remain hopeless. In the area of legitimate authority, it is proposed that public policy concerning drugs be removed from the domain of criminal justice officials. Efforts to reduce drug use would better be directed by public health, education, and economic advisors who together can propose social realignments that contribute to the fulfillment of inherent human needs and potentials (Welch, Bryan, & Wolff, 1999).

Although the Office of National Drug Control Policy (2003) proposes several admirable goals intended to establish a right intention, there exist several hidden intentions. The war on drugs significantly contributes to an expanding criminal justice-industrial complex that benefits private interests along with numerous government agencies. Coercive antidrug tactics have been accelerated partly because it is profitable to do so. Due to the availability and cost-effectiveness of nonbelligerent measures (i.e., treatment, education, prevention), however, a militarized drug strategy is clearly not a last resort. In assessing the two remaining requirements of just war theory, this chapter finds that the militarized drug strategy lacks proportionality since its reliance on hard measures of control merely deepens problems associated with drugs. For instance, the war on drugs perpetuates inequality by disproportionately penalizing the poor and people of color. Finally, coercive drug control policies are carried out in ways that are indiscriminant, causing innocent people to be victimized by an overzealous criminal justice system and corrupt police.

In proposing an alternative to the war on drugs, it is clear that medicalization—much like militarization—suffers from institutional biases in that it is aimed at individuals rather than the social arrangements. One thing is certain—drug dependencies are not likely to be contained by relying solely on rehabilitation. A strategy exclusively based on treatment not only would divert attention from its fundamental causes (e.g., repression and alienation rooted in social and economic inequality) but also would transfer authority from law enforcement agencies to a medical establishment. Whereas the medicalization of drug abuse is widely viewed as a humane alternative to criminalization, there remains a dark side of rehabilitation as a form of public policy. That is, the medical model empowers a class of experts and professionals acting as agents of social control but under the guise of humane intervention (Lesieur & Welch, 1991, 1995, 2000). The medical model is further confounded by socioeconomic considerations, since its experts and professionals derive their financial well-being and status from the same economic system as those who carry out state mandates. Consequently, medical personnel may not be any less inclined to use their authority to manage and regulate those whom the system casts an evil eye upon.

The critical perspective expressed herein does not oppose substance abuse treatment; on the contrary, it supports rehabilitation fully on the condition that it is voluntary and not coerced by the state or by a class of professional experts and technicians. The larger goal of reducing dependency on drugs will not be achieved by taking strictly a medical and individualistic approach. Attention must be directed at injustices produced by social hierarchies and political-economic infrastructures that obstruct the fulfillment of inherent human needs. Contradictions in the social structure foster the need for people to consume drugs while simultaneously becoming addicted to state control. In reconceptualizing the drug problem, it is important to realize that social, political, and economic reforms are necessary to reverse the ironies of criminal justice, particularly those that reproduce inequality, exploitation, and repression.

End-of-Chapter Questions

1. In what ways has American drug policy become increasingly militarized?

2. Describe the four moral reasons used to justify the war on drugs.

3. Describe the means that are utilized in the war on drugs.

4. How would a public health approach to drug dependency benefit society?

5

Health Care Crisis Behind Bars

Keith Carter is doing time for armed robbery. He is also HIV positive and understandably concerned about taking his medications as prescribed, not an easy task in the Florida prison system. Crixivan, one of his daily drugs, has strict instructions dictating food intake since it can interfere with its absorption. Ironically, the prison staff distributed his medication at mealtime. Carter explains his predicament: "I can't eat till an hour after I take it. If I eat, I have to wait two hours. For the longest time, they would wake us up at 8:30 in the morning, give us our medication, then take us directly to breakfast" (Cusac, 2003, p. 198). Carter was forced to choose between eating breakfast and taking his medication properly. Anxious about maintaining his health, Carter began skipping breakfast and would later purchase extra food at the prison canteen. The meal schedule at night also conflicted with Crixivan. "So, I would keep it in my cheek and not swallow it, then get out of there and put it in my pocket. I did this for months. It was very risky. I could have been locked up in disciplinary confinement for trying to save my own life" (Cusac, 2003, p. 198).

Throughout key periods in correctional history, prison reformers have labored to improve the conditions of confinement. However, the current penal harm movement, a campaign to make prison conditions harsher, threatens to offset humane progress by lobbying for longer sentences and eliminating or scaling down what they call amenities, such as personal clothing, televisions, recreation, and educational programs (Clear, 1994; Cullen, 1995; Welch, 1997b). Polarizing matters, some penal harm enthusiasts believe medical care ought to be viewed as a luxury, suggesting that prisons roll back their commitment to health care so as to maximize the punitive purpose of incarceration (Vaughn & Carroll, 1998; Welch, Weber, & Edwards, 2000). The issue is subject to intense debate. There are many health care professionals who advocate the principle of equivalence, drawing no differences between patients in the free world and those under lock and key (Anno, Faiver, & Harness, 1996; Harding, 1987). Proponents of penal harm conversely argue that prisoners ought to receive fewer benefits in terms of medical care than persons residing in the free world. But critics insist that denying medical treatment to prisoners as a means of inflicting pain and suffering violates the Hippocratic oath, raising serious ethical questions in the administration of correctional health care (Vaughn & Smith, 1999).

As addressed in the previous chapter, the war on drugs continues to import a larger number of addicts into prisons, many of whom are in dire need of health care. The incarceration of IV drug addicts infected with HIV/AIDS is straining the medical capabilities of corrections. Moreover, due to the drug war's lengthy mandatory minimum sentences, corrections officials must contend with the daunting task of administering health care to an aging prison population. This chapter explores those concerns, illuminating further the ironies of imprisonment. It begins by considering that metaphors abound in conservative interpretations of morality, particularly in the realm of sickness. Those perspectives affect tremendously the ways in which persons with HIV/AIDS are treated in prison. While focusing on HIV/AIDS and tuberculosis (TB), the chapter also examines the long-term budgetary and programmatic prospects for an elderly prison population. It concludes with insights into the phenomenology of imprisonment, suffering, and illness.

HIV/AIDS: Metaphors and Morality

In *AIDS and Its Metaphors* (1989), Susan Sontag delivers an interpretive narrative of HIV/AIDS, blending historical and literary references that parallel the sociologies of knowledge, medicine, and deviance. Much of her discussion underscores the processes and consequences of stigma and social control by illuminating the potency of metaphors, the tendency to give a thing a name that belongs to something else. Sociologically, the construction of metaphors is an initial process of labeling; that reification allows those who are perceived as different from so-called normal people to be stigmatized and marginalized (Becker, 1963; Goffman, 1963; Schur, 1971). Sontag, drawing on her previous work *Illness as Metaphor* (1980), reminds us of society's propensity to interpret diseases through the prism of morality and punishment. HIV/AIDS has not been confined to moral and punitive connotations, but rather is subject to an array of metaphors.

> AIDS has a dual metaphoric genealogy. As a micro-process, it is described the way cancer is, as an invasion. When the focus is transmission of the disease, an older metaphor, reminiscent of syphilis, is invoked: pollution. (One gets it from the blood or sexual fluids of infected people or from contaminated blood products.) (Sontag, 1989, p. 17)

That particular metaphor for HIV/AIDS moves in opposite directions. Inwardly, the disease attacks the body of the infected, while outwardly it poses a threat to others. Not only is stigma imposed on those infected, the outward threat (contagiousness) posed by HIV/AIDS spawns another form of societal reaction, namely moral panic—a turbulent and exaggerated response to a social problem (Cohen, 1985, 2003). HIV/AIDS is subject to demonization, evangelical condemnation, and moral judgments. In a nationally televised sermon, Jerry Falwell of the Moral Majority proclaimed that HIV/AIDS affecting homosexuals represented a "lethal judgment of God on America for endorsing this vulgar, perverted and reprobate lifestyle" (Bayer & Kirp, 1992, p. 34). In a more nuanced form of moral judgment, the Florida Department of Health in 2003 published an AIDS information brochure featuring biblical references and telling people to "answer Jesus' call" by reaching out to people with HIV and AIDS. The American Civil Liberties Union complained to the state of Florida, demanding that the brochure be recalled (Canedy, 2003). Integrating such moral metaphors with medical constructs suggests that the illness is brought on by the lack of moral hygiene, insinuating that homosexual sex is both immoral and unhealthy (see Welch, 2000b).

An understandable public reaction to HIV/AIDS is fear. Thus, it is crucial to turn to the scientific community so as to understand the nature of the illness, not only in the hope of eventually developing a cure but also to reduce the fear and paranoia as well as guard against infection. Regrettably, not all members of the scientific community have acted responsibly. Some researchers have inaccurately characterized HIV/AIDS only to inflame fears and incite hysteria among the public. For example, the famous sex researchers Masters and Johnson published a popular book about HIV/AIDS in 1988. In *Crisis: Heterosexual Behavior in the Age of AIDS,* the authors made false statements about the nature of the transmission of HIV, claims that ran counter to what was known about the disease at the time. They asserted that the illness had "clearly broken out" among heterosexuals and that it could be contracted from saliva and hard surfaces such as toilet seats. When confronted by the Presidential Commission on AIDS about such claims, Masters and Johnson conceded that they had no independent data to support their conclusions (Sirica, 1988). Critics charged that Masters and Johnson had knowingly disseminated false information about HIV/AIDS in an effort to capitalize commercially on book profits; in doing so, they stoked fear among the public and reinforced the myths and misconceptions about HIV/AIDS (see Thomas, 1985; Welch, 1989).

Originating from the traditional enforcement of conventional morality, stigma is a mark of social disgrace. In ancient Greece, unusual bodily markings were construed as signs of moral inferiority; similarly, law-breakers were physically branded for the purpose of exposing their moral defects. During early Christian times, bodily signs in the form of eruptive blossoms on the skin were interpreted as being emblematic of holy grace, suggesting supernatural qualities. However, less aesthetic imperfections were believed to be indicative of physical and moral defects. Nathaniel Hawthorne's novel *The Scarlet Letter* (1850/1962) remains a compelling example of how colonial American communities publicly punished and humiliated women for moral—especially sexual—transgressions. Contemporary understanding of stigma is largely indebted to the work of sociologist Erving Goffman, author of *Stigma: Notes on the Management of Spoiled Identity* (1963). Goffman demonstrates how stigma devalues and disqualifies some people from full social acceptance. Stigma has numerous sources: physical (e.g., illnesses, injuries, disfigurements), documentary or character (e.g., mental illness, chronic unemployment, a prison record), and contextual (e.g., keeping "bad company"). Stigma that is ascribed or assigned to a person at birth is known as tribal (or class) stigma, tainting all members of a particular race, ethnic group, or religion. Tribal stigma also connotes moral transgressions because it is inherited from the sins of one's parents.

Complex stigma attached to prisoners with HIV/AIDS actually is a configuration of several attributes—physical, documentary or character, contextual, and tribal—all of which are interpreted through the lens of morality. Physically, inmates with HIV/AIDS are devalued because they are afflicted with a contagious and potentially lethal illness. Prisoners with HIV/AIDS typically became infected by injecting illicit drugs into their bodies with unclean needles or by having sexual contact with infected partners, either heterosexually or, even more stigmatizing, homosexually. Due to the ways they contracted HIV/AIDS, those inmates are further discredited for lack of moral character and for keeping "bad company." The stigma of HIV/AIDS is potent, explaining why many of those infected refuse testing and treatment. Sheila Morris, an HIV-positive prisoner in Washington, D.C., concurs: "You have a lot of people who know they're [HIV] positive who are in denial. I am surprised by people who are sick and won't admit it. They're more willing to admit they're drug addicts or murderers or pedophiles than admit they're sick and get care for it" (Purdy, 1997, p. 28). Compounding their stigma, prisoners with HIV/AIDS are convicted felons and since many of them are impoverished people of color from the inner city, they are ascribed a tribal (class) stigma.

Throughout history, the interpretation of plagues and epidemics has been typically twofold. First, plagues have been depicted in moral terms—sent by a higher power as a punishment for society's sins; second, plagues have been depicted as coming from a foreign place. Sontag (1989) notes that the syphilis epidemic in Europe during the 15th century, the bubonic plague during the 18th century, and the outbreaks of cholera during the 19th century were all characterized as dreaded foreign diseases. Plagues were commonly viewed as pollution from alien and exotic lands. HIV/AIDS "is thought to have started in the 'dark continent,' then spread to Haiti, then to the United States and to Europe, then . . . It is understood as a tropical disease: another manifestation from the so-called Third World" (Sontag, 1989, pp. 51–52). Popular beliefs about the origin of HIV/AIDS—often inaccurately described as a plague—have fueled anti-African (black) prejudice in the Americas, Europe, and Asia.

> The subliminal connection made between HIV/AIDS and notions about a primitive past, and the many hypotheses that have been fielded about possible transmission from animals (a disease of green monkeys? African swine fever?) cannot help but activate a familiar set of stereotypes about animality, sexual license, and blacks. (Sontag, 1989, p. 52; see also Huber & Schneider, 1992)

Throughout history, urbanization also has been blamed for plagues, epidemics, and the spread of numerous diseases. Whereas rural communities have been long cherished as pure, simple, and wholesome, cities are symbolic of crime, vice, and disease—aggravated by an influx of minorities and immigrants. Not surprisingly, conservative extremists proclaim that HIV/AIDS is another symptom of the immorality of urban life, specifically homosexuality and illicit drug use (see Shilts, 1987; Welch, 2000b).

Prisoners With HIV/AIDS
as a Problem Population

In corrections, the term "problem population" is frequently used to refer to prisoners who require special, in many cases medical, attention, including the infirm, the elderly, the pregnant, and inmates with various psychiatric needs. Among the most pressing medical issues in correctional management is HIV/AIDS. According to the Bureau of Justice Statistics, in 1999, 2.3% of state prisoners, 0.9% of federal prisoners, and 1.7% of local jail inmates were known to be infected with HIV. Overall, correctional authorities reported that 24,607 state prisoners, 1,159 federal prisoners, and 8,615 local inmates were known to be HIV positive. Of those known to be HIV positive in all U.S. prisons, 6,642 were confirmed AIDS cases, while 17,718 either showed symptoms of HIV infection or were asymptomatic. Of those in jail, 3,081 had confirmed AIDS. The nationwide rate of confirmed AIDS cases among the prison population (0.60%) was five times greater than the rate in the general population (0.12%) (Maruschak, 2001).

The percentage of the custodial population known to be HIV positive has remained relatively stable from 1995 (2.3%) to 1999 (2.1%); however, the number of AIDS-related deaths has dramatically declined from 1,010 in 1995 to 242 in 1999. It is important to stress that there are large differences in rates of HIV infection between male (2.1%) and female prisoners (3.4%). In nine states, more than 5% of all female inmates were known to be HIV positive, and in three states, over 20% of female inmates were known to be HIV positive: Nevada (30.6%), the District of Columbia (22.4%), and New York (21.5%). Other differences in the pattern of HIV infection are found regionally. In the state of New York, more than a quarter of all prison inmates (7,000) are known to be HIV positive; similarly, New York City (the second-largest jail jurisdiction) holds the most jail inmates known to be HIV positive, 1,165 (7% of its prison population). Three states house nearly half of all HIV-infected inmates in state prisons, namely New York (7,000), Florida (2,633), and Texas (2,520). Those states also had the largest number of confirmed

AIDS cases among its prisoners: New York (1,170), Texas (994), and Florida (804) (Maruschak, 2001). Finally, HIV is more prevalent among black and Latino prisoners (of low socioeconomic status) than among white prisoners (see Flavin, 2002; Inciardi, 2002).

Myths and Misconceptions

After years of medical and scientific research demonstrating that HIV/AIDS cannot be transmitted through casual contact, many criminal justice and security personnel still behave according to myths and misconceptions. In 1995, fifty gay and lesbian officials were invited to the White House where four security guards wore plastic gloves while conducting routine security checks on the officials' briefcases and other personal belongings (Kappeler, Blumberg, & Potter, 2000). In corrections facilities, many staff members also stray from medical and scientific knowledge and rely more on exaggerated fears in shaping their views of HIV/AIDS; contributing to those misconceptions are deep-seated anxieties and prejudices against the impoverished, urban minorities, IV drug users, and homosexuals. A common fear among correctional officers is that they will contract HIV while performing their duties, even though the Centers for Disease Control and Prevention (CDC) have not documented a single case of occupational transmission among correctional officers (or police officers) (Hammett, Harmon, & Maruschak, 1999; see also Flavin, 1998). Nevertheless, some offenders with HIV have been sentenced harshly by the courts for engaging in behaviors while incarcerated that in fact pose relatively little health risk to others; appellate courts in Georgia, Indiana, New Jersey, and Texas have upheld attempted homicide charges against HIV-infected prisoners who bit or spit on correctional staff.

In scenarios involving spitting, laboratory tests reveal that HIV is present in saliva but only in a very few infected persons; moreover, tests indicated that the quantity of HIV in saliva is minute, making transmission extremely unlikely (Centers for Disease Control and Prevention, 1997). In Texas, an HIV-positive prisoner was convicted of attempted murder for spitting in the face of a correctional officer and was sentenced to life imprisonment (*Weeks v. Texas,* 1992). Curtis Weeks testified at trial that he was provoked to spit at the guard after being denied bathroom facilities while being transported between two prisons. To no avail, an expert witness for the prisoner testified that it is impossible to transmit HIV by spitting and reported that there had never been a documented case of such transmission.

Risks of contracting HIV through biting also are remote. Researchers conclude that "the transmission of HIV through human bites is biologically possible but remains unlikely, epidemiologically insignificant, and as yet, not well documented" (Richman & Richman, 1993, p. 402). But in New Jersey, an HIV-positive prisoner was convicted of attempted murder for biting a correctional officer and was sentenced to 25 years (*New Jersey v. Smith,* 1993). The Appellate Division was not concerned whether HIV can be transmitted by biting as long as the inmate believed that it could. During the scuffle in which the officer was bitten, the inmate was reported to have shouted, "Now die, you pig! Die from what I have" (Sullivan, 1993, p. B-7). The trial judge instructed the jury: "Impossibility is not a defense to the charge of attempted murder. That is because our law, our criminal statutes, punish conduct based on state of mind" (Sullivan, 1993, p. B-7). The prosecution maintained that whether the biting could transmit HIV was legally irrelevant, but the appellants argued that Smith "was as likely to have caused the death of [corrections officers] by biting them as he was to have caused their deaths by sticking pins in dolls bearing their likenesses" ("NJ Inmate Argues for Reversal," 1992, p. 1). Attorneys for the inmate insisted that the guilty verdict and 25-year sentence were not founded on current medical evidence or sound legal reasoning but rather were driven by public hysteria regarding HIV/AIDS. Biting occurrences have led to other tragic incidents. Following a confrontation in which an HIV-positive prisoner bit a corrections officer, nine officers retaliated with a severe beating of the prisoner. Later, the prisoner attempted suicide and bled to death while chained to a bed in the psychiatric unit (Dougherty, 1998; see also Siegal, 2002b).

Regarding altercations with infected persons, transmission of HIV through open wounds has been documented in the medical literature (O'Farrell, Tovey, & Morgan-Capner, 1992). Although such cases are rare and have not involved criminal justice personnel, public safety workers are advised to follow CDC (1997) guidelines by keeping all open wounds bandaged and wearing gloves when anticipating contact with blood (or body fluids containing visible blood). Being wounded by HIV-contaminated needles also remains a concern of those working in criminal justice because such injuries do present a risk—albeit a relatively low one—of HIV transmission; experts recommend that safety procedures be followed to reduce the likelihood of these incidents (Richman & Richman, 1993).

Another popular myth suggests that HIV/AIDS is spreading rapidly within the correctional population. That myth is driven by the concerns over homosexual rape and IV drug use among inmates, as well as by a general misunderstanding of how HIV is transmitted. As will be discussed in Chapter 6, the prevalence of homosexual rape in correctional facilities is greatly exaggerated. While transmission can occur during incarceration, it is a relatively infrequent event, and at this time there is no evidence to support the claim that there is widespread transmission of HIV/AIDS among inmates while behind bars (Hammett et al., 1999).

Confronting myths about HIV/AIDS is crucial because misinformation inflames fear and hysteria, resulting in discriminatory management practices. Louise K. Nolley, a prisoner with AIDS, was awarded $155,000 for what a judge called humiliating and improper treatment at the Erie County Jail, where she was held on charges of forgery and passing a check without sufficient funds. Staff placed Nolley in a forensic unit usually reserved for suicidal and mentally disturbed inmates, required that she wear plastic gloves when she used the typewriter in the jail library, and denied her regular attendance at Roman Catholic services. Jailers also attached red stickers to all her belongings indicating that she had AIDS, a violation of New York State law that prohibits the disclosure that a person has tested positive for HIV. Judge John T. Curtain concluded, "There is no question that the red sticker policy was developed, not in response to contagious diseases in general, but specifically in response to the hysteria over HIV and AIDS" (Sullivan, 1992, p. B-4). The judge also cited the Erie County Jail for violating regulations adopted by the New York State Department of Correction Services in 1987, under which prisoners who test positive for HIV cannot be isolated from the general prison population. The ruling and award were based on compensatory and punitive damages for AIDS discrimination (*Nolley v. County of Erie*, 1991). Norman Siegel, executive director of the New York chapter of the American Civil Liberties Union (ACLU), added, "We applaud Judge Curtin for his courageous and legally correct decision. It sends a strong message that such stigmatization will not be tolerated by the courts and that once and for all we must end this kind of hysteria" (Sullivan, 1992, p. B-4).

The red-sticker alert controversy in the *Nolley* case is reminiscent of other correctional practices that overtly stigmatize and humiliate unpopular prisoners. For more than 15 years, homosexual inmates held at the Polk County Jail in Florida were segregated and required to wear pink bracelets symbolizing their sexual preference. Facing legal action, jail officials discontinued the practice of tagging and segregating homosexuals. Six lesbians had complained to the ACLU that being "pink-tagged" had limited their privileges and brought harsh treatment from jailers. According to ACLU attorney Jim West, "It reflects homophobia. . . . Labeling people's clothing based on a sexual preference seems an extreme response that [isn't] warrant[ed]" ("Pink Bracelets for Homosexuals," 1989, p. 35; "Red Tags for Gays," 1990). Red-tagging homosexual prisoners also should be understood in a larger social and historical context. During the Third Reich of the 1930s and 1940s in Germany, Nazis held between 10,000 and 15,000 homosexuals in concentration camps for violating Paragraph 175 of the German criminal code that called for the imprisonment of any "male who commits lewd and lascivious acts with another male." Under Nazi rule, homosexuality was characterized as sinfully deviant and sexually subversive. While in the camps, homosexuals wore uniforms bearing pink triangles. Many were tortured and castrated; overall, 60% of the incarcerated homosexuals died in the camps (Dunlop, 1995; Heger, 1972; Plant, 1986, 1989).

Inadequate Medical Care

Due in large part to the penal harm movement, proposals to allocate health care dollars to corrections have become increasingly unpopular, especially when those who require expensive medications and services are infected with illnesses brought on by IV drug use or homosexual sex. Efforts to generate greater public concern for treating prisoners with HIV/AIDS often are hampered by lack of awareness, apathy, and in some instances, hostility. Special officer for the Court of the District of Columbia released a document describing the abominable conditions concerning the delivery of medical care for inmates with HIV/AIDS. In particular, the report featured an account of a male prisoner with AIDS who—after being neglected in his cell for 10 days—died while being transported to the hospital, strapped in a wheelchair and wrapped in a bed sheet stained with urine and feces (Perez, 1996). According to Ronald Bogard, a former general counsel of the New York City Health Department, there has been little effort to determine the extent of the problem: "Not only do we not know, we don't really care, because of the people that are involved and the money that is involved" (Purdy, 1997, p. 28; see also Alexander, 2003).

An important feature of HIV/AIDS intervention is the distribution of azidothymidine (AZT), a medication that is believed to retard the progression of the disease in some patients. Due to its high cost, however, correctional systems may not properly distribute AZT in ways required for effectiveness, at times improperly rationing dosages (see Cusac, 2003;

Purdy, 1997). A similar treatment gaining interest inside and outside of prison is the so-called HIV cocktail, a combination of medications designed to prevent the reproduction of the virus. Still, financial barriers abound. In New Jersey, the annual expense for treating one prisoner with the HIV cocktail is $10,000 to $15,000, and the expense jumps to $70,000 for prisoners with full-blown AIDS. These and other medical costs have prompted New Jersey's Correctional Health Services, a private contractor, to renegotiate part of its contract. The medical plan covers annual expenses to the tune of $2,900 per inmate. Correctional Health Services requested an additional $5 million to meet HIV-related expenses (Sforza, 1998b).

While the quality of medical services varies from state to state and prison to prison, even under the best circumstances it is marred by inconsistent care. Often medical care for inmates is compromised by budgetary constraints; many administrators deal with those financial obstacles by lobbying state officials for additional funding. In some cases, litigation geared toward increasing spending for medical services in corrections has obtained support from the courts. Attorneys representing prisoners with HIV/AIDS, often in class action suits, insist that the denial of adequate care constitutes cruel and unusual punishment, and thus is unconstitutional under the Eighth Amendment of the U.S. Constitution. "A sick person on the street can go to an emergency room. But these people can't because they're under lock and key, so that puts a big responsibility on the person holding the key" says Maddie LaMarre, clinical services coordinator for the Georgia prison system (Purdy, 1997, p. 28). Despite some important legal victories, financial obstacles combined with larger social forces (e.g., political apathy) and organizational forces (e.g., lack of equipment, supplies, and staff) continue to strain medical attention for inmates with HIV/AIDS (Courtenay & Sabo, 2001; Polych & Sabo, 2001). Michael Wiseman of the Prisoners' Rights Project of the Legal Aid Society of New York comments, "Prisons were never designed to deliver medical treatment, they were designed to keep people locked up. Before HIV prisons never gave good care. But with HIV, it's turned a lot of them into death camps" (Gross, 1993, p. A12).

For years, prisoners with HIV/AIDS have formally complained to the courts that they have been denied adequate medical care. As a result of litigation, some medical services have improved. Nevertheless, disparities in treatment for HIV/AIDS persist because prisoners do not have a constitutional right to "every potential beneficial medical procedure" (Friedman, 1992, pp. 933–934; Adams v. Poag, 1995; Vaughn & Carroll, 1998). In Harris v. Thigpen (1991), the district court ruled that inmates are not entitled to state-of-the-art medical care and that reasonable care (determined by community standards) is constitutionally sufficient. Questions persist as to whether many prisoners with HIV/AIDS are receiving even basic medical attention. Prisoners with AIDS live about half as long following diagnosis as individuals with AIDS in the community (Committee on the Judiciary, 1991, p. 86; U.S. General Accounting Office, 1994; Vaughn & Carroll, 1998). Admittedly, the accelerated death rate among inmates also may be related to the poor health of inmates before entering prison (Marquart, Merianos, Cuvelier, & Carroll, 1996). Still, it is commonly argued that denial of medical care is the result of deliberate indifference to the prisoners' medical needs, or a form of retaliation against prisoners for exercising their right to contest the charges against them (*Proctor v. Alameda County*, 1992; Vaughn & Smith 1999).

In developing the term penal harm medicine, researchers have found that in some instances hostility toward prisoners with HIV/AIDS manifests in ill treatment, such as withholding medical care (Dabney & Vaughn, 2000; Vaughn, 1999; Vaughn & Smith, 1999). In one such case, a prisoner asked jail medical officials to distribute his AIDS medication but was told that it was too much trouble. The jail officials added, "[Y]ou are in jail not a hotel; if you don't like it bond out" (Vaughn & Smith, 1999, p. 202). In a more serious incident, a prisoner with advanced AIDS received permission to receive medical attention in the community. However, the prisoner was forced to wait two months before seeing an outside physician, and during that time all of his medication and medical care was discontinued inside the jail (Vaughn & Smith, 1999). In a similar case, a pretrial detainee, whose health status was rapidly declining due to AIDS and Karposi's sarcoma, was losing his vision. Despite being told that he would be promptly examined by a free-world physician, the prisoner waited four months for such attention. The detainee complained, "I haven't been found guilty of anything, but it seems like I have already been sentenced to die in jail" (Vaughn & Smith, 1999, pp. 202–203; see also Maeve & Vaughn, 2001).

Finally, the ongoing controversy over the distribution of condoms has become an ideological battleground in corrections. Many criminal justice officials oppose condom distribution, often citing reasons of morality. "It's ludicrous. If we issue condoms, then it would send a message that the Sheriff's Department would be responsible for illegal or immoral behavior," said Jack Quigley, Bergen County, New Jersey, undersheriff. Having revealed his belief that homosexuality is wrong and that gays should be converted to heterosexuality, Quigley continued, "The most basic concept of rehabilitation is to accept responsibility for one's behavior" (Sforza, 1998a, p. A12). Many public health experts, however, favor condom distribution, including the New Jersey Governor's Advisory Council and the HIV Prevention Community Planning Group (PCPG) that offers recommendations to the state's health department. Gisele Pemberton of the HIV PCPG argues, "This is one of the populations already marginalized and discriminated against. They of all people should have access to condoms" (Sforza, 1998a, p. A12). Currently, only five correctional systems make condoms available to inmates; administrators in those systems defend the practice by arguing that they are not condoning the behavior but simply recognizing that sexual contact does occur in institutions (Hammett et al., 1999).

Tuberculosis in Corrections

Tuberculosis (TB) has a long history in corrections. In the mid-19th century, TB, or "consumption," accounted for up to 80% of all prison deaths in the United States; in Boston, New York, and Philadelphia, 10% of all prisoners died of the disease (Greifinger, Heywood, & Glaser, 1993; Reyes & Coninx, 1997). Nowadays, TB remains a public health threat to jails and prisons. TB is a highly contagious disease spread by bacteria that become airborne when an infected person coughs or sneezes and others inhale the bacteria, becoming infected. TB most often affects the respiratory system and even today may sometimes lead to death. Correctional facilities are particularly vulnerable to the spread of TB due to overcrowded conditions and poorly ventilated cells and dormitories. "Expansion of physical facilities has not kept pace with the doubling of prison and jail populations in the past decade, nor did it contemplate the risk of transmission of airborne disease" (Greifinger et al., 1993, p. 333). While prisoners and staff are at risk of developing TB, it should be noted that the disease also can be carried into the community, posing a wider public health threat (Abramsky, 2002; "Tuberculosis Can Spread," 2001).

The makeup of jail and prison populations figures prominently in the high risk for TB outbreaks. TB is associated with HIV/AIDS as well as other medical conditions. Persons born in foreign countries, alcoholics, IV drug users, blacks, and Latinos also are particularly vulnerable to the illness (Hammett et al., 1999). "HIV further fueled these prison epidemics. The explosion of TB in prisons was even more intimately tied to government policies, most notably those of the Reagan and Bush administrations. In addition to dismantling the country's system to guard against TB—budgets were slashed and the drug war was declared" (Farmer, 2002, p. 244). Indeed, the war on drugs has increased the risk of TB in correctional institutions. Due to their emphasis on security and not public health, jails and prisons have difficulty managing infectious diseases, especially illnesses that are imported from the community due to mandatory drug sentencing. Dr. Robert Cohen concedes that his experience as medical director at Rikers Island jail complex (NYC) forever changed his view on drug policy: "The problem of drug abuse is much better approached with a medical model than with a crime-and-punishment model" (Skolnick, 1993). Compounding matters, as TB has intersected with HIV, further medical complications have developed. Most notably is the emergence of a new, drug-resistant form of TB (Farmer, 2002).

Although the incidence of TB disease has declined in recent years, both in the total U.S. population and among correctional inmates, the rates remain much higher among inmates than in the general population. Experts report that most state and federal prison systems are following CDC recommendations regarding the screening of inmates and staff and the isolation and treatment of persons with TB disease. However, substantial improvement is needed in city and county jail systems. "Continuing problems with adherence to regimens for the treatment of TB disease following release to the community may be amenable to improvement by better education, discharge planning, linkages with health departments and community-based providers, incentives to appear for follow-up appointments (for example, food coupons and bus tokens), and shorter courses of therapy" (Hammett et al., 1999, p. 90; Tulsky et al., 1998).

The judiciary has empowered correctional facilities to take aggressive measures in detecting and controlling TB, including the mandatory screening of inmates. Moreover, courts have held correctional systems liable for neglecting to implement such measures, thereby placing inmates at risk of acquiring TB (Gostin, 1995; Hammett et al., 1999). In Colorado, a parolee sued a county jail and the Department of Health after developing TB during his incarceration (Abbott, 1998). Despite improvements in controlling TB, such health-related problems persist, especially in jails that hold INS (Immigration and Naturalization Services) detainees. At the Sarasota County jail (Florida), a female immigration detainee with TB was not seen by a doctor after urinating blood for 24 hours and despite multiple requests for medical attention (Saewitz, 2002). In another case, an INS detainee held at DuPage County Jail (Illinois) was discovered to have active tuberculosis. The jail notified the INS that it did not have proper facilities to keep someone with active tuberculosis and recommended that the agency transfer him to another facility. Because the INS could not locate another facility that would take custody, the infected detainee was simply released. Remarkably, the INS dropped the detainee off at a local homeless shelter without any medicine and without notifying public health officials. The INS also never notified the detainee's attorney of his client's release, "instead allowing the young man with an active infectious disease to wander off with no resources" (Human Rights Watch, 1998, p. 69). The warden at DuPage County Jail later said: "The Health Department finally tracked him down at a local hospital," but his lawyer, who has not heard from his client again, wonders: "For all I know, he could be dead" (Human Rights Watch, 1998, p. 69; Welch, 2002a).

Aging Prisoners

While the war on drugs, mandatory minimum sentences, three-strikes laws, and other tough-on-crime measures have remained politically popular, experts have been reminding us that locking up more offenders for longer periods means that increasingly large numbers of prisoners are aging behind bars (Flanagan, 1996). Moreover, the socioeconomic and racial factors are evident insofar as prisoners are disproportionately drawn from groups that have the poorest health status in free society (e.g., low income, urban dwellers, and minorities). Prisoners also tend to have lengthy histories of engaging in unhealthful risk behaviors such as drug and alcohol use along with smoking tobacco. While incarcerated, prisoners are subjected to institutional conditions that further undermine their health and present opportunities for the spread of infectious disease. Health care costs comprise 10 to 20% of prison operating costs and are the fastest growing item of corrections budgets, due in large part to an aging prison population that requires greater and more expensive medical attention (Lamb-Mechanick & Nelson, 2000; McDonald, 1999). Due to mounting health care expenses, it costs more than $60,00 per year to house one elderly (or infirm) prisoner in a facility that functions as both a penitentiary and nursing home (Leone, 2002; Morton, 2001).

In 1999, U.S. prisons housed more than 43,000 prisoners over the age of 55, a 50% increase since 1996. Overall, approximately 12% of male prisoners and 14% of female prisoners report a chronic physical impairment, while 25% of all inmates aged 45 or older report a physical impairment. Nearly 40% of state prisoners aged 45 and older report chronic medical problems and have surgery rates that are twice that of the general inmate population (Maruschak & Beck, 2001). Expenses stemming from medical services for aging inmates extend beyond the exorbitant costs of medication and routine laboratory work; administrators also have to alter the physical features of the institution to make them accessible for wheelchairs and less mobile inmates. The aging prison population has dumbfounded many administrators: "We've not been in the geriatric business," said Gary Hilton of New Jersey's Department of Corrections. "I know how to run prisons, not old-age homes" (Malcolm, 1988, pp. A1, 6; see also Drummond, 1999).

Program needs also change as the prison population ages. Older inmates are less interested in GED classes and other educational programs, and more interested in learning how to secure Social Security benefits upon their release. Indeed, preparing them to return to the community might be the most pressing problem facing the correctional system. Having grown old in prison, they must return to a society that often does not meet the needs of the lower income elderly (Nieves, 2002). Like their lower income aging peers in the community, elderly ex-cons have few family members to support them, and are likely to have difficulty surviving on benefits available from an overburdened social service system. In another of the ironies of imprisonment, aging prisoners will continue to place a huge financial burden on correctional systems while presenting little public safety threat (Auerhahn, 2002; Mauer, 2002).

The Phenomenology of Imprisonment and Suffering

Historically speaking, imprisonment replaced corporal punishment and its public spectacle; as a result, retribution became concealed behind prison walls where its aim shifted from the body to the mind. That shift in punishment produced a qualitatively different form of suffering (Foucault, 1979). Since then, inflicting emotional pain on lawbreakers has remained the prevailing rationale for incarceration, where anguish is achieved by the deprivation of liberty, goods and services, heterosexual relationships, autonomy, and security (Sykes, 1958; see also Johnson & Toch, 1982; Welch, 2004a). Suffering inherent to the prison experience also is compounded by the length of time a convict spends incarcerated; indeed, a prominent feature of contemporary sentencing is its quantification, measuring prison terms by years, months, and days. That construction of punishment, termed the penal calculus by Foucault, demonstrates the significance of the temporality of imprisonment, allowing for a greater appreciation of phenomenology, as discussed below.

As a framework for studying the diversity of consciousness and experience, phenomenology has benefited from the richly layered works of philosophers and sociologists, especially those interested in the pertinence of time. Husserl (1962) theorized that temporality significantly shapes the way people apprehend the world around them. Likewise, Heidegger (1949) offered an existentially informed interpretation of the temporal field, noting that perceptions of time direct the course of future actions. Drawing on both of those insights, Sartre (1966) reasoned that futureness—the projected plans of action—creates meaning for the present. The role of time remains an integral part of the life-worlds that extend beyond personal to social experience; in that context, the construction of time becomes a shared reality, offering a unity of meaning (Schutz & Luckmann, 1973). Summarizing those ideas, Meisenhelder contends, "all human activity, as seen phenomenologically, is then temporally structured through and is a casting of oneself toward the future" (1985, p. 42). That perspective is reminiscent of an old adage—life is what happens while you are making other plans.

The prison world is structured to be distinct and separate from the free world, deliberately adopting the model of institutionalization in routinizing, scheduling, and controlling the lives of inmates (Goffman, 1961; Rothman, 1990; Sykes, 1958). "Prisoners are effects, rather than causes: That is, they perceive themselves as being nearly wholly determined by the institution" (Meisenhelder, 1985, p. 43). Foucault (1979) similarly concluded that modern imprisonment transforms prisoners from subjects to objects. The unique shift of the temporal field further contributes to the nature of the prison world in that time is experienced as a burden rather than a resource. Looking toward the future gives meaning to one's life: "Without a definite sense of attainable future, time is likely to be experienced as meaningless, empty, and boring" (Meisenhelder, 1985, p. 45). Farber (1944) also advanced our understanding of the phenomenology of the prison world, proposing that suffering is heightened by making prisoners feel that their future is uncertain. Given the gravity of the temporal field and its significance to perceptions of the future, the phenomenology of suffering has particular relevance to aging prisoners and those with serious illness, most notably HIV/AIDS.

Compared to other inmates, it is important to realize that elderly prisoners and those with terminal diseases experience a more complex form of penal suffering, especially considering the basic human tendency of looking toward the future in creating meaning for life and personal existence. For the typical prisoner, a sense of futurelessness is temporary because they resume their meaningful lives upon returning to the free world. Often that is not the case for those who are aging or seriously ill; they must cope with a permanent sense of futurelessness. While incarcerated, all prisoners tend to alter their sense of self, developing a heightened self-consciousness due to continuous and intense introspection (Meisenhelder, 1985). For old and ill inmates in particular, that reflection can produce an alarming awareness of their own physical deterioration, thus compounding their suffering (Welch, 1991).

To ward off the burden of a shifting temporal field in the prison world, the typical inmate engages in consuming activities such as education and work. By making time pass quickly, inmates can partially alleviate their suffering. That coping mechanism, however, may not be useful for elderly and seriously sick prisoners, presumably due to their fear of death. Paradoxically, experiencing time slowly prolongs their suffering and compounds their sense of futurelessness. Depending on the circumstances of the illness, suffering can be portrayed as either honorable or dishonorable. Sontag reminds us that etymologically, *patient* means "sufferer" and that "it is not suffering as such that is most deeply feared but suffering that degrades" (1989, p. 37). Rarely are elderly and ill prisoners depicted as patients, an identity that might bring them dignity and honor. Rather they face the late stages of their lives as prisoners, an identity spoiled by degradation and dishonor.

Conclusion

This chapter has explored growing concerns facing correctional health care, particularly in light of problems produced by the war on drugs. Critical attention is turned to the incarceration of addicts with HIV/AIDS and other serious illnesses such as TB. The influx of prisoners with serious medical needs promises to burden—financially and otherwise—prisons and jails for the near and distant future. That strain on the correctional apparatus is multiplied by warehousing elderly prisoners who have their own health care needs.

Not discussed in this chapter are other issues that must be considered when looking at the totality of the health care crisis behind bars, including hepatitis C (Talvi, 2003b), mental health (Wisely, 2003), suicide (Welch & Gunther, 1997a, 1997b), the unique medical needs of female prisoners (Herivel, 2003), and shady correctional health care companies, physicians, and health care personnel (Sherwood & Posey, 2003; St. Clair, 2003; Young, 2003).

To make sense of such unenlightened policies, it is useful to consider the social impact of the penal harm movement. In the realm of HIV/AIDS, retribution is driven largely by moral and punitive conceptions of the illness, perpetuating the belief that victims of AIDS are being judged and punished by a higher power for having indulged in illegal drugs or homosexuality (Welch, 2000b). As Sontag notes, HIV/AIDS is "a theodicy as well as a demonology, it not only stipulates something emblematic of evil but makes this the bearer of a rough, terrible justice" (1989, p. 57). The stigma attached to prisoners with HIV/AIDS is amplified further by their status as lawbreakers, at times producing ill treatment and denial of adequate medical care. Those problems are compounded by a lack of general awareness, apathy, and in worse cases, hostility. According to John Miles, a special assistant for corrections and substance abuse at the Centers for Disease Control, "This is not just a hidden population. This is an invisible population. The public doesn't like to spend the money" (Purdy, 1997, p. 28).

Due to coercive drug control policies, many penal institutions are being transformed partially into infirmaries where suffering is aggravated rather than alleviated. Those developments illuminate the ironies of imprisonment, particularly the self-defeating campaign of locking up nonviolent offenders who grow old or become chronically sick behind bars. In addition to exorbitant financial cost of caring for that population, there remain grave concerns over the ethics of penal policies that overincarcerate and do not contribute to public safety. Perhaps society—and justice—would be better served by transferring elderly and seriously ill prisoners to the medical facilities, halfway houses, or even their own homes so that their health care needs could be more suitably met.

End-of-Chapter Questions

1. What are the metaphors used to interpret HIV/AIDS?

2. Describe the myths and misconceptions of HIV/AIDS.

3. Why does TB pose a serious medical threat to correctional environments?

4. How has an aging prison population altered correctional management?

6

Reproducing Prison Violence

In 2002, John J. Geoghan, a defrocked priest, was sentenced to a prison term of 9 to 10 years for groping a young boy in a Massachusetts swimming pool. Geoghan stood accused of more than 130 cases of sexual abuse dating back to his early days as a priest in the mid-1960s, and his conviction had a cascading effect on the Roman Catholic Church as it faced its darkest crisis in modern history. "In many ways he was a worst case scenario because he was a serial predator whose behavior was facilitated by the hierarchy of the Archdiocese of Boston, and the worst judgments were made in his case," explained Stephen Pope, a professor of theology at Boston College (Wakin & Zezima, 2003, pp. 1, 26). Geoghan's extensive pattern of sexual abuse was evidence that Church officials knew of his criminal behavior. But in an effort to protect the reputation of the Archdiocese, bishops elected to shuttle Geoghan among parishes where he continued to accumulate victims. While incarcerated in a protective custody unit with 23 other prisoners, Geoghan never felt safe. Eventually his deepest fears were realized when he was attacked by another prisoner and dragged into his cell where he was beaten and strangled to death. His assailant, Joseph Druce, is a self-proclaimed neo-Nazi serving a life sentence for the murder of a gay bus driver. In that case, Druce abducted his victim, stuffed him into the trunk of a car, and drove to a secluded wooded area where the victim was strangled. Druce admitted to the lethal attack of Geoghan, adding that he, too, was a victim of sexual abuse as a child. In the aftermath of the incident, many observers turned attention to the nature of violence in prisons. "It was troubling that an inmate convicted of one of the most despised crimes among prisoners—sexual abuse of a child—was left vulnerable," said Professor Pope, adding: "It's an irony that his criminal behavior was facilitated by a church that was negligent, and now his death was facilitated by a criminal justice system that was negligent" (Wakin & Zezima, 2003, p. 26).

Traditional criminology has often taken cues from broader sociological notions, particularly the idea that crime stems from the absence of social control (Hirschi, 1969; Reiss, 1951). However, the presence of social control has also been blamed for inadvertently contributing to crime. In a word, social control becomes ironic when it escalates the very behavior it intends to deter (Marx, 1981). Departing from functionalist sociology, labeling theorists in the early 1960s began to acknowledge the role that authorities play in creating crime, deviance, and various forms of rule breaking (Becker, 1963; Kitsuse, 1962; Scheff, 1966; Wilkins, 1965; see also Hawkins & Tiedeman, 1975; Lemert, 1972; Schneider, 1975). Gary Marx (1981) developed further this sociological perspective by setting out to identify and explain the ironies of social control, directing greater attention to particular situations that generate rule breaking. In doing so, Marx underscored Blumer's (1969) key sociological observation: While some actions are motivated, others are situated and structured (see Colvin, 1982; Gil, 1996; Young, 1982).

By examining the contradictions of social control, Marx (1981) and like-minded symbolic interactionists offer valuable insights into the creation of lawlessness by authorities; still, those analyses tend to be limited primarily to such social-control agents as law enforcement officers. Penologists also have recognized patterns of irony in corrections, noting that rule breaking, often with violent overtones, is frequently reproduced in prisons. Porporino (1986), for instance, pointed out, "It is ironic that the most violent individuals in society, once apprehended and convicted, are isolated within settings where violence is especially commonplace" (p. 213). In a similar vein, Lowman and MacLean (1991) insist that "Prison seems to either produce or reinforce the very behavior it is supposed to correct" (p. 130). Some have gone so far as to claim that prison managers take a more insidiously utilitarian approach to the ironies of social control in corrections in that "Violence and tension between prisoners are encouraged by prison managers as a tool to control and distract prisoners from the conditions of their confinement" (Coalition for Prisoners' Rights, Santa Fe, NM, as quoted in Welch, 2004a, p. 287; see also Fleisher, 1989; Silberman, 1995).

Although examples of seemingly contradictory correctional practices are scattered throughout the penological literature, few attempts have been made to integrate those ironies within a coherent conceptual structure. In this chapter, Marx's model of the ironies of social control is applied to the world of corrections, thereby introducing a sense of order to an understanding of the dialectical nature of incarceration and the reproduction of violence behind bars. Drawing on the three components of Marx's framework (i.e., escalation, nonenforcement, and covert facilitation), two types of violence are examined: inmate-versus-inmate violence, and staff-versus-inmate violence. Overall, the chapter sheds light on the interdependence between keepers and the kept, with particular emphasis on institutional violence.

Ironies of Social Control

Marx (1981) organized his approach to the ironies of social control around three types of situations that contribute to, and at times generate, rule-breaking behavior. In the first, escalation, authorities unintentionally encourage rule breaking by taking enforcement action. In the second situation, nonenforcement, agents of social control, by taking no enforcement action, intentionally permit rule infractions. In the third situation, covert facilitation, the authorities engage in hidden or deceptive enforcement action that intentionally encourages rule breaking. In the following sections, those concepts are applied to institutional corrections and its realm of violence.

Escalation

The ironies stemming from escalation invite questions over the effectiveness of law enforcement in general and corrections in particular. According to Marx (1981), escalation is the clearest illustration of self-defeating measures of social control in which intervention contributes to rule breaking and violence. Escalation produces increases in the frequency and seriousness of the original violations; likewise, it creates new categories of violators (e.g., gangs, toughs, gorillas, peddlers) and victims (e.g., snitches, punks, short-eyes). It also denotes a commitment to violence as evidenced in forms of rule breaking that stand as reactions to social control (e.g., taking down the man, busting up the joint, sticking a pig). Those challenges to authority almost invariably provoke strong-armed tactics by corrections officers who punish inmates for failing to show proper deference to their keepers, thereby perpetuating a vicious cycle of rebellion and abuse of authority (see Adams, 1998; Useem & Reisig, 1999; Welch, 1999b, 1996c).

The interdependence of rule enforcers and rule breakers in correctional facilities is reproduced at the situational level by three key factors: lack of expertise, self-fulfilling prophecies, and sanctions that increase secondary gains for rule breaking (Marx, 1981). Lack of expertise remains a crucial problem in prisoner management because violence by officers against inmates is likely to escalate when the situation involves staff who are unprofessional, insensitive, insecure (e.g., racist and bigoted), and poorly trained in dealing with interpersonal conflicts—sometimes resulting in "oilin' the fire" (Marx, 1981; Stark, 1972). Poor institutional conditions and poor facility design also contribute to the escalation of violence.

Lack of Expertise

Consider the 1971 uprising at Attica penitentiary in New York. The chronology of events began the day before the riot when a misunderstanding between guards and prisoners escalated into a confrontation in which an inmate assaulted an officer. Later that night, two inmates were removed from their cells and placed in administrative detention, further escalating the incident. Fellow inmates vowed revenge, and the next morning the guard who was situated at the center of the controversy was attacked. At that same moment, prisoners attacked officers, took hostages, and destroyed property. By 10:30 A.M., prisoners had seized control of four cell blocks, including the yards and tunnels. Soon, 1,281 inmates and over 40 hostages gathered in the D Yard. The lack of training and expertise among corrections personnel became increasingly evident. Prison officials who did not have a riot control plan and relied on an antiquated communications system were unable to quell the disturbance. Contributing to the magnitude of the disturbance was overcrowding. Attica contained more than 2,200 prisoners. More accurately, the inmates were simply warehoused since few meaningful programs of education and rehabilitation were offered, even though such programs function to reduce tension and frustration among prisoners. It should also be noted that the riot was able to spread due to a key structural flaw in the institution's security fortress. Prisoners broke through a defective weld in the gate located in the institution's main intersection, nicknamed "Times Square," enabling the inmates to take control of the entire prison (Mahan, 1994; New York State Special Commission on Attica, 1972; Useem, 1985; Useem & Kimball, 1987, 1989; Wicker, 1975; see also Oswald, 1972, and the 1991 commemorative issue of *Social Justice* devoted to the Attica riot [Weiss, 1991]).

The eventual storming of the prison by the authorities, however, did not end the violence. For many of the kept, it marked the beginning of a sequence of brutal acts committed by officers. Hundreds of inmates were stripped naked and beaten by corrections officers, troopers, and sheriffs' deputies. The agony of the prisoners and hostages was prolonged because prison officials withheld immediate medical care for those suffering from gunshot wounds and injuries stemming from the widespread reprisals. There were only 10 medical personnel (only 2 of whom were physicians) available to treat more than 120 seriously wounded inmates and hostages. Doctors at local hospitals who could have assisted the wounded were not dispatched by prison officials until 4 hours later. Reprisals by officers against inmates became brutal spectacles of humiliation. Injured prisoners, some on stretchers, were struck, prodded, or beaten with sticks, belts, bats, or other weapons. "Many more inmates were injured when guards and troopers took over the yard and set up a gauntlet in which naked inmates were beaten with clubs as they were herded back into the cellblocks" (Jackson, 1992, p. 122). Some prisoners were dragged on the ground, marked with an "X" on their backs, spat upon, burned with matches, and poked in the genitals or arms with sticks (Deutsch, Cunningham, & Fink, 1991; *Inmates of Attica v. Rockefeller,* 1971).

A class action suit, *Al-Jundi v. Mancusi* (1991), was filed on behalf of the 1,200 prisoners who were wounded, denied medical care, beaten by officers, or killed. The jury found Deputy Warden Pfeil liable for violent reprisals following the riot, for permitting police and corrections officers to beat and torture inmates. Five years later, a federal court ordered Pfeil to pay a $4 million award to Frank B.B. Smith, one of the prisoners beaten by guards. But in 1999, a federal appeals court overturned that ruling, saying that the 1992 liability finding against Pfeil was invalid. Then in 2000, a federal judge announced that the inmates who were beaten and tortured during the riot would receive an $8 million settlement from New York State (Chen, 2000). The judge determined that prison managers not only had failed to contain the violence but, ironically, had escalated it.

Lack of expertise also has contributed to other institutional disturbances, most notably at the New Mexico State Prison. Apparently, lessons were not learned from Attica, for a containable incident rapidly erupted into a brutal riot in 1980, in which 33 prisoners were killed by fellow inmates. The incident began after midnight when an officer approached two rowdy inmates who were intoxicated on prison hooch (prisoner-made alcohol). The situation escalated when an altercation ensued and prisoners overpowered the officer and his two backups. The incident could have been contained, but the inmates snatched the prison keys and entered other sections of the institution. Meanwhile, the three officers were taken hostage, raped, and beaten into unconsciousness. As was the case in the riot at Attica, the officials at New Mexico were not prepared to deal with a large-scale riot. The institution was overcrowded and inexcusably understaffed. There were only 22 guards supervising 1,157 inmates in a prison built to hold 800. The riot could not be prevented from spreading because other officers were unable to locate a complete set of prison keys. Compounding the problems at New Mexico was a major architectural flaw—the failure of so-called shatterproof glass installed at the control center, the prison's life-line. By breaking the protective glass and seizing the control center, the inmates gained complete, unobstructed access to the facility and electronically opened all interior gates. The violence spread rapidly, manifesting in a degree of brutality rarely witnessed in American penal history (Colvin, 1982, 1992; Mahan, 1994; Morris, 1983; Rolland, 1997, 2002; Saenz, 1986; Stone, 1982; Useem, 1985; Useem & Kimball, 1989).

Another more recent incident of escalation involving the lack of expertise and harsh conditions of confinement occurred in Elizabeth, New Jersey, at an Immigration and Naturalization Services (INS) detention center. The facility, operated by a private contractor called ESMOR, had been open less than a year when officials learned of physical abuse by staff against detainees. INS Commissioner Doris Meissner ordered a review of the ESMOR facility, but before the investigation could begin, a riot broke out. The scope of the investigation was consequently expanded to include probable causes of the disturbance, adequacy of response by ESMOR and INS personnel, and emergency plans that were in effect at the time of the disturbance (INS, 1995; see also Welch, 1998b, 2002a).

The INS assessment team concluded that ESMOR officers and their mid-level supervisors failed to exhibit proper control during the disturbance. Moreover, there was considerable evidence to support the allegations of abuse and harassment of detainees by corrections officers. Many incidents of abuse were serious. According to the assessment team's report, officers were implicated in numerous acts of physical abuse and theft of detainee property. Women detainees complained that they had been issued male underwear on which large question marks had been scrawled on the crotch. Other accounts of harassment included the unjustified waking of detainees in the middle of the night under the guise of security checks (INS, 1995). It was determined that ESMOR did not have sufficient personnel and had resorted to inappropriate uses of overtime. The facility suffered from considerable staff turnover due to low wages, producing a revolving-door policy of hiring poorly qualified officers placed on duty without mandatory training required by INS (INS, 1995; see also Peet & Schwab, 1995). Due to poor personnel training, the staff failed to implement its emergency plan. At the onset of the riot, 14 ESMOR staff and 1 INS officer were supervising 315 detainees. The disturbance commenced at 1:15 A.M. and was brought under control at 6:30 A.M., following a tactical entry by local law enforcement officers. It was concluded that many detainees participated in the disturbance in reaction to harassment by ESMOR staff, harsh treatment in confinement, prolonged periods of detention, lack of communication about their cases, and the inefficient hearing process.

With the subsequent closing of the INS facility at Elizabeth, detainees were transferred either to other INS detention centers or to county jails in New Jersey and Pennsylvania. For many of those detainees, unfortunately, the harshness of treatment not only continued but in some cases worsened. Twenty-five detainees (who had not participated in the riot) were sent to the Union County Jail (NJ) where they were confronted by a group of officers who formed a gauntlet, punching and kicking them in an ordeal that lasted more than 4 hours. "The guards broke one detainee's collarbone, shoved other detainees' heads in toilets, used pliers to pull out one man's pubic hair and forced a line of men to kneel naked on the jail floor and chant, 'America is No. 1'" (Sullivan, 1995a, p. A1). Initially, six guards were arrested and charged with the beatings of INS detainees, but prosecutors contended that at least two dozen officers participated in the beatings (Misseck, 1995; see also Hassel & Misseck, 1996; Welch, 1997e). Three jailers were convicted of assault, misconduct, and conspiracy to obstruct the investigation; two of them were sentenced to 7 years in prison and a third received a 5-year sentence ("Prison Terms for Officers," 1998; Smothers, 1998).

In addition to internal conditions that contribute to escalation (e.g., lack of expertise and poor institutional conditions), it is important to acknowledge external forces that complicate those problems. The punitive stance of political leaders and the criminal justice establishment has led to an increase in prison overcrowding as more offenders (typically nonviolent) are sentenced to prison for longer periods of time. Overcrowding is exacerbated further by the abolition of parole in some jurisdictions. At the federal level, such structural changes have contributed to the increase in violence evident in prisons. Due to stricter sentencing and parole requirements, offenders are serving longer prison terms with little opportunity to earn "good time." Federal prisoners are currently required to serve 85% of their sentence before being eligible for parole. Traditionally, the use of parole was an important method of imposing control over inmates in that violating institutional rules would lead to a forfeiture of the "good time" they had earned. Nowadays, correctional officers who serve on the front line of institutional control possess fewer management devices. The influx of a growing number of felons contributes to prison tensions, threatening the stability of the facility. That destabilization becomes a key source of aggression and violence (see Crews & Montgomery, 2002; May, 2000; Wooldredge, Griffin, & Pratt, 2001).

Another external force contributing to escalation is a social movement devoted to making prison life harsher by eliminating amenities (e.g., weight rooms, televisions) and programs (e.g., education) and in some cases deliberately humiliating prisoners (e.g., chain gangs and striped prison uniforms) (Welch, 1997b, 2003f). Campaigns to harshen prison life tend to aggravate tensions behind bars. Moreover, the absence of programs reduces prosocial opportunities for inmates to alleviate stress, thereby increasing prisoner frustration, boredom, and in many instances, violence.

Self-Fulfilling Prophecies

Self-fulfilling prophecies also contribute to the escalation of deviance and violence. Marx (1981) reminds us that "The appearance of deviant behavior may stem from 'self-fulfillment' of initially erroneous beliefs by authorities about a group or an individual" (p. 234). The effects of labeling are easily detected in prison, partly because convicts previously have been subjected to the formal degradation ceremony of the criminal justice apparatus (Becker, 1963; Garfinkel, 1956; Goffman, 1961). Behind prison walls, correctional officers are trained not to trust inmates under any circumstances and are told, "*Con*victs will *con* you." More to the point of escalation, the labeling of prisoners contributes to violence, especially when perceptions of "us versus them" are imbued with racist stereotypes. Many states rely on rural prisons to house offenders who are members of racial minority groups transported from urban centers; correspondingly, those institutions are staffed by white people from small towns and rural communities where they have little contact with racial and ethnic minorities.

Attica prison is located in Wyoming County, in upstate New York, where "most people there work in the prison, work in service industries connected to the prison, or are related to the white rural guards who staffed the prison at the time of the rebellion" (Jackson, 1992, p. 124). At the time of the riot, the majority of Attica's prisoners were black (54%; 37% of the prisoners were white, and 8.7% were Spanish-speaking), and nearly 80% of the black inmates were from urban ghettos (New York State Special Commission on Attica, 1972). Contrary to popular belief, prisoners—not the staff—eventually contained the violence at Attica. Following a period of random destruction, inmate leaders organized fellow prisoners in an effort to reach a peaceful resolution. The group of prisoners taking the initiative was not involved in the initial violence; they included Muslims, Black Panthers, and Young Lords, groups the authorities labeled, distrusted, and routinely hassled. The atmosphere surrounding the negotiation was later riddled with rumors that inflamed the situation. Drawing on stereotypes of violent criminals, prison officials manufactured a disinformation campaign, deliberately reporting unfounded rumors to the media. Specifically, officials announced that "hostages had died because their throats had been slit by the inmates and that several hostages had been found with their genitals stuffed in their mouths" (Jackson, 1992, p. 123). For the record, the Rochester medical examiner reported to journalists days after the riot that except for Officer William Quinn, who later died of injuries sustained in the initial violence at the Times Square section of the prison, "All guards had been killed by police and guard bullets; none had their throats cut, and none had their genitals removed and stuffed in their mouths" (Jackson, 1992, p. 123). Despite the truth, the disinformation campaign already had dominated the prison officials' narrative. Local newspapers ran full-page articles with false accounts describing guards with slit throats and genitals stuffed in their mouths. The momentum of the labeling process proved difficult to correct, for the belief that the riot had been "precipitated by a number of down-state violent 'niggers' never lost currency" (Jackson, 1992, p. 125).

In the end, it was the authorities that stoked the violence, reacting with deadly force as state police ambushed the prisoners. During 15 minutes of gunfire, 39 inmates were killed, and 80 others were wounded; in all, 43 people lost their lives during the riot. One out of every 10 persons in D Yard that morning was struck by gunfire, and more than a quarter of the hostages died of bullet wounds. "With the exception of Indian massacres in the late 19th century, the state police assault that ended the four-day prison uprising was the bloodiest one-day encounter between Americans since the Civil War" (New York State Special Commission on Attica, 1972, p. 130).

At the New Mexico state penitentiary, the effects of labeling also reinforced hostility and distrust between officers and prisoners. Unlike the inmates of Attica, who had joined forces across race to challenge the prison regime, prisoners at New Mexico became deeply—and dangerously—divided against each other, even within ethnic groups. During a critical era leading up to the riot, officers initiated a system of "snitching" based on involuntary rather than voluntary informing, placing prisoners in a classic "Catch 22." Officers privately told inmates that they must snitch on fellow prisoners; if they did not cooperate, officers would falsely announce to other inmates that they had informed. Either way, inmates were "screwed."

The involuntary snitch system pressured convicts to become increasingly suspicious of their peers. Mistrust among prisoners gradually stratified inmates into small cliques. In effect, the staff divided and conquered the inmate society by turning inmates against each other. For the purpose of protecting themselves from snitches, many prisoners adopted violent reputations along with public displays of aggression. Criminologist Hans Toch found that "Prisoners who achieve notoriety as fighters are much less likely to be attacked [and snitched on] than those who appear to fear overt conflict" (1992, p. 64; Robertson, 1995). As violence grew more prevalent, the administration, seemingly oblivious to its own role in escalation, began to think that it was dealing with a so-called new breed of prisoner who could be controlled only through coercive measures. The New Mexico prison riot serves as a potent example of how labeling and self-fulfilling prophecies can escalate violence by creating a new class of perpetrators (i.e., new breeds) who preyed on a new class of victims (e.g., snitches and sex offenders, especially pedophiles). Moreover, perpetrators became more skillful in their use of violence.

Small cliques of felons sought revenge against those labeled prison outcasts, including snitches and convicted child molesters known as "diddlers" or "short-eyes." Preparing themselves for skillful acts of revenge, inmates confiscated prison records identifying informers and those convicted of sex offenses—the two most despised criminal types in the prison world. Enraged prisoners armed themselves with hammers, meat cleavers, and blowtorches stolen from the prison maintenance supply room. The impending rampage would exceed by far the usual forms of prison violence. For the next several hours at the New Mexico penitentiary, inmates stalked, raped, burned, decapitated, castrated, and eviscerated their victims. A reporter asked an inmate, "What was it like in there?" to which the prisoner anxiously replied, "Man, what can I tell you? It was like the Devil had his own butcher shop, and you could get any cut you wanted" (Morris, 1983, p. i). Consider the following incident involving the systematic torture of Jimmy Perrin, serving a life sentence for raping and murdering two little girls and their mother. Four executioners blowtorched his door open, dragged Perrin out of his cell, "tied him spread-eagle to the bars and cooked him slowly with the roaring flame of the acetylene torch, melting his three hundred pounds of flesh to bone" (Stone, 1982, p. 127). For 30 minutes, the executioners tortured Perrin, "first burning his genitals, then his face, moving the torch up and down his body, bringing him around with smelling salts when he drifted into the comfort of unconsciousness" (Stone, 1982, pp. 127, 129; see also Akerstrom, 1986; Morris, 1983; Rolland, 1997, 2002).

Other prisoners suffered similar acts of torture, shocking investigators who had the grim task of uncovering human remains. Many victims were burned to death when rioters threw flammable liquids through the bars and ignited them with matches and blowtorches. Some inmates were burned so extensively that their race could not be determined. Three bodies were not conclusively identified until anthropologists reassembled the bone fragments (Morris, 1983). Dozens of inmates suspected of being informants were found slashed to death in their cells. One prisoner was found with a steel rod driven completely through his skull, and another was stomped to death and had the word "RATA" (the Spanish word for rat) carved into his abdomen. Several other victims had whisker-shaped gashes on their faces, signifying the stigma of prison "rats." In one brutal snitch killing, a prisoner was beaten to death with metal pipes. His lifeless body was thrown off the two-story tier, and an accomplice planted "a shovel into the corpse, cutting off his genitalia" (Morris, 1983, p. 100). The rage continued long after the rioters' victims perished: "As an afterthought, [rioters] broke the fingers of one hand on an already burned, dismembered body. Several corpses were mutilated, then sodomized, the torsos left at grotesque angles" ("The Killing Ground," 1980; Morris, 1983, p. 105).

Secondary Gains

Sanctions creating secondary gains also provide another key source for escalation. Under such conditions, punishment reproduces rather than deters rule breaking. "Prohibiting something can make it more attractive for those with rebellious needs or in search of excitement and 'kicks'" (Marx, 1981, p. 234; see also Ferrell, 1996; Katz, 1988; Welch & Bryan, 2000). Public condemnation of deviance may arouse curiosity and generate a "forbidden fruit" effect. That phenomenon especially applies to juveniles who experience an increase in peer status when arrested, verifying the rebellious belief that "It's good to be bad." In prison, secondary gains are attached to numerous forms of rule breaking, including violence and the contraband trade.

Secondary gains engender a type of violence that is said to be "instrumental." The rational and calculative nature of instrumental violence makes it distinguishable from expressive violence that is motivated by the need to reduce annoyances. As a form of incentive-motivated aggression, instrumental violence facilitates the pursuit of rewards. That phenomenon is particularly evident as inmates threaten or assault other prisoners for the purpose of garnering power, enhancing status, or promoting a particular self-image within the prison society. In their quest to dominate fellow prisoners, convicts may threaten or exact violence to obtain a more desirable living situation, sexual contact, commodities (e.g., cigarettes, junk food, sneakers), contraband (e.g., drugs, weapons), and various services (e.g., laundry tasks, paper work for legal matters) (see Wooldredge et al., 2001; Welch, 1995b, 1996c, 1999b).

Instrumental violence is not confined to individual violence. It is also evident in collective incidents (e.g., riots, disturbances, hostage taking, gang banging), particularly when rebellion against authorities produces in-group solidarity. Secondary gains are payoffs for those who resort to violence. As sanctions generate alternative status, rule breakers wear their punishment as a badge of honor. Given the very nature of correctional institutions, demands for illegal goods and services (e.g., weapons, drugs, sex) become immense, and when the demand for contraband is met with penalties, the underground economy adopts a crime tariff (Packer, 1968). Efforts to ban certain commodities increase not only the risk but also the gain for peddlers. Under those circumstances, the dialectical relations between rule enforcers and rule breakers fuel the underground economy. "Cost and benefit exist in an equilibrium not found in other situations. Classical deterrence theory assumes that increasing the penalty will decrease the activity. This does not hold when the rule-breaking decision flows from rational calculation and the potential gain from the deviance remains constant" (Marx, 1981, p. 235). Failed attempts to reduce the supply of illegal drugs (both inside and outside of prison) should also be understood within the context of market forces. Simply put, prices attached to illegal drugs are contingent upon demand and scarcity. Therefore, reducing the supply merely drives up the price of the drug, which makes trafficking more profitable, attracting those willing to take such risks (Wilkins, 1994).

Some staff members also participate in the underground economy. Officers might attempt to be "nice guys," giving inmates items believed to be harmless, such as junk food. But on occasion, officers import drugs for personal profit or to lure inmates into performing sexual favors. The most prevalent form of participation in the underground economy stems from officers "looking the other way" and not reporting such violations (a form of nonenforcement discussed in the next section). In doing so, officers create another form of leverage that can be used as bargaining power to control inmates informally; as a result, staff directly and indirectly perpetuate the *sub-rosa* economy (Kalinich, 1980; Kalinich & Stojkovic, 1985, 1987; McCarthy, 1995; Ross & Richards, 2002, 2003).

Secondary gains in the underground economy are patterned by the struggle for power, contributing to violence in several ways. As mentioned, a tariff placed on contraband serves to entice those interested in peddling. For example, drugs create the need for weapons, another form of contraband. Weapons are used to protect the enterprise against competition (e.g., turf wars) and to threaten or injure those who might consider snitching to authorities. All of those activities offer secondary gains to those who can rise to the top of the underground economy, enhancing their peer status and power. Ultimately, that hierarchy invites further violence by those interested in challenging and conquering the elite (e.g., gang-banging) (May, 2000).

Nonenforcement

As another irony of social control, nonenforcement shows how authorities intentionally permit rule breaking by strategically taking no enforcement action. In nonenforcement, the authorities' contribution to rule breaking is more indirect. While nonenforcement extends to an array of prison violations (e.g., possession or selling of various types of contraband), the focus of this section is on two major forms of institutional violence: inmate-versus-inmate and staff-versus-inmate.

Inmate-Versus-Inmate Violence

As previously reviewed, numerous institutional traits contribute to nonenforcement, which can lead to violence, especially the lack of adequate supervision by officers. As overcrowding outpaces the hiring of security staff, opportunities for violence increase, especially if the interior architecture limits supervision (Welch, 2004a). Security lapses also contribute to the proliferation of weapons. When officers conclude that they do not have the ability to control prisoners, they are prone to nonenforcement, which allows convicts to protect themselves by any means necessary (see Abbott, 1981; Colvin, 1982; Robertson, 1995; Welch, 2003g).

In greater conceptual terms, nonenforcement involves an exchange relationship between rule enforcers and rule breakers. For instance, nonenforcement may be offered as a reward to selected prisoners who are allowed to control and victimize weaker inmates (see Sykes, 1958). Classic illustrations of the exchange between authorities and selected prisoners have been found in the Arkansas and Texas prison systems. Like many states until the 1970s, Arkansas had instituted an elaborate prison-management structure by transferring authority to convict-guards, known as trustees. Those elite inmates ruled the institution and were rewarded for controlling—often with the use of force—the inmate population. Trustees enjoyed better living arrangements, clothing, food, and numerous privileges. They were permitted to gamble, consume alcohol and drugs, and even live in shacks outside of the institution where they entertained girlfriends. Prison administrators realized that using trustees rather than hiring additional staff reduced operating costs.

The Texas Department of Corrections (TDC), often referred to as "America's toughest prison," also relied on trustees, known as building tenders, to discipline the inmate population. BTs were hardened convicts deputized by the administration, making them elite prisoners. "They were the inmates who really ran the asylum: the meanest characters the administration could co-opt into doing the state's bidding" (Press, 1986, p. 46). Although Texas law forbids inmates from serving in supervisory and administrative roles, corrections officials ignored those restrictions.

Moreover, some BTs were furnished with weapons to bolster their control of other convicts. Often with the tacit approval of the staff, BTs armed with homemade clubs brutally beat stubborn or aggressive inmates, a form of victimization called "counseling" or "whipping them off the tank" in the prison vernacular (Marquart & Crouch, 1985).

The BT system was elaborate, featuring its own hierarchy of high-, medium-, and low-level convict guards—a structure of social control that insidiously pitted convicts against convicts. That form of nonenforcement cultivated an atmosphere of fear and distrust among the inmate population (Marquart & Crouch, 1985). In the 1970s and 80s, TDC was notorious for its institutional problems: enormous overcrowding (230% of capacity), lengthy sentences (brought about by several mandatory sentencing laws), poor chances for parole, and excessive violence. During a 7-day stretch in 1981, 11 inmates were killed by fellow prisoners, and 70 prisoners and officers were severely injured. Although some administrators believed that BTs reduced aggression at TDC, researchers found that BTs actually escalated violence (Marquart & Crouch, 1985; Martin & Ekland-Olson, 1987). In *Ruiz v. Estelle* (1980), federal judge William Wayne Justice declared the operations at TDC unconstitutional and abolished the BT system. The judicial order also called for measures to reduce overcrowding and improve medical, mental health, and educational services. Although such court orders create a sense of optimism, litigation rarely leads to immediate or smooth changes in correctional reform. In the case of TDC, years passed before any noticeable reforms occurred; meanwhile, overcrowding, physical abuse, poor services, corruption, graft, mismanagement, and especially violence persisted.

Another important type of nonenforcement leading to violence among prisoners is deliberate indifference, a legal concept advanced significantly by *Farmer v. Brennan* (1994; *Farmer v. Moritsugu,* 1990). Dee Farmer was sentenced to federal prison upon his conviction for credit card fraud. At the time of his incarceration, the 18-year-old Farmer was undergoing medical treatment to change his sex to female. As a preoperative transsexual, Farmer exhibited feminine traits and mannerisms, commonly wearing a T-shirt off one shoulder. Federal Bureau of Prisons officials classified Farmer as a biological male and designated him to the Federal Correctional Institution at Oxford, Wisconsin. For his safety, Farmer was confined to protective custody during much of his incarceration at Oxford. Upon a disciplinary infraction in 1989, Farmer was transferred to a higher-security institution within the system, the U.S. penitentiary in Terre Haute, Indiana. At Terre Haute, Farmer resumed serving his sentence in administrative segregation but was later transferred to the general population. Approximately a week later, he was raped and physically beaten in his cell after he spurned the sexual advances of another prisoner.

Farmer filed suit against corrections officials, complaining that "placing a known transsexual with feminine traits in the general population within a male prison with a history of violent inmate-against-inmate assaults" amounts to "deliberate indifference" (Vaughn, 1995, p. 3). In his suit, Farmer contended that such action violates the Eighth Amendment's ban on cruel and unusual punishment. The U.S. District Court for the Western District of Wisconsin ruled that prison officials did not demonstrate deliberate indifference by failing to prevent the assault. On appeal, the U.S. Court of Appeals for the Seventh Circuit affirmed without comment. However, the U.S. Supreme Court agreed to hear the case in order to resolve a dispute among the circuits regarding the definition of deliberate indifference in cases of assault between inmates. In a 9–0 ruling, the High Court ruled in *Farmer* that prison officials could be found liable for failing to protect a prisoner from attacks from other inmates if administrators did not act when they knew of a substantial risk of serious harm. Justice Souter, writing for a unanimous court, ruled that because imprisonment deprives inmates of the means to protect themselves, prison officials cannot let the state of nature take its course (*Farmer v. Brennan,* 1994). *Farmer* offers a glimpse of how correctional staff members, by taking no enforcement action, permit sexual violence in prisons and jails. In a classic study of prison rape, Daniel Lockwood concluded that sexual violence illustrates the need of some prisoners to dominate weaker inmates. "The primary causes of violence are subcultural values upholding men's rights to use force to gain sexual access" (Lockwood, 1982, p. 257; see also Lockwood, 1980). To take the argument a step further, staff nonenforcement reinforces those subcultural beliefs (Donaldson, 2001; Kupers, 2001; Page, 2002).

Although sexual attacks occasionally occur, experts insist that rape in correctional institutions is not a common event. Several studies suggest that the frequency of sexual assault in correctional institutions often is exaggerated (Lockwood, 1980, 1982; Nacci, 1982; Nacci & Kane, 1984). Still, the nature of sexual assault in prisons remains poorly understood, largely because the authorities, through nonenforcement, generally refuse to acknowledge the problem. Reported estimates may underrepresent the prevalence of institutional rape because correctional officers may inhibit reporting by treating victims insensitively or by ignoring assaults altogether (Eigenberg, 1994; Mariner, 2003). What is far more common than homosexual rape in correctional institutions is sexual harassment in which the threat of sexual assault emerges as a form of incentive-motivated aggression. The overarching fear—real and imagined—of sexual assault reveals the consequences of nonenforcement since it con-tributes to a predatory atmosphere of mistrust that can lead to violence (Donaldson, 2001; Kupers, 2001). According to Robertson (1995),

> Incarceration exposes male inmates to a "world of violence" where staff cannot or will not protect them from rape, assault, and other forms of victimization. To make matters worse, retreating in the face of danger is neither normative nor feasible; in prison your back is always against the wall. Most inmates have but two options: to fight in self-defense or become passive victims of a predatory subculture. (p. 339)

Given that nonenforcement allows prisoners to prey on weaker victims, the vulnerable are left to their own devices and must either "fuck or fight" (Eigenberg, 1994, p. 159; Robertson, 1995, 1999, 2000). Under those conditions, nonenforcement contributes to four configurations of violence: (a) The aggressor sexually assaults his victim; (b) during the attack, the victim wards off the aggressor with violence; (c) the potential victim carries out a preemptive strike against the aggressor as a measure of self-protection; (d) the victim later retaliates against the aggressor. Interestingly, nonenforcement tends to blur the line between aggressor and victim (Robertson, 1995; see also Abbott, 1981). Consider the following testimony:

> Well, the first time [a potential sexual aggressor] says something to you or looks wrong at you, have a piece of pipe or a good heavy piece of two-by-four. Don't say a damn thing to him, just get that heavy wast-ing material and walk right up to him and bash his face in and keep bashing him till he's down and out, and yell loud and clear for all the other cons to hear you, Mother fucker, I'm a man. I came in here a mother fucking man and I'm going out a mother fucking man. Next time I'll kill you. (Thomas, 1967, quoted in Robertson, 1995, p. 340)

Nonenforcement leading to predatory violence between inmates also is evident in the victimization of prison outcasts, most notably convicted sex offenders. A defining component of the prison social world is its hierarchy, prompting inmates to compare themselves to other offenders on the basis of their respective crimes. Generally, nonviolent offenders feel superior to inmates convicted of violent and sexual offenses, and convicted rapists and child molesters occupy the lowest strata in the inmate caste system. The mistreatment of sex offenders by other convicts tends to exceed mere harassment. At times, outcasts are assaulted, prompting some sex offenders to serve their sentences in isolation for their own protection. Whereas attacks on sex offenders are sometimes limited to minor injuries, other incidents have involved severe beatings and torture (e.g., James Perrin during the New Mexico state prison riot). While working as a correctional counselor in a Southern jail, I witnessed the aftermath of a brutal beating of a convict by approximately 20 prisoners. The episode was precipitated by a jail officer who announced to a crowded tank of detainees that the inmate was being charged with raping two young girls. In a ruthless act of nonenforcement, the officer smirked and vacated the area, returning to the scene an hour later to transfer the severely injured prisoner to solitary confinement. To no avail, I tried to persuade the staff to hospitalize the injured prisoner. The incident shows that authorities have the power to create situations that are interpreted as "open season" on selected inmates. Likewise, prisoners often take cues from staff members who tacitly grant them license to commit violence against despised convicts.

Staff-Versus-Inmate Violence

By not taking enforcement action against staff members who commit violence against prisoners, authorities intentionally encourage that type of rule breaking, so that it emerges as a form of informal control. Several court cases have brought to light the degree to which corrections officials have turned their backs on violence carried out by their custodial staff. As mentioned previously, in a class action suit filed against Attica's corrections administration, Deputy Warden Pfeil was found liable for violent reprisals that followed in the wake of the riot and for permitting police and correctional officers to beat and torture inmates (*Al-Jundi v. Mancusi*, 1991).

In *Hudson v. McMillian* (1992), prisoner Keith Hudson charged that beatings inflicted by officers constituted a form of cruel and unusual punishment. The High Court concurred, ruling that when officers maliciously and sadistically assault inmates, contemporary standards of decency are violated. More importantly, the decision confirmed that assaults do not have to be as severe as broken bones or concussions to be considered unconstitutional. Even assaults involving injuries as minor as a split lip or a broken dental plate, as in *Hudson,* are unconstitutional. The beating of Hudson clearly reveals the extent of nonenforcement, considering that a supervisor reportedly watched and quipped, "Don't be having too much fun, boys" (Elvin, 1992, p. 6).

In a more recent case involving nonenforcement, a corrections officer at the Nassau County Jail (New York) pleaded guilty to acting as a lookout while two other officers entered a cell and severely beat an inmate who died in custody days later. The victim, Thomas Pizzuto, was serving a 90-day sentence for driving while intoxicated and other traffic violations. Pizzuto, a recovering heroin addict, is believed to have angered the correctional officers by clamoring for his methadone treatment (Cooper 2000).

In a rare examination of unofficial force as informal social control, James Marquart (1986) explored the contours of nonenforced violence against prisoners. In particular, Marquart focused on verbal intimidation (racial and ethnic slurs), minor incidents of physical abuse (known as "tune-ups," "attitude adjustment," or "counseling"), and severe acts of violence (known as "ass whipping"). Marquart learned that unofficial force, as a mechanism of informal control, serves key sociological and organizational functions. First, coercion maintains control and order; prisoners who challenge authority are commonly subjected to informal punishment. Second, unofficial force maintains status and deference by instilling fear and an attitude of subordination among inmates toward the prison staff. Third, unofficial force provides an opportunity for young ambitious officers to prove themselves in order to move upward in the prison organization.

As special populations, women (as well as juveniles) behind bars are particularly vulnerable to violence and abuse (Friedman, 2003; Herivel & Wright, 2003). The Women's Rights Project at Human Rights Watch issued an extensive report detailing the abuse of women inmates in California, Georgia, Michigan, New York, and Washington, D.C. "We found that in the course of committing such gross misconduct, male officers have not only used actual or threatened physical force, but have also used their near total authority to provide or deny goods and privileges to female prisoners to compel them to have sex or, in other cases, to reward them for having done so" (Human Rights Watch, 1996, p. 1; see also Amnesty International, 1999).

Covert Facilitation

In covert facilitation, authorities intentionally encourage rule breaking by taking hidden or deceptive enforcement action (Marx, 1981). Covert facilitation involves "setting up" or framing rule breakers, sometimes in the form of sting operations, considered by their proponents to be lawful entrapment. Compared to the passive tactics of nonenforcement, authorities become more active in covert facilitation by consciously enticing their target to violate a rule. Still, covert facilitation and nonenforcement are often reciprocally connected. For example, authorities may grant rule breakers license to commit violence to further the objectives of covert facilitation. Consider the previous examples in which authorities relied on BTs and snitches, contributing to escalation, nonenforcement, and covert facilitation.

In prisons, covert facilitation has been linked to various tactics of trickery, including the infiltration of gangs and creation of opportunities in which rule breakers can more easily "get busted."[1] Covert facilitation also extends to cases in which officers target certain prisoners and plant contraband in their cells, providing justification to transfer prisoners to solitary confinement. Maintaining our focus on institutional violence, we turn to a major incident allegedly involving covert facilitation at Soledad Prison in California. In 1969, corrections officers at Soledad Prison singled out eight white and seven black inmates to be searched for weapons. In the process, the inmates were ordered outdoors to the exercise yard, where the already tense situation escalated into a brawl between the groups of convicts. Although controversy continues to obscure the actual sequence of events, it was reported by inmates that a tower guard—without warning—fired pinpoint strikes at the black prisoners. Three black inmates were fatally wounded. Inmates accused the officers of contributing to the death of one of the injured prisoners who lay bleeding but was not allowed to be moved for more than 20 minutes, thereby delaying crucial medical attention that might have saved his life (Jackson, 1970).

Days following the shooting, a grand jury in Monterey County ruled that the officers' use of force was justifiable. News from the court aggravated angry prisoners at Soledad. Later that day, a white officer was beaten to death by inmates. Following an investigation, authorities charged three black convicts with murder, Fleeta Drumgo, John Clutchette, and George Jackson. Many prisoners insisted that Drumgo, Clutchette, and Jackson were not involved in the killing, arguing that prison officials targeted them for their black militancy. Amid a highly controversial public campaign of support for the prisoners, charges against Drumgo, Clutchette, and Jackson were dismissed (Jackson, 1970). In 1971, George Jackson, radical leader and author of *Soledad Brother,* was killed by officers during an alleged prison escape. Jackson's death remains shrouded by suspicion of covert facilitation.

A similar incident of alleged covert facilitation occurred in a Southern jail where a prisoner was seemingly enabled to escape. While still handcuffed after being fingerprinted, the prisoner was left unattended in the processing room, seemingly "set up" or enticed to escape. As the prisoner fled through the unlocked back door, he was immediately spotted by an armed police officer who shot the escapee in the back of the head. The bullet exited the escapee's cheek as he continued to flee, running into traffic where he was struck by a van. The escapee managed to regain his balance only to be hit again by another vehicle. Astonishingly, he was alive and conscious. Law enforcement officers escorted him to a hospital, where he was treated for several injuries and then returned to the county jail and placed in solitary confinement. Within an hour, a trustie discovered him committing suicide. The attending officer initially refused to open the cell, but when urged by the trustie, he unlocked the cell, and the trustie removed the prisoner from a hanging position. The officer refused to perform CPR, so the trustie desperately attempted, albeit unsuccessfully, to revive the prisoner, who was pronounced dead on the floor of the jail.[2]

As another form of covert facilitation, some corrections officers have been known to instigate "cock fights" by putting together prisoners who have deep personal conflicts with each other and allowing them to "duke it out" without interference from staff. Similarly, the organizing of prison gladiator matches demonstrates how authorities play a direct role in institutional violence. It has been reported at various prisons around the nation that correctional officers orchestrate fights between convicts for sport and wagering. In a widely publicized incident, a convict—due to his size and strength—was repeatedly coerced by officers to participate in gladiator games at the institution. During one particularly brutal contest in the exercise yard, the prisoner was shot without warning from an officer in the watchtower. The bullet lodged in his spine, permanently paralyzing him below the waist. The crippled prisoner insists he was victimized by staff, first by being forced to fight as a gladiator and second by the marksman's bullet (Nieves, 1998).

The controversy over a premeditated rape at California's Corcoran State Prison sheds light on the degree to which officers will engage in covert facilitation. State prosecutors alleged that four corrections officers deliberately transferred prisoner Eddie Dillard to the cell of Wayne Robertson, nicknamed the "Booty Bandit," knowing that the smaller, younger inmate would be raped. At the trial, Robertson told jurors that he had assaulted and sodomized his victim for two days because officers said Dillard needed to "learn a lesson" (Parenti, 2003a, p. 253). The acquittal of the corrections officers in 1999 triggered a wave of criticism aimed at the California Correctional Peace Officers Association, a group that paid the defendant's legal fees along with launching a media campaign to support the officers. In their defense, the officers insisted that they were unaware that Robertson was a rapist. Many observers of the trial, however, viewed that testimony with enormous skepticism. According to Tom Quinn, a private investigator who specializes in such cases,

> Fundamentally, the claim that the guards didn't know that Robertson was a rapist is totally implausible. The SHU [Special Housing Unit] is a unique social experiment designed to generate information. Furthermore, the CO's [corrections officers] are constantly working with snitches. They know who's who. And they knew . . . that Robertson was a rapist. (Parenti, 2003a: 253)

Failure to convict the four officers has been attributed largely to the code of silence pressuring staff members to not cooperate with state investigators and prosecutors. In a similar incident of covert facilitation and sexual abuse, three women prisoners at Federal Correctional Institution at Dublin (California) were sold as sex slaves to male inmates in an adjoining unit. To resolve the civil suit that followed, the Federal Bureau of Prisons paid the women a settlement of $500,000 (see Burton-Rose, 2003; Siegal, 2002a; Talvi, 2003c).

To summarize, the concept of covert facilitation captures a key irony of social control, exposing tactics in which authorities take hidden or deceptive enforcement action that in turn encourages rule breaking. As the examples discussed clearly illustrate, covert facilitation contributes to the reproduction of violence in penal institutions.

Conclusion

Admittedly, the ironies of social control described here are ideal types, and although they are useful as analytical categories, they have limitations when used to attend to empirical evidence. Escalation, nonenforcement, and covert facilitation commonly overlap, thereby blurring their conceptual boundaries. The secretive nature of those activities also makes it difficult to gather data, especially in situations involving nonenforcement and covert facilitation. Indeed, such actions occur within closed systems—most notably prisons—where official wrongdoing remains conveniently concealed from public, legal, and scientific scrutiny.

Another limitation of this conceptual framework is the uncertainty of correctly arranging the causal order of official actions and their perceived consequences. Is it possible that violence is escalated by the activation of special operations response teams (SORTs) during institutional disturbances? Perhaps. But once again, the causal sequence of events is not always evident. Despite its drawbacks, the chapter sheds crucial light on factors contributing to institutional violence, namely lack of expertise (e.g., lack of training, poor institutional conditions, poor facility design), self-fulfilling prophecies (e.g., labeling), and secondary gains. The penological literature is replete with vivid examples of ironies of social control; still, there are few available conceptual frameworks that systematically link and explain incidents of escalation, nonenforcement, and covert facilitation. Fittingly, Marx's (1981) model—though initially applied to law enforcement—offers a heuristic device for correctional research. By exploring the paradoxes of social control in corrections, it becomes clear that there is much to learn about the dynamics and consequences of managing penal institutions.

A sociology of irony enables researchers to situate authorities and their interdependent relations with rule breakers at the crux of social control analysis, thereby illuminating the dialectics of regulating individual and collective behavior (Schneider, 1975). That framework is particularly relevant in the face of evidence that social control is becoming increasingly dispersed, penetrating, and intrusive, as well as more specialized and technical (Cohen, 1979; Garland, 2001; Staples, 1997). Foucault referred to that phenomenon as the modern state's "subtle calculated technology of subjection" (1979, pp. 220–221). However, that does not necessarily mean that measures of social control are becoming more coercive. "If Hobbes is correct that there are two basic forms controlling others, force and fraud, then it is not surprising that a decrease in the former is accompanied by an increase in the latter" (Marx, 1981, p. 239). Marx reminds sociologists that they should give more than a passing thought to deception, paradox, incongruity, trade-offs, and irony. Not only are those concepts apparent in modern life, but they also have become prominent themes in the correctional apparatus of social control (see Bottoms, 1999; Camp, Gaes, Langan, & Saylor, 2003).

Notes

1. Covert facilitation also is found in the controversial prison "catchall" rules that give authorities blanket authority over institutional conduct. "Catchall rules deny inmates fair warning of punishable behavior and provide prison staff with unwarranted discretion in distinguishing permissible from punishable conduct" (Robertson, 1994, p. 153). Ironically, "catchall" rules facilitate rule breaking, thereby permitting staff to penalize inmates. However, these rules (e.g., disrespect, insubordination, insolence) are "so vague and indefinite that it is difficult to differentiate between what might be permissible conduct and what might constitute a violation" (Robertson, 1994, p. 153; 1996a).

2. While investigating that incident, I interviewed several eye witnesses, including the trustie who intervened.

End-of-Chapter Questions

1. How does escalation contribute to prison violence?

2. How does nonenforcement contribute to prison violence?

3. How does covert facilitation contribute to prison violence?

4. Describe the controversy surrounding George Jackson.

7

Ironies of Capital Punishment

On the day of his execution, Robert Brecheen, a condemned Oklahoma inmate, slipped into a self-induced drug stupor. Facing a life-threatening situation, Brecheen was rushed to a nearby hospital where physicians pumped his stomach. His suicide was averted. But as soon as Brecheen regained consciousness, state corrections officials returned him to death row so as to keep his execution on schedule. Two hours later, Brecheen was prepped in the prison medical unit and put to death with state-approved drugs. The paradox was obvious. "This shows the absurdity of the situation. The idea that they're going to stabilize him and bring him back to be executed is plainly outrageous," said the prison chaplain. The director of the state's corrections department conceded: "Certainly, there's irony" ("Revived From Overdose," 1995, p. 6; see also Mauro, 1999).

Due to an expansion of what constitutes capital crimes, a reduction of appeals, and political pandering to public opinion, capital punishment has become increasingly common. From 1977 to 2002, the number of prisoners put to death in the United States totaled 820. Two-thirds of those executions took place in five states: Texas (289), Virginia (87), Missouri (59), Oklahoma (55), and Florida (54) (Bonczar & Snell, 2003). Currently, 38 states and the federal government have enacted legislation allowing for death sentences. At the end of 2002, a total of 37 states and the federal prison system held 3,557 prisoners under sentence of death

(Bureau of Justice Statistics, 2003; see also Bonczar & Snell, 2003). In efforts to streamline and mechanize the death penalty process, state officials have adopted techniques mirroring the work of Frederick Taylor. A key figure in the industrial revolution, Taylor pioneered scientific management as a model for maximizing efficiency by improving the use of time and motion. In 1997, a triple execution was carried out in Arkansas, only the second of its kind since capital punishment was reinstated in 1976. Prison officials insist that "Such multiple executions minimize overtime costs and reduce stress on prison employees" (Kuntz, 1997, p. E7). Also in 1997, a total of 74 prisoners were put to death, the most executions in a single year since the 76 inmates executed in 1955. That year, Texas carried out 37 executions—the most by a single state in U.S. history (Snell, 1997). Executions in Texas have been rescheduled from midnight to the early evening "to make it easier on everyone involved" (Verhovek, 1998a, p. A4). Convenience has become a prominent feature of capital punishment. As R. J. Parker, an assistant warden in the Texas Department of Corrections, simply put it, "I don't know too many people who like to stay up after midnight. People have to get up and work the next day" (Verhovek, 1998a; see also Janofsky, 2003).

With an eye on efficiency, many law-and-order politicians criticize the appeals process as an obstacle that slows capital punishment, prompting lawmakers to gut legal protections intended to guard against wrongful convictions. Like other states, Texas has reduced the number of appeals, cutting the stay on death row from 9 years to half that or less. Executions in Texas have become not only increasingly efficient, frequent, and routine, but also virtually uneventful; newspapers in the state's largest cities no longer send reporters to cover them. Whereas the death penalty is portrayed by its supporters as a precise, reliable, and necessary armament of criminal justice, opponents often point out that it is a punishment fraught with error and contradiction (Waldo & Paternoster, 2003). Turning again to Marx's (1981) notions of escalation, nonenforcement, and covert facilitation, this chapter explores capital punishment by attending to its many ironies, including counterdeterrent effects, new categories of violators, and false convictions. The significance of race and class in shaping patterns of executions is observed throughout.

Escalation

As defined in the previous chapter, escalation refers to situations in which, "by taking enforcement action, authorities unintentionally encourage rule breaking" (Marx, 1981, p. 222). Throughout this analysis, it is shown that executions not only fail to deter homicide but, ironically, also serve to promote such violence. To support that claim, there is a growing body of research documenting that capital punishment produces counterdeterrent effects. The most compelling research in this field concentrates on the theory of brutalization and the contradictions of executions.

Brutalization Versus Deterrence

Despite the volumes of empirical studies showing no conclusive evidence linking deterrence with capital punishment, the myth persists. Focusing on the adverse effects of the death penalty, Walker (2001) characterizes deterrence theory as a crime control theology—a belief resembling a religious conviction more than an intellectual position because it rests on faith rather than on facts. Still, the issue is not whether the death penalty offers greater deterrence than no penalty at all—of course it does. Rather, the issue is whether the death penalty deters more than other severe penalties, such as life imprisonment without parole. The debate over deterrence stems from a 1975 article by Isaac Ehrlich, an economist who claimed that each execution prevented seven or eight murders. Understandably, Ehrlich's research was celebrated by supporters of the death penalty (see Welch, 2002a; Yunker, 1976). Adding to its political significance, Ehrlich's study was cited in *Gregg v. Georgia* (1976) in which the U.S. Supreme Court permitted states to resume executions. Ehrlich reinvigorated deterrence theory following Zimring and Hawkins' (1973) persuasive criticism of deterrence propositions. Despite the popularity of Ehrlich's research, its high-level statistical analysis was not free of methodological problems. Several reexaminations of Ehrlich's data failed to replicate what he claimed was a deterrent effect (Bowers & Pierce, 1975; Forst, 1983; Passell, 1975; see also Bowers, 1984; Klein, Forst, & Filatov, 1978; Peterson & Bailey, 1991; Stack, 1987).

Proponents of deterrence theory argue that publicizing executions is a necessary component of capital punishment because it is through such publicity that the tough law-and-order message of death sentences is widely communicated. Conversely, a competing theory of publicized executions has challenged the notion of deterrence. Brutalization theory suggests that publicized executions not only fail to deter violence but, paradoxically, increase it. To appreciate brutalization theory fully, it is important to attend to a central assumption of deterrence theory: Potential killers are restrained from committing murder because they identify with those who have been executed. Brutalization theory suggests that some persons, rather than identifying with the condemned, identify with the executioner (Bowers & Pierce, 1980b). It is crucial here to return to the principal message inherent in capital punishment; that is, those who commit heinous crimes deserve to die. Supporting that perspective, advocates of the death penalty view executions as a "public service" performed by the state, ridding society of its despicable members (see Katz, 1988, for a discussion of righteous slaughter).

According to brutalization theory, publicized executions create an alternative identification process that promotes imitation, not deterrence. Bowers and Pierce (1980b) found an increase in homicides soon after well-publicized executions, suggesting that some murderers liken their victims to the condemned. That finding was presented as evidence of a counterdeterrent effect (see also Bailey, 1983, 1998; Bowers, 1988; Cochran, Chamlin, & Seth, 1994; Decker & Kohfeld, 1990; Forst, 1983; King, 1978). Bowers and Pierce specified that publicized executions have a brutalization effect on individuals who are prone to violence, not on persons who are generally nonviolent; in the former case, the publicized execution reinforces the belief that lethal vengeance is justified. Executions devalue human life and "demonstrate that it is appropriate to kill those who have gravely offended us" (1980b, p. 456).

Brutalization theory has been subject to further research. Cochran, Chamlin, and Seth (1994) studied the return of capital punishment in Oklahoma and found evidence of a brutalization effect. They took into account various types of murder and discovered that brutalization was more prevalent in stranger homicides in which social ties (or social controls) are much weaker for persons not known to one another. Cochran et al. contend that, in general, if inhibitions against the use of lethal violence to solve problems created by "unworthy" others are reduced by executions, "such a brutalization effect is most likely to occur in 'situated transactions' . . . where inhibitions against the use of violence are already absent or considerably relaxed" (1994, p. 110). In a widely cited replication, Bailey (1998) confirmed Cochran et al.'s findings, and corroborated their analysis of the different types of murder indicating that the impact of capital punishment in Oklahoma was much more extensive than previously suggested.

Creation of New Categories and Net Widening

According to Marx (1981), escalation leads to the creation of new categories of violators and victims that, in turn, reproduce the ironies of social control. Following this form, capital punishment is escalated by the development of new categories, resulting in a net-widening effect. Several states have recently amended their death penalty statutes. Florida added as aggravating factors the commission of a capital felony by a convicted felon under sentence of imprisonment; commission of a capital felony while engaged in abuse of an elderly or disabled adult, resulting in bodily harm or permanent disability or disfigurement; commission of a capital felony against a person in a vulnerable state due to advanced age, disability, or the defendant's position of familial/custodial authority; and commission of a felony by a criminal street gang member (Snell, 1997).

Other states have also expanded their death penalty statutes (Bessler, 2003). Indiana, for instance, amended its penal code to include as an aggravating factor burning, mutilation, or torture of the victim while the victim was alive. Pennsylvania added to its penal code as an aggravating factor killing a woman who was in her third trimester of pregnancy when the defendant had knowledge of the victim's pregnancy. South Carolina revised its death penalty statute to include as an aggravating factor murder of a witness or potential witness committed for the purpose of impeding or deterring prosecution of any crime. Murder of emergency medical or rescue workers, paramedics, or firefighters engaged in official duty when the defendant knew or reasonably should have known the occupation of the victim was attached to the Tennessee penal code. Virginia also weighed in to the matter, amending its definition of capital murder to include, among enumerated kidnapping offenses, intent to defile the victim and the killing of more than one person within a 3-year period (Snell, 1997).

These new categories of violators and victims add to an array of existing conditions for capital punishment, including treason (Arkansas, California, Georgia), train wrecking, perjury causing execution (California), capital drug trafficking (Florida), aircraft hijacking (Georgia), aircraft piracy, capital rape (Mississippi), contract murder, and solicitation by command or threat in furtherance of a narcotics conspiracy (New Jersey). At the federal level, the death penalty has been extended to, among other things, murder related to the smuggling of illegal aliens; destruction of aircraft, motor vehicles, or related facilities resulting in death; murder committed during a drug-related drive-by shooting; murder committed at an airport serving international civil aviation; murder of a member of Congress, an important executive official, or a Supreme Court Justice; espionage; genocide; and assassination or kidnapping resulting in the death of the president or vice president of the United States (Snell, 1997).

Juvenile Offenders

Increasingly, the application of the death penalty has expanded to include juvenile offenders convicted of homicide. Although 7 states do not specify a minimum age at which the death penalty may be imposed, 14 states and the federal system require a minimum age of 18, and 17 states indicate an age of eligibility between 14 and 17 (Snell, 2001). While serving as California Governor, Pete Wilson reported that he would consider a state law allowing executions of 14-year-olds, similarly Cruz M. Bustamante, a key California politician, said he might support executions for "hardened criminals" as young as 13 (Verhovek, 1998b, p. A7). Texas State Representative Jim Pitts proposed the death penalty for 11-year-old killers. Pitts reasoned, "This is a drastic step. . . . But some of the kids are growing up today, they just aren't the 'Leave it to Beaver' kids that I grew up with" (1998b). Reacting to the 1998 Arkansas schoolyard killings, Pitts argued that the state needs "to send a message to our kids that they can't do these kinds of crimes" (1998b).

In 2002, Toronto M. Patterson, who was 17 years old when he killed his cousin in 1995, was put to death in Texas. The U.S. Supreme Court declined to stay the execution, but three justices issued an unusual dissent, urging the court to reconsider the issue of juvenile offenders being sentenced to death. Justice John Paul Stevens, who dissented when the court last reviewed the issue in 1989, said he remained convinced that it is unconstitutional to execute people for crimes committed when they are younger than 18. "I think it would be appropriate to revisit the issue at the earliest opportunity," added Stevens (Liptak, 2002, p. A1).

Mentally Ill Offenders

New categories of offenders eligible for the death penalty include the mentally ill. While the U.S. Supreme Court has prohibited the execution of emotionally disturbed capital defendants (*Ford v. Wainwright*, 1986; see Miller & Radelet, 1993; Paternoster, 1991), such restrictions have been not been uniformly enforced. Varnall Weeks, a convicted murderer diagnosed by psychiatric experts as a paranoid schizophrenic, was executed in 1995 in Alabama. Weeks was clearly disturbed. Living in a maze of delusions, he believed that "he would come back to life as a giant flying tortoise that would rule the world" (Bragg, 1995, p. 7). At one of his hearings, Weeks described himself as God, wore a domino on a band around his shaved head, and responded to the court's question with a "rambling discourse on serpents, cybernetics, albinos, Egyptians, the Bible, and reproduction. . . . [He also] sat in his cell naked in his own feces, mouthing senseless sounds" (Shapiro, 1995, p. A29). Although prosecution and defense acknowledged that he suffered from paranoid schizophrenia, the courts contended that he was sane enough to be executed. The U.S. Supreme Court unanimously rejected his appeal.

In 2002, the U.S. Supreme Court granted a last-minute reprieve to James Blake Colburn, a death row prisoner in Texas who suffers from severe mental illness. By intervening, the High Court halted the execution one minute before Colburn was to be led to the death chamber. Colburn's lawyers petitioned the court on the grounds that Colburn was incompetent to be executed and had been denied his constitutional rights during proceedings in state court. Colburn confessed to the 1994 stabbing and strangulation of Peggy Murphy, but his case was complicated by his long psychiatric history. At age 14, Colburn was diagnosed as having paranoid schizophrenia. At 17, he was raped and soon began hearing voices and suffering from delusions. Colburn told his mother that he saw a devil slither out of his stomach. He frequently heard voices instructing him to commit suicide. Records show that Colburn attempted suicide at least 15 times, and often he tried to be admitted into public mental health units only to be discharged with a bottle of pills. Once Colburn was voted out of a support group when he disclosed his suicide ideation (Yardley, 2002a).

Defense attorneys pointed out that Colburn had been so heavily medicated with antipsychotic drugs that he dozed through much of his trial. His lawyers argued that Colburn's proceedings were unconstitutional because his condition rendered him incompetent to stand trial. Prosecutors showed a videotaped confession in which Colburn, void of emotion, chewed a sandwich while he recounted the grizzly details of the killing. Prosecutors portrayed Colburn as a person who was simply mean rather than mentally ill. At least two jurors have expressed doubts about the death sentence. One juror now says that she would not have voted for the death penalty had she realized that Colburn's demeanor was caused by chronic schizophrenia (Yardley, 2002a, 2002b). To date, legislators and the courts have not established a consistent or humane definition of how sane or competent a capital defendant needs to be in order to be executed.

Mentally Retarded Offenders

Until recently, the Supreme Court did not interfere with executions involving mentally retarded offenders (those scoring below 70 on a standardized intelligence test). It has been speculated that throughout history, mildly retarded offenders have been commonly executed, but their level of intelligence was never revealed to the courts because such tests were not conducted. Nowadays, defendants are routinely administered intelligence tests; therefore, the courts are fully aware of the defendant's level of intelligence. In 1989, the High Court ruled in *Penry v. Lynaugh* that states have the right to execute mentally retarded persons convicted of capital murder. Critics argue that executing mentally retarded (even mildly retarded) offenders raises serious moral and ethical issues, especially because mental retardation constitutes a serious liability affecting every dimension of that person's life. Persons with mental retardation are often quite susceptible to suggestion and have enormous difficulty in logic, planning, and understanding consequences. Professor of Special Education Ruth Luckasson asks, "Can you imagine anyone easier to execute? I have seen people with mental retardation sitting in their own capital trials, with their lives at stake, who had absolutely no understanding of what was going on" (Harlow, Matas, & Rocamora, 1995, p. 1; see also Reed, 1993; Talbot, 2003).

In 1992, Bill Clinton, then governor of Arkansas, refused to halt the execution of Ricky Ray Rector, who had blown away part of his brain in a suicide attempt just after he had killed a police officer. At the time of his trial, Rector was so mentally retarded that "he did not understand that death was permanent" (Ridgeway, 1994, p. 23). On the day of his death, he told his lawyer that "he planned to vote for Mr. Clinton that November" (Shapiro, 1995, p. A29) and asked the guards to "save his dessert for a snack before bedtime" (Terry, 1998, p. 22). In a similar case, Mario Marquez was executed by the state of Texas after being convicted of double murder and rape. Marquez, a grade-school dropout with an IQ of 65, was the 10th of 16 children born to a migrant farmworker. As a child, he was beaten with a horsewhip by his father and abandoned to the streets and a life of drug abuse at the age of 12. During the trial, Marquez asked his lawyer "if he [Marquez] was going to have a good job when he goes to heaven" and wanted his lawyer to tell him "if he could get a job being a gardener, or taking care of animals" (Hentoff, 1995, p. 30).

The U.S. Supreme Court, in 2002, barred the execution of mentally retarded offenders. The landmark decision, *Atkins v. Virginia,* was based on the court's view that a national consensus rejects such executions as excessive and inappropriate. Of the 38 states that have reinstated the death penalty, 18 prohibit executing the retarded, up from 2 states when the court last considered the question in 1989. The case involves Daryl

R. Atkins, who was convicted of committing a murder and robbery at the age of 18 and is known to have an IQ of 59. The ruling could move 200 or more mentally retarded prisoners from death row. It is estimated that as many as 10% of those convicted of capital murder are mentally retarded (see Human Rights Watch, 2002). One study contends that at least 44 mentally retarded inmates have been executed since 1976 (Keyes, Edwards, & Perske, 2002).

Demonstrating the international significance of *Atkins v. Virginia*, the 15 countries of the European Union filed a brief on behalf of Atkins, as did a group of senior American diplomats who told the court that "the practice of executing retarded offenders was out of step with much of the world and was a source of friction between the United States and other countries" (Greenhouse 2002, p. A14). Amnesty International reported that since 1995, only three countries were known to have executed mentally retarded people: Kyrgyzstan, Japan, and the United States. While *Atkins v. Virginia* dramatically alters the landscape of capital punishment, the Supreme Court offered the states virtually no guidance on who must be considered retarded and who gets to make that determination. The ruling will produce complicated legal activity on two fronts. In the judiciary, some defendants accused or convicted of capital crimes will argue that they are mentally retarded in order to escape the death penalty. Similarly, legislatures will have to establish procedures to determine whether someone is mentally retarded (Liptak & Rimer, 2002; Talbot, 2003).

Nonenforcement

Nonenforcement refers to situations in which authorities, by taking no enforcement action, intentionally permit rule breaking (Marx, 1981). Among the clearest examples of nonenforcement in American history is vigilante justice, most notably lynching— by refusing to intervene or impose sanctions on the perpetrators, authorities encouraged such attacks. Lynching is rooted in racism in that African-American males were specifically targeted, serving as scapegoats for white anger and frustration. Following the Civil War, "black codes" were formally established to perpetuate the economic subordination of former slaves; those codes employed harsher penalties for crimes committed by blacks and led to a disproportionate number of black executions. Informally, black men also were subject to unlawful executions by vigilante mobs. In the 1890s, there were more lynchings (1,540) than legal executions (1,098) in the United States. Although the number gradually declined, nearly 2,000 illegal executions occurred in the early part of the 20th century. Between 1900 and 1909, there were 885 reported lynchings; between 1910 and 1919, there were 621 lynchings, and in the 1920s, there were 315 (Bowers, 1984; see also Brundage, 1993; Dray, 2002; Jackson, 1996; Jackson & Jackson, 2001; Tolnay & Beck, 1992, 1994).

Despite efforts to make the administration of the death penalty less discriminatory, it continues to have a recognizable pattern of racial bias. It is commonly assumed that capital punishment is racially discriminatory simply because black murderers, compared to white murderers, are disproportionately sentenced to death. That assumption, however, is not entirely accurate. In determining racial bias, the race of the victim must be considered along with the race of the offender. Nationwide, approximately half of those murdered each year are black. However, since 1977, about 85% of capital defendants who are executed had killed a white person, whereas only 11% had murdered a black person (Baldus, Woodworth, & Pulaski, 1990). A large body of research demonstrates that killers of whites are more likely than killers of blacks to be sentenced to death. Paternoster (1983) revealed that blacks convicted of killing whites have a 4.5 times greater chance of facing the death penalty than blacks who kill blacks. When the race of the victim is ignored, the chances of blacks and whites receiving a death sentence are almost equal. Keil and Vito (1989) found that when controlling for seriousness of the murder (in Kentucky), "Prosecutors were more likely to seek the death penalty in cases in which blacks killed whites and juries were more likely to sentence to death blacks who killed whites" (p. 511). Baldus et al. (1990) concluded that when the murder victim was white, the chance of a death penalty was roughly doubled in certain kinds of cases—in particular, those incidents in which the victim was killed during the commission of a felony (e.g., homicide during a robbery). In a study on racial disparities in capital punishment, Baldus (1998) reported that in Philadelphia, black defendants in murder cases are 4 times more likely than other defendants to be sentenced to death, even when the circumstances of the killings are the same (see Blume, 1998; Butterfield, 1998; Garvey, 2000).

Numerous other studies have found that blacks charged with murdering whites are more likely to be sentenced to death than are other combinations of race, offender, and victim (Baldus, Pulaski, & Woodworth, 1983; Baldus et al., 1990; Bowers, 1980; Bowers & Pierce, 1980a; Foley & Powell, 1982; Lewis, 1978; *McClesky v. Kemp,* 1987; Radelet & Pierce, 1985; Riedel, 1976; Zimring, Eigen, & O'Malley,

1976). A report by the General Accounting Office presented to the Senate and House Committees on the Judiciary further documents the racial bias in capital punishment:

> In 82% of the studies, race of the victim was found to influence the likelihood of being charged with capital murder or receiving the death penalty, i.e., those who murdered whites were more likely to be sentenced to death than those who murdered blacks. (1990, p. 5)

More recent research continues to reveal a racial bias in the administration of the death penalty. Sorensen and Wallace (1999, p. 559) found that "Homicide cases involving black defendants and white victims fared worse than other racial combinations in all of the pretrial decisions made." Specifically, Sorensen and Wallace revealed that those cases were more likely to result in first-degree charges, to be served notice of aggravating circumstances, and to proceed to capital trial. In a similar study, Brock, Sorensen, and Marquart (1999) discovered disparities, based on race of the offender and victims, resulting from decisions made by both prosecutors and juries. "Blacks who killed whites fared worst in these decisions" (p. 159; see also Baldus, Woodworth, & Pulaski, 1994, 1990; Bright, 2002; Liptak, 2003).

The racial bias points to a key contradiction of the death penalty, especially in the realm of nonenforcement. The fact that only 11% of all executions involve capital defendants convicted of killing a black person gives the appearance that the lives of white victims are more valuable than those of black victims. From 1977 to 1995, a total of 88 black men were executed for murdering whites, whereas only 2 white men were executed for killing blacks (Eckholm, 1995). To date, the state of Texas—the all-time leader of executions with 586 since 1930 and 289 since 1977—has never executed an offender for killing a black person (Bonczar & Snell, 2003). By taking less (or no) enforcement action, that is, by failing to impose death sentences and carry out executions for such a crime, is it possible that authorities—intentionally or unintentionally—encourage the murder of blacks? Even the most cynical of critics would probably say they do not. Still, more than half of all homicide victims in the United States are black. Thus, it seems that there is less retribution for black murder victims than for those who are white. In Virginia, Louis Ceparano pleaded guilty to burning alive a black man, Garnett P. Johnson, and chopping off his head with an ax. Ceparano was one of two white men accused of soaking Johnson with gasoline and subjecting him to racial slurs, then setting fire to him. Receiving two consecutive life terms without possibility of parole, Ceparano was spared the death penalty ("White Man Pleads Guilty," 1998).

Those who believe that the death penalty can be modified to eliminate its racial bias (e.g., see van den Haag & Conrad, 1983) are likely to encounter an even greater irony. In most murders, the assailant and the victim are of the same race; therefore, eliminating the disparity linked to the race of the victim would be likely to result in a higher proportion of blacks sentenced to death. "If killers of black people were executed at the rate of killers of whites, many more blacks would receive death sentences. If, on the other hand, killers of whites were executed at the same rate as killers of blacks, many whites would be spared" (Eckholm, 1995, p. B4). Nationwide, whites make up slightly less than half the total number of murder victims, but 80% of those executed are murderers of white victims (Dow & Dow, 2002; see also McAdams, 1998).

The history of black lynchings serves as a reminder of blatant acts of nonenforcement that authorized and perpetuated the racist practice of unlawful executions. Today, incidents of nonenforcement are not as clear-cut and obvious. Admittedly, it is unlikely that authorities intentionally encourage lethal violence against blacks. Nevertheless executions remain significantly patterned by the race of the victim, suggesting that in the eyes of the state, white murder victims are inherently more valuable than their black counterparts.

Covert Facilitation

Ironies of capital punishment are most evident in cases in which innocent people are falsely convicted, and worse, executed. The problem may be the result of error, wrongdoing, or a combination of the two. Whereas the former serves as evidence of an imperfect criminal justice system, the latter reveals an insidious side of capital punishment. The deliberate prosecution of innocent people represents covert facilitation in that hidden or deceptive enforcement action is taken by authorities who intentionally encourage rule breaking (Marx, 1981). In this context, rule breaking refers to wrongdoing by the prosecutors and police that is facilitated by the state for the purpose of securing capital convictions, even if the suspect is innocent. Such infractions are evident in the framing of suspects, prosecutorial misconduct, and the allowing of perjured testimony. Covert facilitation sheds further light on racism and classism, since people of color and the impoverished are more susceptible to false convictions.

Capital punishment experts have long speculated that numerous innocent persons have been convicted, and in some instances, executed; still, a general understanding of the problem was based previously on anecdotal reports. Then, in 1987, Hugo Bedau and Michael Radelet published a systematic study of 350 defendants believed to have been wrongly convicted in capital (or potentially capital) cases between the years 1900 and 1985. It is important to note that Bedau and Radelet did not simply include any case that appeared suspect. Rather, they applied strict standards of miscarriages of justice and accepted cases only on the basis of *overwhelming* evidence that an innocent person had been falsely convicted. An expanded volume of their work, *In Spite of Innocence: Erroneous Convictions in Capital Cases,* was released by Radelet, Bedau, and Putnam in 1992, cataloguing 416 cases of falsely convicted capital defendants between 1900 and 1991. Approximately one-third of those defendants were sentenced to death, and the authors persuasively documented 23 cases in which innocent people were executed. Most of the remaining defendants eventually escaped execution. Radelet et al. referred to them as the lucky ones. Still, they experienced years of incarceration and their lives were virtually ruined (see also Huff, 2002; Huff, Rattner, & Sagarin, 1996; Scheck, Neufeld, & Dwyer, 2000).

Covert facilitation is commonly found in the most egregious cases of false convictions, many of which resonated with racism and classism. Consider the case of Walter McMillian who eventually was released after spending 6 years on Alabama's death row. Upon further investigation, different prosecutors conceded that the state had withheld evidence from defense lawyers and had relied on perjured testimony to falsely convict McMillian, a low-income African American. The crime involved Ronda Morrison, an 18-year-old white female clerk who was murdered by a black male during a robbery. (Coincidentally, the incident occurred in Monroeville, Alabama, the hometown of Harper Lee, author of *To Kill a Mockingbird* [1960], a story of race and injustice in the Jim Crow South). While being interrogated in connection to another killing, Ralph Myers, an ex-con with a lengthy criminal record, accused McMillian of murdering Morrison. In an unusual move, McMillian was assigned to death row before his trial. After a one-and-a-half-day trial, McMillian was convicted on the testimony of three witnesses, including that of Myers and another criminal suspect. The defense lawyer called a dozen witnesses who each testified that McMillian was at home the day of the murder, socializing with friends at a fish fry. Prosecutors offered no physical evidence linking McMillian to the murder. The trial became widely known for its racist overtones. McMillian had been dating a white woman and one of his sons had married a white woman, an enduring racial taboo in the South (Dieter, 1997).

The Alabama Bureau of Investigation eventually discredited the prosecution's case against McMillian. All three witnesses recanted their testimony, and Myers also reported that he was pressured by law officers to accuse McMillian. Interestingly, the case emerged at a time when federal appeals for capital defendants were becoming increasingly restricted, a reminder of how flawed—and corrupt—the machinery of death can be. Bryan Stevenson, McMillian's attorney, said, "It's clear that he had nothing to do with this crime. There are other folks in prison who don't have the money or the resources or the good fortune to have folks come in and help them" (Applebome, 1993, p. B11).

In a similar case, all charges were dropped against three black men who were incarcerated in an Illinois prison from 1978 to 1996 for a double murder they did not commit. Dennis Williams spent much of that sentence waiting on death row. His case not only underscores the weaknesses of the criminal justice system, but also turns attention to the controversy over the restriction of federal death penalty appeals recently affirmed by the U.S. Supreme Court. The reduction of federal appeals for capital defendants is expected to cut in half the time between conviction and execution (from approximately 8 to 4 years). Richard C. Dieter, director of the Death Penalty Information Center, warns that those restrictions mean that the length of appeals would "fall well below the average time it takes to discover new evidence of innocence. . . . This rush to get on with the death penalty by shortening the appeals process will raise the danger of executing innocent people" (Terry, 1996, p. A14).

The case against Williams, Jimerson, and their codefendants, Willie Rainge and Kenneth Williams, stems from the murder of a white couple in suburban Chicago in 1978, but new DNA evidence, witness recantations, and a jailhouse confession led to their release. Cook County State's Attorney Jack O'Malley said his office was trying to determine how the original investigation "got derailed and why it is the wrong people were charged" (Terry, 1996, p. A14). To answer that, Dennis Williams pointed to racism: "The police just picked up the first young black men they could and that was it. . . . They didn't care if we were guilty or innocent. . . . We are victims of this crime too" (p. A14).

Dishonest and unethical prosecution leading to execution is clearly the most obvious form of covert facilitation. Consider the case of Jesse DeWayne Jacobs who was put to death on January 4, 1995. Because 87 other prisoners have been executed in Texas since it reinstated the death penalty in 1976, Jacobs' execution looked routine. But Jacobs' case is plagued by serious problems, most notably his innocence. His innocence was widely acknowledged even by the prosecutor who convicted him. While prepped for lethal injection, he optimistically believed that the courts would intervene at the last moment. Just before Jacobs was put to death, he announced, "I have news for all of you, there is not going to be an execution. This is premeditated murder by the state of Texas. I am not guilty of this crime" (Hentoff, 1995, p. 22).

Events leading to Jacobs' execution began in 1986 when he and his sister Bobbie Jean Hogan were arrested for the fatal shooting of Etta Ann Urdiales. At the time, Hogan was intimately involved with Urdiales' estranged husband. Separate trials were ordered, and Jacobs confessed that he had abducted Urdiales at his sister's request so that those women could have a meeting. Hogan had hoped to persuade Urdiales to cease contact with her ex-husband and to give up custody of her children. In addition to confessing that he abducted Urdiales, Jacobs initially claimed responsibility for shooting her as well. Although it was true that he kidnapped the victim, the fact remained that Jacobs did not murder her. It was Hogan who shot Urdiales, but Jacobs took the rap because he was already facing life imprisonment for the kidnapping. Moreover, Jacobs also had a previous conviction for murder and was out on parole at the time of the incident. Jacobs later reconsidered his confession and decided not to take the rap for his sister. He then told the truth—that he had abducted Urdiales and took her to an abandoned farmhouse so that his sister could meet with her. Jacobs left the house to sit on the porch when he heard gunfire; quickly returning, Jacobs saw his sister with a gun, and on the floor was a fatally wounded Urdiales. Jacobs explained to the jury that he "'did not know [the murder] was going to take place' and that he 'would not have had anything to do with it if he would have known his sister was armed'" (Hentoff, 1995, p. 22). Despite his plea, the prosecutor insisted that Jacobs shot Urdiales. The jury concurred and Jacobs was convicted and sentenced to death.

Seven months later, during the Hogan trial, Peter Speers, the same prosecutor who secured the conviction of Jacobs, presented to the jury a different version of the killing. Speers accurately placed Hogan in the role of the shooter, thereby eliminating Jacobs as the assailant. Referring to the previous trial, Speers said he "changed his mind 'about what really happened. And I'm convinced . . . that Bobbie Hogan pulled that trigger'" (Hentoff, 1995, p. 22). Speers even went so far as to declare Jacobs innocent, insisting that "Jacobs was telling the truth when he testified that he did not in any way anticipate that the victim would be shot" (p. 22). Furthermore, since Jacobs was not aware of his sister's intention to shoot Urdiales, he was free from accomplice liability under state law. Hogan was convicted of involuntary manslaughter, sentenced to a 10-year prison term, and was likely to be paroled in a few years. Her conviction and the prosecutor's admission that Jacobs was falsely imprisoned changed nothing for Jesse Jacobs. The state of Texas refused to vacate Jacobs' conviction; nor did he receive legal relief from the court of appeals.

Eventually, Jacobs' case reached the U.S. Supreme Court, but it, too, refused to keep him from being executed. In his five-page dissent opinion, Supreme Court Justice John Paul Stevens argued that it was "fundamentally unfair for the state of Texas" to put Jacobs to death (Hentofff, 1995, p. 22; see also Verhovek, 1995). The Jacobs case is strikingly similar to that of *Herrera v. Collins* (1993) in which the United State Supreme Court also ruled that "actual innocence" is not enough to avert execution. In *Herrera,* Justice Harry Blackmun retorted, "Nothing could be more shocking than to execute a person who is actually innocent." Jacobs lamented, "I have committed a lot of sins in my life. . . . Maybe I do deserve this. But I am not guilty of this crime" (Verhovek, 1995, p. E6). Despite the injustice of Jacobs' execution, capital punishment still receives unwavering support, even by some criminologists. Laurin A. Wollan, Jr., an associate professor of criminology at Florida State University who advocates the death penalty, while openly conceding that the criminal justice system makes mistakes. In the words of Wollan, "The value of the death penalty is its rightness vis-a-vis the wrongness of the crime, and that is so valuable that the possibility of the conviction of the innocent, though rare, has to be accepted" (Verhovek, 1995, p. E6).

Forced Confessions

An examination of covert facilitation and the death penalty would not be complete without confronting the practice of deceptive interrogations and forced confessions. Many police interrogators are trained to talk suspects through the *Miranda* warning in ways that reduce the chance that they will request a lawyer, and once suspects waive their rights, courts permit interrogators to use tricks, deceptions, and lies to extract confessions. Moreover, some interrogators simply roar past the suspect's rights and continue the questioning (Leo, 2001; Scheck et al., 2000).

According to Peter Schoenburg, a defense lawyer, "When people assert the right to counsel, that's being dismissed by police in the field as, 'Well, O.K., you'll get a public defender down the road, but first answer my question'" (Hoffman, 1998, p. A1). Law professor Charles D. Weisselberg adds, "When detectives tell a suspect who has invoked his rights that they still want to question him, an ominous message is sent: 'We won't obey the law we just described to you, and the only way you're going to get out the door is to talk to us'" (Hoffman, 1998, p. 40).

Persistent attacks on *Miranda* rights have generated grave injustices. In *Miranda v. Arizona* (1966), Chief Justice Earl Warren warned that police interrogators, wearing a badge of intimidation, could produce untrustworthy confessions even in capital cases (Welch, 2002a). Following the brutal massacre of nine people, including six Buddhist monks, outside Phoenix, Arizona, in 1991, police subjected four suspects to grueling interrogations lasting as long as 20 continuous hours and threatened the suspects that they might wind up in the "gas chamber" or "in a lake with an anchor around their neck" (Whiting & Kelly, 1991, p. A1). The forcefulness of those interrogations became apparent. Each suspect eventually confessed to the killings. After spending 3 months in jail, the suspects were released when police captured the real murderers ("4 Cleared in Massacre," 1991).

Some suspects, especially the emotionally disturbed and the mentally retarded, are exceedingly vulnerable to covert facilitation in the form of unlawful interrogation tactics. Oklahoma City police subjected Robert Lee Miller to an 8-1/2-hour interrogation, resulting in a bizarre confession in which he claimed to have had a dream vision about the rape and murder of two elderly women. Miller's confession was riddled with 112 inconsistencies. He had also told investigators that he was the Lone Ranger, that he was an Indian warrior, and that his family had visionary powers. Miller was convicted and placed on death row, but in 1995, DNA testing cleared him, and he was finally released from prison in 1998. Similarly, Rolando Cruz was convicted of the rape and murder of a 10-year-old Chicago girl, even though investigators could not produce any physical evidence linking Cruz to the crime and prosecutors could not establish a motive. Without much of a case against Cruz, prosecutors and the police claimed that during the interrogation, he had recounted a dream complete with specific details of the murder. Although the recorded interrogation did not include the so-called dream confession, Cruz was convicted and sentenced to death row. Eleven years later, Cruz was released when a new DNA test exonerated him. The man who actually committed the murder had confessed to the crime 8 years earlier (Dieter, 1997; Kolarik, 1996).

Law enforcement officers know all too well the need to be protected against unlawful interrogations; indeed, when police themselves become suspects, they enjoy rights that far surpass those specified by *Miranda*. In New York City, for example, police officers implicated in the death of a civilian are granted two business days to consult attorneys prior to a departmental investigation. Joseph McNamara, former police chief in Kansas City and San Jose, captures the essence of suspects' rights: "When it comes to police, then suddenly rights are precious because they know the danger of being innocently convicted. . . . This is the great irony of the police who resist Miranda" (Hoffman, 1998, p. 40).

Conclusion

Drawing critical attention to the ironies of capital punishment, this chapter has explored a host of ethical and legal problems that produce escalation, nonenforcement, and covert facilitation. Still, the death penalty suffers from other contradictions. Consider the alliance between the state and certain physicians and psychiatrists willing to participate in the execution protocol. Although the American Medical Association's (AMA) standard of medical ethics prohibits physicians from participating in executions (AMA, 1992, see especially "Physician Participation in Capital Punishment," Resolution 5, I-91), the state has little difficulty in recruiting medical personnel needed to carry out its executions (Davis, 1995; see also Bayer, 1984; Weiner, 1972). The state's case often rests on the expert testimony of a psychiatrist—commonly known as Dr. Death—to convict capital defendants (Rosenbaum, 1990). In Texas, Dr. James Grigson, dubbed "the hanging shrink," has offered more than 1,400 condemning testimonies that have resulted in 118 people convicted of murder being sentenced to death row. Grigson has presented so-called expert testimony against a number of defendants who were later exonerated. In his testimony against Randall Dale Adams, Grigson "guaranteed" that Adams "will kill again" (Rosenbaum, 1990, p. 142). Adams, the subject of Errol Morris's documentary *The Thin Blue Line,* was later released from prison when it became known that prosecutors relied on perjured testimony to convict him.

States are required by law to have physicians present at executions to supervise the injection of lethal doses of drugs and document the time of death—a procedure that, paradoxically, takes place in the prison's hospital unit (Trombley, 1992). Recently, critical attention has been directed at pancuronium bromide, the chemical used in lethal injections.

Medical experts insist that pancuronium bromide, marketed under the trade name Pavulon, "paralyzes the skeletal muscles but does not affect the brain or nerves. A person injected with it remains conscious but cannot move or speak" (Liptak, 2003, p. A18). Simply put, the paralysis masks intense distress, leaving a wide-awake prisoner unable to speak or cry out for help while slowly suffocating. In 2001, veterinarians in Tennessee were banned from using pancuronium bromide to euthanize pets (Liptak, 2003). Physicians and psychiatrists who participate in executions serve valuable social functions, adding to the enduring nature of capital punishment in American society. While perpetuating the myth of humane executions, they contribute to the legitimacy of the state and its coercive apparatus of social control (Bohm, 1999; Johnson, 1998; Marquart, Ekland-Olson, & Sorensen, 1994).

Opponents of capital punishment are hoping that their concerns will soon reach critical mass, particularly given the number of innocent people recently released from death row. Since many of those exonerations have been confirmed by DNA, it is difficult to retain a high level of confidence in the criminal justice system's ability to convict only the guilty. In 2002, Illinois Governor George Ryan, a conservative Republican committed to law and order, suspended all executions in his state after DNA had cleared 13 death row inmates. A year later, Ryan stunned the political establishment by commuting all 167 Illinois death sentences to life imprisonment. "The facts that I have seen in reviewing each and every one of these cases raised questions not only about the innocence of people on death row, but about the fairness of the death penalty system as a whole," said Ryan (Wilgoren, 2003, p. A1; see also Liebman, Fagan, West, & Lloyd, 2000).

End-of-Chapter Questions

1. Describe brutalization theory.

2. How has the death penalty contributed to the creation of new categories of violators and net widening?

3. Describe the nature of racial bias evident in capital punishment.

4. How do forced confessions corrupt the criminal justice process?

8

War on Terror and the Misuse of Detention

In the days following the attacks on the World Trade Center and the Pentagon, hundreds of Middle Eastern men—across the United States—were swept up by law enforcement agents in search of persons involved in terror-related crimes. Muhammad Rafiq Butt was one of those individuals caught in the dragnet. Butt, a native of Pakistan, was arrested in South Ozone Park, Queens, New York, for overstaying his visitor visa. Swiftly he was transported to New Jersey where he was detained in the Hudson County Correctional Center. It took the FBI a day to determine that it had no interest in him for its investigation into terrorism. He chose to appear at his deportation hearing without a lawyer, even though he spoke virtually no English and had little education. From jail, he made no calls to his relatives or to the Pakistani Consulate in New York. Days later, Butt was found dead in his jail cell. An autopsy revealed that Butt, 55, whose one-year stay in the United States seems to have been hapless from the very start, had coronary disease and died of a heart attack. His death forced the INS to do something it had not had to do during the 33 days it had him in custody: talk about him publicly and explain the circumstances behind his arrest, detention, and death (Sengupta, 2001a, pp. EV1–2; 2001b).

The war on terror, particularly in the wake of the events of September 11th, has assumed a new resonance not only in the United States, but also in nations around the globe. Ironically, many democratic governments are adopting antiterrorism legislation that has traditionally been associated with repressive states, including the criminalization of peaceful activities, clampdown on asylum seekers, and detention without trial (Amnesty International, 2003; Jilani, 2002; Schuster, 2003). While realizing the importance of protecting national security, critics argue that such tactics violate civil liberties and human rights.

Compounding those problems is evidence of profiling in which members of certain ethnic and religious groups are stereotyped and labeled as possible terrorists (Cole & Dempsey, 2002; Welch 2003a, 2003b). As we shall see, such profiling has fueled several questionable measures in the war on terror. This chapter focuses specifically on two of those controversies: the special registration program and detention, both of which are complicated by government secrecy.[1] While maintaining a human rights perspective, the discussion explores issues of race and ethnicity. It concludes by drawing parallels between the war on drugs and the fight against terrorism, calling into question the effectiveness of current law enforcement and detention practices.

Profiling in the War on Terror

In response to the attacks of September 11th, the Federal Bureau of Investigation (FBI) and the Immigration and Naturalization Service (INS) immediately embarked on a sweeping process that involved the questioning of thousands of persons in the United States who might have information about terrorist activity (Welch, 2004a, 2004b). While the search for information was frequently haphazard and random, Middle Eastern males (and those who appeared to be Middle Eastern) became profiled in the course of the investigation. In its report, *Presumption of Guilt: Human Rights Abuses of Post-September 11th Detainees*, Human Rights Watch (2002) discovered a growing use of profiling on the basis of nationality, religion, and gender. Being a male Muslim non-citizen from certain countries was viewed as a basis for suspicious behavior. Those cases suggest that where Muslim men from certain countries were involved, law enforcement agents presumed some sort of a connection with or knowledge of terrorism until investigations could subsequently prove otherwise. The questioning led to the arrest and detention of as many as 1,200 non-citizens, although the precise number is unknown due to the Justice Department's unwillingness to divulge such information. Of those arrested, 752 were charged not with terror-related crimes, but with immigration violations (e.g., overstaying a visa) (Human Rights Watch, 2002).

Using nationality, religion, and gender as a proxy for suspicion is not only unfair to the millions of law-abiding Muslim immigrants from Middle Eastern and South Asian countries, it may also be an ineffective law enforcement technique. The U.S. government has not charged a single one of the thousand-plus individuals detained after September 11th for crime related to terrorism. Such targeting has also antagonized the very immigrant and religious communities whose cooperation with law enforcement agencies could produce important leads for the investigation (Human Rights Watch, 2002, p. 12).

It should also be noted that a series of cases in which there is more substantive evidence of links to acts of terror clearly demonstrates that a national origin terrorist profile is flawed. Most notably, Zacarias Moussaoui, the so-called "twentieth" hijacker, is a French citizen; the "shoe bomber," Richard Reid, is a British citizen; and José Padilla (a.k.a. Abdullah Al Muhajir), "the dirty bomber," is a U.S. citizen of Puerto Rican descent.

Special Registration Program

Despite objections from civil liberties and human rights organizations, the Department of Justice expanded its use of profiling in the war on terror by introducing a special registration program in December 2002. The plan, intended to produce vital information about terrorist activity, required the registration of all non-immigrant male visitors who are over the age of 16 and entered the United States before September 30, 2002. Specifically, special registration applied to those males from countries which, according to the U.S. government, have links to terrorism, including 12 North African and Middle Eastern countries plus North Korea, affecting more than 82,000 students, tourists, businessmen, and relatives. Those who complied with special registration were required to complete a personal information form, then be fingerprinted, photographed, and interviewed by the FBI. Justice Department spokesman Jorge Martinez believes that this information is necessary intelligence for the war against terrorism. "These people are considered a high risk," he said. "The goal of the system is to know who is coming in and out, and that they are in fact doing what they said they would do" (Gourevitch, 2003, p. EV2).

In the first few months of special registration, the Justice Department failed to discover any links to terrorism, raising questions of its effectiveness. Initially, about 1,000 people were detained, but only 15 were charged with a criminal violation and none was charged with a terrorism-related crime. Most of those detained were in violation of immigration laws, most commonly overstaying their visas in hopes of finding a job and eventually adjusting their status to legal resident. From its start, the program was confusing both for registrants and the immigration service, suggesting that the initiative was poorly planned. The Justice Department neglected to issue a press release or post information on its website until 10 days before the first deadline, explaining why many foreign nationals did not know they had to register and were subsequently arrested for showing up late. In another mishap, an Arabic rendering of the rules for registering was embarrassingly mistranslated to say that individuals under the age of 16 rather than over the age of 16 must register (Gourevitch, 2003, p. EV3).

Many immigration officials and immigration lawyers are perplexed over the precise meaning of the law. The special registration program states that "foreign citizens and nationals" must register; but the language of the requirements does not clearly define the difference between a "citizen" and a "national," or even clearly state what a "national" is. The only available guidance is a phrase from a 50-year-old statute that defines a "national" as "a person owing permanent allegiance to a state" other than the United States. Even Justice Department spokesman Jorge Martinez, when interviewed, did not know how to define "national" (Gourevitch, 2003, p. EV3). Due to the confusion, several foreign nationals not covered by the program (e.g., those from Canada, Liberia, and Norway) showed up to register. Immigration officials did not know how to interpret the procedures, so they arrested them. Similarly, two Canadian citizens, who were born in Iran but emigrated when they were children, were detained for several days. They were in the United States on work visas for the high-tech industry, and had appeared at an INS office uncertain whether they were required to register. The special registration program also created problems for the INS, an agency already strained by other operations in the war on terror. INS employees complained that they received very little special training; moreover, they frequently had to work overtime to process the thousands of registrants. The Arlington (Virginia) immigration office became so inundated with registrants that it had to send many to the Dulles International Airport office for processing (Gourevitch, 2003).

Among the most controversial incidents occurred in Los Angeles where more than 400 foreign nationals who appeared for registration were handcuffed and detained. Soheila Jonoubi, a Los Angeles-based attorney representing several of the men, said that the detainees spent the next several days (and in some cases weeks) in custody. Many of them were strip searched; verbally accosted; deprived of food and water, bedding and adequate clothing; and denied information as to why they were being detained. The Justice Department reported that the men were detained because their visas had expired; after completing background checks, all but 20 of them were released. Many of those detained held legal immigration status and were waiting to receive work permits that had been delayed by the INS due to a backlog in processing a high volume of applications (Talvi, 2003a, 2003b).

While the registration of more than 82,000 people failed to uncover any major links to terrorism, the Justice Department has moved forward with plans to deport as many as 13,000 Arab and Muslim men whose legal immigration status had expired. Many of the men had hoped for leniency since they had cooperated fully with the program. Detentions coupled with deportations have sent shock waves through immigrant communities across the nation, producing unprecedented levels of fear. Many Middle Eastern men and their families—many of whom are U.S. citizens—have fled the country, particularly to Canada where they intend to apply for political asylum (Cardwell, 2003; Elliott, 2003).

These developments bring to light the problem of human rights violations in the realm of immigration, criminal justice, and the war on terror. Understandably, government officials stationed in the Department of Homeland Security (DHS) and the Bureau of Immigration and Customs Enforcement (BICE, the newly reorganized INS) point to the need for national security. Jim Chaparro, acting director for interior enforcement at the DHS, emphasizes, "We need to focus our enforcement on the biggest threats. If a loophole can be exploited by an immigrant, it can also be exploited by a terrorist" (Swarns, 2003a, p. A9). Even so, civil liberties and human rights groups denounce the government for using the immigration system as a weapon in the war on terror. Similarly, they complain about selective enforcement since the government focuses on immigrants from Arab and Muslim nations while ignoring similar violations by those from Mexico and Central America.

The overall logic of implementing the special registration program as a tactic in the war on terror raises serious doubts among criminologists and legal scholars. Why would a terrorist risk detection and detention by appearing before the special registration program, especially since the exhaustive procedure involves fingerprinting, photographing, and interrogation by FBI agents? "And if intelligence officials are right that Al Qaeda sleepers generally lead quiet, unremarkable lives in conformity with legal requirements, the INS would have no way of knowing even if an Al Qaeda member *were* to walk in" (Cole, 2003b, p. 5). Moreover, experts point out that deportation is among the worst antiterrorism maneuvers. According to David Cole, Professor of Law at Georgetown University, "The last thing you want to do with a real terrorist is send him abroad. . . . What we want to do is charge him and lock him up. Which, of course, would also spare the innocent thousands caught in the middle" (Gourevitch, 2003, p. EV5; see also Cole & Dempsey, 2002, Welch, 2003b).

Even government agencies have weighed in to the debate over the utility of the special registration program. The General Accounting Office (2003a) issued a report that left many questions unanswered as to the value of the project. That report included interviews with officers, many of whom expressed doubts over the usefulness of registration in the campaign against terrorism. Still, the Justice Department defended the special registration program. "To date, the program has not been a complete waste of effort," replied Jorge Martinez, who points out that it has led to the arrest of "a wife beater, narcotics dealer, and very serious violent offenders" (Gourevitch, 2003, p. EV6). To this, critic Alex Gourevitch countered, "But that isn't exactly the same as catching terrorists. And if what we really want is to catch wife beaters, narcotics dealers and violent offenders, the Justice Department should simply require everyone in America to show up and register" (2003, p. EV6; see also Swarns, 2003b).

To reiterate, issues of profiling and human rights figure prominently in the war on terror, producing an array of contradictions that undermine efforts to detect terrorist activity.

> The racist component to these directives is hard to overlook. The escalation of selective registration, detention and deportation of immigrants has taken the form of a large, very poorly guided fishing expedition. One of the great ironies of this kind of social control is that it erodes the cooperation of these immigrant communities. When a government embarks on a fishing expedition like this one, they're admitting that they don't have a lot of clues to begin with. (Welch, quoted in Talvi, 2003a, p. 3)

Civil liberties organizations, such as the American Civil Liberties Union and the Center for Constitutional Rights, caution against the government's claim that in order to effectively fight the war on terror, people must surrender some of their freedoms. That reasoning marks a false paradigm in that national security is not predicated on diminishing civil liberties. Mass detention produced by the special registration program is dysfunctional and ineffective. Former executive director of the ACLU, Ira Glasser, reminds us, "No one can be made safe by arresting the wrong people. In focusing on them [wrong targets], the government certainly violated their civil rights but, more important to most Americans, abandoned public safety as well" (2003, p. WK12).

In a major development in June 2003, President Bush announced guidelines barring federal agents from relying on race or ethnicity in their investigation. One exception to that policy, however, is terrorism, allowing agents to use race and ethnicity aimed at identifying terrorist threats. Officials in the immigration service will continue to require visitors from Middle Eastern nations to undergo registration and special scrutiny. Civil rights groups swiftly denounced the policy since it perpetuates stereotyping and provides authorities with legal justification to single out Arabs, Muslims, and other ethnic groups who may fall under suspicion. The initiative also falls short of what Bush had claimed to do about racial profiling. In a February 2001 national address, Bush declared that racial profiling was "wrong, and we will end it in America" (Lichtblau, 2003a, p. A1). Ibrahim Hooper of the Council on American-Islamic Relations also complained about the policy, especially in light of a recent government report criticizing the Justice Department for rounding up and detaining hundreds of Middle Eastern men following the September 11th attacks. As we shall see in the next segment, the misuse of detention prompts serious questions about the penal features of the war on terror.

Misuse of Detention

In addition to problems posed by profiling, particularly evident in its special registration program, the government continues to face similar charges of human rights violations, especially in the realm of detention. Shortly after the Justice Department began its post-September 11th sweeps and roundups, allegations surfaced involving arbitrary detention, abuse of detainees, and a host of other procedural infractions. Civil liberties and human rights organizations issued stern warnings to the government that, despite the unique circumstances caused by the attacks on the Pentagon and the World Trade Center, such abuses would not be tolerated. Several groups released reports documenting serious violations of civil liberties and human rights (American Civil Liberties Union, 2001;

Amnesty International, 2003; Lawyers Committee for Human Rights, 2003). Chief among the complaints among civil liberties and immigration attorneys is that the government, in waging its war on terror, misuses immigration law to circumvent its obligations under the criminal justice system. Moreover, the Department of Justice has established new immigration policies and procedures that undermine previously existing safeguards against arbitrary detention by the INS. Those violations are catalogued into three key areas: denial of access to counsel, arbitrary detention, and harsh conditions of detention (Human Rights Watch, 2002). As we shall see, each of those problems has been exacerbated by the government's reliance on secrecy, in that the Department of Justice refuses to divulge information concerning the persons being detained.

Denial of Access to Counsel

In line with the U.S. Constitution as well as international human rights law, all persons, citizen or non-citizen, have the right to be represented by legal counsel after being deprived of liberty for alleged criminal or immigration law violations. Human Rights Watch (2002) discovered that "special interest" detainees (those the government suspected of being involved in terrorism-related activity) were questioned in custody as part of a criminal investigation, even though they were subsequently charged with immigration violations. Many of those detainees were interrogated by FBI and INS agents concerning criminal matters as well as their immigration status. Immigration attorneys complain that the government relies on administrative proceedings under the immigration law as a proxy to detain and interrogate terrorism suspects without affording them the rights and protections that the U.S. criminal justice system provides. Among those safeguards is the right to have a lawyer present during custodial interrogations, including free legal counsel if necessary (Cole, 2003b; Cole & Dempsey, 2002).

Abusive Interrogations

The right to have an attorney present during custodial interrogations serves to prevent coercion. As the war on terror escalated in the aftermath of the September 11th attacks, detainees were not only denied access to attorneys, but were subjected to abusive treatment in violation of federal and international law. Both the U.S. Constitution and Principle 21 of the *United Nations Body of Principles for the Protection of*

All Persons under Any Form of Detention or Imprisonment (1988) specifically prohibit abusive interrogations since such mistreatment impairs a person's judgment and capacity to make decisions. Similarly, abusive interrogations produce false confessions.

Consider the case of Abdallah Higazy, a 30-year-old Egyptian graduate student with a valid visa, who was detained as a material witness on December 17, 2001. A pilot's radio had allegedly been found in the New York City hotel room where he had stayed on September 11th. Higazy was placed in solitary confinement at the Metropolitan Correctional Center (MCC) in Manhattan. Eager to establish his innocence, Higazy volunteered to take a polygraph examination. He then was subjected to a grueling five-hour interrogation during which he was not given a break, food, or drink. Due to some unusual restrictions concocted by the Justice Department, Higazy's attorney was forced to remain outside the interrogation room, unable to advise his client. Higazy reported that from the beginning of the interrogation, the agents threatened him and his family. Yielding to intense emotional and physical fatigue as a result of the abusive interrogation, Higazy eventually said that the radio belonged to him. The Justice Department charged Higazy with lying to the FBI, but three days later, an American pilot went to the hotel to claim it. Charges against Higazy were dropped and after one month in solitary confinement, he was released from the MCC onto the streets of New York City wearing a prison uniform and given three dollars for subway fare. Months later, Ronald Ferry, the former hotel security guard who had found the pilot's radio, admitted that he had fabricated the story accusing Higazy. Ferry was sentenced to six months of weekends in prison for lying to the FBI. He admitted that he had known that the device was not in a safe belonging to Higazy. Ferry, who is a former police officer, said that he lied during a "time of patriotism, and I'm very, very sorry." The judge said that his conduct was "wrongly motivated by prejudicial stereotypes, misguided patriotism or false heroism" (Human Rights Watch, 2002, p. 39; see also Weiser, 2002).

Arbitrary Detention

Civil liberties and human rights organizations remind us that physical liberty is a fundamental human right affirmed in international law and in the U.S. Constitution, in the due process clauses of the Fifth and Fourteenth Amendments. Correspondingly, arbitrary detention violates that right. "An individual who is arbitrarily detained is rendered defenseless by the coercive power of the state. While arbitrary detention is a hallmark of repressive regimes, democratic governments are not immune to the temptations of violating the right to liberty" (Human Rights Watch, 2002, p. 46; Amnesty International, 2003). Regrettably, many detainees swept up during the early phase of the post-September 11th investigation were subjected to arbitrary detention and held for lengthy periods of time. Such violations were not merely inadvertent due to the confusion surrounding the events of September 11th. Rather, arbitrary detention became a systematic tool in the Justice Department's campaign against terror under which new procedural rules had been created. Those rules provided greater power to the government and undermined previously existing protections for detainees. As noted previously, the new rules enabled the government to use immigration detention as a form of preventative detention (Lawyers Committee for Human Rights, 2003).

Harsh Conditions of Detention

According to the *International Covenant on Civil and Political Rights* (ICCPR, 1966) (Article 10), "All persons deprived of their liberty shall be treated with humanity and with respect for their inherent dignity of the human person." Correspondingly, the ICCPR forbids cruel, inhuman, or degrading treatment or punishment. In the aftermath of September 11th, human rights advocates complained that INS detainees were subjected to abuse and inadequate conditions of confinement, even though they had not been accused of criminal conduct, much less convicted of it. Simply put, from the early stages of the investigation on, those detainees were treated as if they were convicted terrorists, locked down in solitary confinement where they were rarely allowed to leave their cells for weeks and sometimes months. In addition, they were subjected to extraordinarily strict security measures that prevented them from communicating with their families and attorneys. Even worse, some were victims of verbal and physical abuse, refused adequate medical attention, and housed with suspected or convicted criminals (Human Rights Watch, 2002; Welch, 2000d, 2002a, 2002d).

Physical and Verbal Abuse

With emotions running high after the attacks on the Pentagon and the World Trade Center, detainees feared reprisals from corrections officers and prisoners who might subject them to a form of violence that can best be described as scapegoating (Welch, 2003a, 2003b). In some instances, those fears were realized. Human rights advocates report numerous incidents in which detainees were subject to physical and verbal abuse by staff and inmates (Amnesty International, 2003; Human Rights Watch, 2002, 2003). In one particular case, Osama Awadallah, a lawful permanent resident of the United States and a citizen of Jordan, was held as a material witness for 83 days during which he experienced a series of humiliating and physically abusive incidents. While at the San Bernardino County jail (California), corrections officers forced Awadallah to strip naked before a female officer. At one point, an officer twisted his arm, forcing him to bow and pushed his face to the floor. After being transferred to a federal facility in Oklahoma City, a corrections officer hurled shoes at his head and face, cursed at him, and issued insulting remarks about his religion.

Later, Awadallah was shackled in leg irons and flown to New York City, and while in transit, U.S. marshals threatened to "get" his brother and cursed the Arabs. At the Metropolitan Correctional Center, he was confined to a room so cold that his body turned blue. Physical abuse continued as one corrections officer caused his hand to bleed by pushing him into a door and a wall while he was handcuffed. The same guard also kicked his leg shackles and pulled him by the hair to force him to face an American flag. In another incident, marshals kicked him and threatened to kill him. Eventually, Awadallah was released on bond. A government investigation corroborated the physical mistreatment. His attorney has filed a complaint on his behalf (Human Rights Watch, 2002; see also Amnesty International, 2003).

Government Secrecy

Contributing to the problems of profiling and the misuse of detention, the government has maintained a policy of secrecy (Dow, 2001). Months following the investigation on the attacks of September 11th, Attorney General Ashcroft repeatedly denied defense attorneys and the press access to basic information about many of those in detention, including their names and current location. Such secrecy has been denounced by human rights and civil liberties advocates as well as by news organizations. Even some political leaders have complained that the Attorney General has failed to explain adequately the need for such drastic measures. Kate Martin, director of the Center for National Security

Studies, stated, "The rounding up of hundreds of people secretly, secretly arresting them and putting them in jail where their families don't know where they are and not telling the public is unprecedented and extraordinary in this country" (Donohue, 2001, p. EV1). Martin added, "This is frighteningly close to the practice of 'disappearing' people in Latin America" where secret detentions were carried out by totalitarian regimes (Williams, 2001, p. 11). An attorney for three other men being held in San Diego likened their detention to the sweeps for communists and sympathizers during the Red Scare of the 1920s; he complained that he was not even told where his clients were being held and was not permitted to contact them (Fox, 2001). Harvey Grossman of the ACLU added, "There's been nothing as massive as this since the day after Pearl Harbor, when they rounded up 700 Japanese immigrants and held them incommunicado and without charges for a protracted period" ("Concerns Rise of Civil Rights," 2001).

Reports that detainees have been subjected to solitary confinement without being criminally charged, as well as being denied access to telephones and attorneys, suggests that detainees are being deprived of due process. Moreover, those deprivations clearly contradict assurances by the Department of Justice (DOJ) that everyone arrested since September 11th has had access to counsel. Key members of Congress have begun to challenge the sweeps of aliens in search of terrorists. Seven Democrats, most notably a coauthor of Ashcroft's antiterror legislation, Senate Judiciary Committee Chairman Patrick Leahy (VT), as well as the only senator to vote against it, Russ Feingold (WI), requested from the Attorney General detailed information on the more than 1,200 people detained since the terrorist attacks. Specifically, the lawmakers asked for the identity of all those detained, the charges against them, the basis for holding those cleared of connection to terrorism, and a list of all government requests to seal legal proceedings, along with the rationale for doing so. The lawmakers stated that, while the officials "should aggressively investigate and prevent further attacks," they stressed the Justice Department's "responsibility to release sufficient information . . . to allow Congress and the American people to decide whether the department has acted appropriately and consistent with the Constitution" (Cohen, 2001, p. EV1).

Similarly, human rights groups have admonished the Justice Department for operating a war on terror behind a thick wall of secrecy, a tactic that "reflects a stunning disregard for the democratic principles of public transparency and accountability" (Human Rights Watch, 2002,

p. 5; Lawyers Committee for Human Rights, 2003; Welch, 2004b). The government has put forth an effort to shield itself from public scrutiny by concealing information that is crucial to determining the extent to which its investigations have been conducted in accordance with the law. Civil liberties advocates also take strong exception to the government's attempt to silence criticism of its antiterrorist efforts, most notably with Attorney General Ashcroft's infamous statement to Congress:

> To those who scare peace-loving people with phantoms of lost liberty, my message is this: your tactics only aid terrorists, for they erode our national unity and diminish our resolve. They give ammunition to America's enemies, and pause to America's friends. They encourage people of goodwill to remain silent in the face of evil. (Ashcroft, 2003)

Legal experts strongly urge the government to amend its tactics in the war on terror so that its actions may be subject to public scrutiny, thus averting civil rights violations. Three areas of accountability are recommended. First, the Justice Department must release information about those it detains, including their names and location. Secret detentions such as those used by the Justice Department in its antiterrorism campaign violate the *Declaration on the Protection of All Persons from Enforced Disappearances,* a non-binding resolution by the United Nations General Assembly in 1992. Second, independent monitoring groups must be granted unrestricted access to detention facilities so as to ensure that detainees are treated in a fair and humane manner. "Such scrutiny is particularly important when dealing with foreigners who for reasons of language, lack of political clout, difficulty retaining counsel, and unfamiliarity with the U.S. justice system may be more vulnerable to violations of these rights" (Human Rights Watch, 2003, p. 23). Third, immigration proceedings must no longer be conducted in secrecy. Open hearings have been the practice at the INS for nearly 50 years, a tradition that is consistent with U.S. constitutional law (Cole, 2003b; Cole & Dempsey, 2002).

In a major blow to civil rights initiatives aimed at striking down the government's use of secret detention, a federal appeals court, in 2003, ruled 2–1 that the Justice Department was within its rights when it refused to release the names of the more than 700 people rounded up in the aftermath of the September 11th attacks. The case stemmed from a campaign by civil liberties groups asserting that the Freedom of Information Act required the Justice Department to disclose the names of those detained on immigration charges. Moreover, such secrecy invites abuse since law enforcement officials are stripped of their accountability. The ruling will likely be appealed, setting the stage for another confrontation over secrecy and the war on terror (Lewis, 2003).

The 2003 Inspector General's Report

As discussed throughout this chapter, much of the criticism over the government's handling of the war on terror has been delivered by human rights and civil liberties organizations relying on their own investigations. In June 2003, their body of knowledge was greatly expanded by the government itself, particularly through a report released by Glenn A. Fine, the Inspector General at the Department of Justice. Civil liberties and human rights advocates hailed the report, especially since it confirmed their complaints that the Justice Department's approach to the war on terror was plagued with serious problems. The report concluded that the government's roundup of hundreds of illegal immigrants in the aftermath of September 11th was a mistake, since it forced many people with no connection to terrorism to languish behind bars in unduly harsh conditions. The Inspector General found that even some of the lawyers in the Justice Department had expressed concerns about the legality of its tactics, only to be overridden by senior administrators. Suggesting that the Justice Department had cast too wide a net in the fight against terrorism, the report was critical of FBI officials, particularly in New York City, who had made little attempt to distinguish between immigrants who had possible ties to terrorism and those swept up by chance in the investigation. Shanaz Mohammed, 39, who was held in Brooklyn for eight months on an immigration violation before being deported to Trinidad in 2002, responded to the report: "It feels good to have someone saying that we shouldn't have had to go through all that we did. I think America over-reacted a great deal by singling out Arab-named men like myself. We were all looked at as terrorists. We were abused" (Lichtblau, 2003b, p. A1; U.S. Department of Justice, 2003a, 2003b; von Zielbauer, 2003a).

Since the Justice Department has maintained a policy of secrecy concerning arrests and detentions, the report was hailed for its openness, offering to the public the most detailed portrait to date of who was held, the delays many faced in being charged or gaining access to a lawyer, and the abuse that some faced in jail. William F. Schulz, executive director of Amnesty International USA, said that the Inspector General's office "should be applauded for releasing a report that isn't just a whitewash of the government's actions" (Lichtblau, 2003b, p. A18). Figures cited in the report show that a total of 762 illegal immigrants were detained in the weeks and months after the attacks on the Pentagon and the World Trade Center. Most of the 762 immigrants have now been deported, and none have been charged as terrorists. The report validated complaints that the 84 detainees housed at the Metropolitan Detention Center in Brooklyn faced a pattern of physical and verbal abuse from some corrections officers. Videotapes, which investigators discovered after being told by prison employees that the tapes no longer existed, showed staff members slamming chained detainees into walls and twisting their elbows. In one episode captured on videotape, a guard was seen ramming a detainee's face into a T-shirt taped to a wall. The shirt featured a U.S. flag and the words "These Colors Don't Run." The detainees were also subjected to unduly harsh detention policies, including a highly restrictive, 23-hour lockdown. Detainees also were handcuffed, and placed in leg irons and heavy chains any time they moved outside their cells (U.S. Department of Justice, 2003a, 2003b; von Zielbauer, 2003a).

Compounding their isolation, detainees were limited to a single phone call per week, and due to a communication blackout, families of some inmates in the Brooklyn facility were told their relatives were not housed there. The report faulted the Justice Department for not processing suspects more rapidly, a procedure that would have determined who should remain in detention and who should be released. In sum, the findings "confirm our long-held view that civil liberties and the rights of immigrants were trampled in the aftermath of 9/11," said Anthony D. Romero, executive director of the ACLU (Lichtblau, 2003b, p. A18; see also Liptak, 2003a; "Report finds U.S. misstated terror verdicts," 2003).

Despite strong evidence of civil rights violations contained in the report, Justice Department officials defended themselves, saying that they believed they had acted within the law in pursuing terrorist suspects. Barbara Comstock, a spokeswoman for the department announced, "We make no apologies for finding every legal way possible to protect the American public from further terrorist attacks" (Lichtblau, 2003b, p. A1). Despite their disagreements with some of the report's conclusions, Justice Department officials said that they have already adopted some of the 21 recommendations made by the Inspector General, including one to develop clearer criteria for the processing of such detentions. Other areas of improvement encompass procedures that would ensure a timely clearance process, better training of staff on the treatment of detainees, and better oversight of the conditions of confinement.

Conclusion

As this chapter demonstrates, ethnicity and human rights are important considerations in antiterrorism campaigns, particularly in light of questionable profiling and detention practices. The war on terror, even in its early stages, is strikingly similar to another major criminal justice movement, namely the war on drugs. Both strategies are intricately linked to race and ethnicity and have produced an array of civil liberties violations compounded by unnecessary incarceration (Talvi, 2003b; Welch 1999a, 2004b, 2004c). Equally important is the evidence that raises serious concerns about effectiveness. While the war on drugs has succeeded in locking up unprecedented numbers of poor people who are disproportionately black or Latino, it has failed to reduce consumption of illegal drugs (Husak, 2002; Welch, Bryan, & Wolff, 1999; Welch, Wolff, & Bryan, 1998). Similar doubts suggest that the current campaign against terrorism also is capturing small fries rather than big fish.

Professor David Burnham, director of the Transactional Records Access Clearinghouse (TRAC) at Syracuse University, released a report showing that the war on terror and its reliance on ethnic profiling have produced small-scale success (TRAC, 2003). That study found that a large proportion of so-called terrorist prosecutions involve minor charges (e.g., document fraud, identification theft, threats, and immigration violations), resulting in jails sentences of only a few months. In the year after the attacks on the World Trade Center and the Pentagon, prosecution of crimes connected with terrorism increased tenfold to 1,208 cases from 115 the previous year. But the sentences dropped significantly, from a median of nearly two years in 2001 to just two months in 2002. Senator Patrick Leahy (D, Vermont) weighed in to the matter, saying, "It raises questions about whether too many resources are being tied up on minor cases that have nothing to do with terrorism" (Lichtblau, 2003c, p. A16).

Contributing to growing skepticism, the General Accounting Office (2003) found that federal prosecutors inflated their success in terrorism-related convictions in 2002 by wrongly classifying almost half of them. Overall, 132 of the 288 convictions reported as international or domestic terrorism (or terrorism-related hoaxes) were determined by investigators to have been wrongly classified (see "Report Finds U.S. Misstated Terror Verdicts," 2003). Similar problems have been discovered in New Jersey, where prosecutors reported handling 62 "international terrorism" indictments in 2002. However, all but two involved Middle Eastern students accused of hiring imposters to take standardized English exams for them. Nearly all of the accused students have been released on bail pending trial, while nine of them already have been convicted, fined between $250 and $1000, and deported ("'Terrorism' Cases in New Jersey," 2003).

As has been the experience with the war on drugs, the government's fight against terrorism promises to be a long-term commitment, demanding vast resources and funding. Still, with the lessons of a failed drug control policy in clear view, it is crucial that the government curb its tendency of blaming racial and ethnic minorities for problems associated with terrorism (see Marable, 2003; Robin, 2003). As Anthony D. Romero of the ACLU observes, "The War on Terror Has Quickly Turned Into a War on Immigrants" (Liptak, 2003b, p. A18). Moreover, citizens ought not to accept the false paradigm that diminished civil liberties is the price to pay for public safety (see Ratner, 2003). Indeed, rather than weakening national security, protection of civil liberties is symbolic of a strong democratic government. As Supreme Court Justice Louis D. Brandeis wrote in 1927, the framers of the U.S. Constitution knew that "Fear breeds repression; that repression breeds hate; [and] that hate menaces stable government" (*Whitney v. California*, 1927; see also Human Rights Watch 2002, 2003; Lawyers Committee for Human Rights, 2003).

Note

1. The scope of this chapter is the misuse of detention within the domestic war on terror. Therefore, the breadth of the topic does not include the current controversy over the detention of the estimated 600 "enemy combatants" in Guantanamo Bay and the U.S. government's unwillingness to comply with the Geneva Convention for the protection of prisoners of war (Cole, 2003a).

End-of-Chapter Questions

1. How does the use of ethnic profiling undermine counterterrorist strategies?

2. Describe the flaws of the special registration program.

3. In what ways is detention misused in the war on terror?

4. Why is government secrecy in the war on terror so detrimental to democratic society?

9

Punitive Profit

High Plains Youth Center in Brush, Colorado, opened in 1993 as a 180-bed facility under the management of Rebound, Inc., a Denver-based company that specialized in housing juveniles. The formula for profit was simple: charge between $140 and $180 per juvenile and refuse to spend money on basic services and programs. As a result, Rebound, Inc. generated considerable revenue while inflicting undue suffering on those trapped behind its locked doors. Many of the juveniles not only had histories of criminal violence but also battled emotional and psychological problems. Although Rebound, Inc. promoted itself as an ideal facility for mentally ill juveniles, the center did not have adequate mental health care and was not licensed to provide such services. It is common for privately run facilities to advertise as having mental health units because they can charge higher fees for housing mentally ill juveniles, even though they frequently do not have the trained personnel necessary to provide sufficient mental health care. Eventually, state authorities launched an investigation into High Plains, following the suicide of a 13-year-old mentally ill youth. Widespread neglect at the institution became evident when investigators concluded that the youth had been dead for more than four hours before being discovered; moreover, only half of the required number of staff was on duty at the time of the suicide. The investigation also revealed a pattern of sexual and physical abuse by the employees at High Plains, including incidents of choking and the misuse of restraints. Faced with compelling evidence of long-term *mismanagement and misconduct, Colorado officials closed the High Plains Youth Center. Similarly, other Rebound, Inc. facilities have been shut down in Florida and Maryland (Friedman, 2003).*

The term enterprise, in everyday language, has come to mean either a project or a business organization. In the realm of corrections, both definitions are fast becoming appropriate. Not only is the continued effort to expand prison construction a massive social project, it also has become a major growth industry. Approaching punishment as an enterprise reinforces the perspective that economic and market forces have an enormous impact on skyrocketing imprisonment rates—even more of an impact than what is uncritically accepted to be the driving cause, namely crime. Whereas popular and political belief suggest that massive reliance on prisons deters crime, research demonstrates otherwise. Lynch (1998) points out that the correlation between imprisonment and deterrence is clouded in mathematical mysticism. In testing the age-old notion that a greater reliance on imprisonment reduces crime, Lynch concluded that "over the long run, imprisonment has no suppression effect on the rate of criminal offending. . . . These data, in short, seem to indicate what drives the rate of criminal offending is external to the crime–punishment nexus" (1998, pp. 10–11; see also Walker, 2001).

Other recent research on the use of prisons shows that incarceration fails to deter repeat offenses. In their 2002 report, Langan and Levin of the Bureau of Justice Statistics reveal that 67% of prisoners released from state prisons in 1994 committed at least one serious new offense within three years, a 5% increase over those released in 1983. Many criminologists acknowledge that putting large numbers of offenders behind bars reduces crime due to an incapacitation effect. However, there is greater debate over whether longer sentences produce a deterrent effect for those released from prison. "The new report, some experts say, suggests that the answer is no" (Butterfield, 2002, p. A11). According to criminologist Joan Petersilia, "The main thing this report shows is that our experiment with building lots more prisons as a deterrent to crime has not worked" (Petersilia, as quoted in Butterfield, 2002, p. A11). Petersilia also says a likely reason for the increase in recidivism is that governments, in an effort to reduce costs and appear tough on crime, have slashed rehabilitation programs such as drug treatment, vocational education, and classes to prepare inmates for life in the free world. Jeremy Travis, former director of the National Institute of Justice, agrees. "Often inmates are released having received very little or no job training, drug treatment or education in how to be a better parent. Many are unable to find jobs and are barred by law from living in public housing projects so they quickly return to crime" (Butterfield, 2002, p. A11; see also Lewin, 2001).

In search of better predictors of imprisonment, scholars turn to economic indicators, such as the impact that unemployment has on incarceration (Dunaway, Cullen, Burton, & Evans, 2000; Lynch, Michalowksi, & Groves, 2000; White, 1999). In his highly regarded work on the subject, Leslie Wilkins (1991, p. 96) reports that "Both between and within countries, unemployment rates tend to be strongly associated with the proportion of the population serving terms of imprisonment," noting that a similar relationship does not exist between unemployment and crime. Moreover, Wilkins finds that additional economic measures, particularly the polarity between extreme wealth and poverty, further refine the prediction of incarceration rates (see also Arvanites & Asher, 1995). Still other economic factors manifesting in market forces are linked to the expansion of corrections. As we shall see in this chapter, prisons have become a lucrative industry, paying financial as well as ideological dividends (Christie, 1994; Reiman, 2004). As one critic puts it, "Recognizing an opportunity to make fortunes off the backs of prisoners and their families, Corporate America—including architects, bankers, building contractors, and telephone companies—lined up at the prison trough" (Pranis, 2003, p. 156).

Especially given the lack of a strong relationship between the rates of incarceration and crime, the expansion of social control in the form of building more prisons promises to have chilling effects on democracy and social equality. "The major dangers of crime in modern societies are not the crimes, but that the fight against them may lead societies towards totalitarian developments" (Christie, 1994, p. 16). This chapter examines punitive profit in a wider conceptual context. In doing so, it explores the role of market forces in the escalating criminal justice apparatus along with the societal and individual casualties they produce. Indeed, the expanding corrections machinery is an ironic and self-defeating mechanism of social—and crime—control, creating profound and negative effects for American society as well as its people.

Production of Prisoners

As previously discussed in Chapter 3, among the contradictions of capitalism is the economic marginalization of a large segment of society, thus creating a surplus population from which deviance and crime is produced. Because those marginalized are significant in both sheer numbers and their perceived threat to the social order, the state invests heavily in mechanisms of social control (Barnett & Cavanaugh, 1994; Spitzer, 1975; Welch, 1998a). Law enforcement and corrections constitute some of the more coercive measures of social control designed to deal with the portion of the surplus population considered a problem. Within the political economy, the criminal justice system functions traditionally as a social-control apparatus by protecting capitalist forms of production. Given the emergence of the corrections enterprise, it is clear that such operations of social control themselves are engaged in the accumulation of capital. Before identifying the structure and composition of the corrections industry, it is fitting that we acknowledge key dimensions of the political economy that contribute to street crime, an activity that produces raw materials necessary for the corrections industry, namely prisoners.

Because large-scale economic marginalization restricts opportunities for legitimate financial survival in a market economy, illegitimate—or unlawful—economic enterprises emerge. Perhaps the most widespread underground economy is the illicit drug industry, a form of financial survival (and mood-altering escape from the harsh conditions of poverty) created by the structural inequality of capitalism (Parenti, 2003b). However, the selling and consumption of illegal drugs has become increasingly criminalized to the extent that vast resources of the state are allocated to control these behaviors. It is crucial to emphasize that additional strategies to prohibit the drug industry (i.e., harsher penalties and mandatory minimum sentences) create an ironic effect due to the prevailing market forces. Even though the drug trade is an outlaw industry, its underground economy conforms to free-world, free-market, capitalist principles insofar as prices attached to illegal drugs are contingent upon supply and demand. Therefore, reducing the supply merely drives up the price of the drug, which makes trafficking more profitable, hence attracting more individuals and groups willing to venture such risks. As noted in Chapter 4, Wilkins (1994) points out that the cost of illegal drugs reflects the risk, not the type or quality of the product; drug peddlers are not so much selling drugs as they are, like insurance companies, trading in risk (see Welch, Bryan, & Wolff, 1999; Welch, Wolff, & Bryan, 1998).

In sum, the criminalization of drugs paradoxically escalates trafficking. Higher penalties increase the risk of selling drugs, making the activity more lucrative and, in the end, recruiting an endless supply of peddlers who already have been marginalized economically. As drug peddlers are apprehended, convicted, and incarcerated, they serve as raw materials for the corrections industry, an economic enterprise considered by many proponents of a free market as legitimate.

As discussed in Chapter 5, the criminal justice machinery has long exhibited equivocal tendencies insofar as relatively harmless lawbreakers (i.e., social junk) are treated like menacing and predatory offenders (i.e., social dynamite) (Spitzer, 1975; see also Adamson, 1984). However, the equivocal nature of the criminal justice system is accentuated by the economic needs of the corrections industry that demands a greater supply of prisoners to remain profitable, even if those offenders are nonviolent and convicted of low-level crimes. That phenomenon is known as net widening, meaning that more and more offenders convicted of less serious crimes are becoming snared in a correctional apparatus that has become increasingly coercive and punitive.

Most prisoners overall are serving time for nonviolent offenses as well as crimes that are not particularly serious. Since 1978, most of the growth in America's prisons can be accounted for by nonviolent offenders, and in 1998 that group reached 1 million. By comparison, the European Union, a political entity of 370 million, has a prison population (including violent and nonviolent offenders) of 300,000. That figure is one-third the number of prisoners that the United States, a nation of 274 million, incarcerates for nonviolent offenses alone (Irwin, Schiraldi, & Ziedenberg, 2000).

New York Governor George Pataki argues that an additional 7,000 prison beds (priced at $635 million) are needed to handle what he claims to be a growing number of violent offenders. Pataki's rhetoric is contradicted by the fact that New York's crime rates are dropping and the fact that in 1996, 60% of those sentenced to prison were convicted of nonviolent offenses. Pataki is accused of grandstanding on the crime issue and placating upstate legislators who see corrections as economic development engines for their districts ("New York's Prison Building Fever," 1997). Manufacturing false claims and manipulating fear are common tactics that politicians rely on to rip off taxpayers. That type of deception represents what Steven Donziger of the National Center on Institutions and Alternatives and the National Criminal Justice Commission calls the political "bait and switch."

A policy that pretends to fight violence by locking up mostly nonviolent offenders is clearly an inefficient use of taxpayer resources. The scam works like the classic "bait and switch" marketing ploy, in which customers are "baited" into a store by an advertisement for an item at an extremely low price. Once in the store, the salesperson "switches" the customer to a higher-priced product than the scheme was designed to promote. In the criminal justice field, the "bait" is citizen fear of violent crime. The "switch" occurs when public officials fight crime by building more prisons *but then fill the new cells with nonviolent offenders.* This scheme profits those who wish to appear "tough" on crime but in reality are failing to make America safe. One consequence of this policy is that the criminal justice system spends tens of billions of dollars on prisons and then underfunds effective drug treatment, educational programs, and violence prevention programs, claiming that there is not enough money (Donziger, 1996b, p. 18).

Undoubtedly, the "bait and switch" tactic works. In 2002, the nation's prison and jail population rose again to 2,166, 269, a new record (Harrison & Karberg, 2003). Between 1990 and 2000, the incarcerated population grew an average of 5.7% annually. Since 1980, the incarceration rate has more than tripled. In 2001, the rate of incarceration (including both prison and jail) reached 699 persons per 100,000 population, making the United States the number one jailer in the world (Sentencing Project, 2002; see also Mauer & Chesney-Lind, 2002). Politicians know intuitively the campaign boost they receive by playing the crime card and capitalizing on the public's fear. John O. Bennett, New Jersey state senator, expressed delight in the amount of public support he receives for sponsoring tough-on-crime legislation: "I many times say that it is too bad that not every year is an election year" (quoted in Peterson, 1997, p. NJ-6). The "bait and switch" scam also benefits other individuals and organizations linked financially to the corrections industry. As mentioned previously, a crucial function of the war on drugs (and other "tough on crime" initiatives resulting from moral panic over perceived "crime waves") is its production of massive quantities of prisoners—raw materials— for the corrections industry. That economic-punishment nexus is further reinforced by lengthy sentences (especially mandatory minimums) that ensure profitability, since long-term occupancy in prison translates into a handsome financial per diem. In a trade publication geared toward investors, the *Cabot Market Letter* compared a private corrections facility (Corrections Corporation of America [CCA]) to "a hotel that's always 100% occupancy . . . and booked to the end of the century" (Bates, 1998a, p. 13).

The Corrections Economy

Imprisonment has become big business, and the bitter "not-in-my-backyard" attacks on prisons have been replaced with proud proclamations, such as the sign in Canon City, Colorado, reading "Corrections Capital of the World." The mayor of Canon City boasts, "We have a nice, nonpolluting, recession-proof industry here" (Brooke, 1997, p. 20). In Leavenworth, Kansas—a community that recently added a private prison to an already extensive corrections system that features a federal penitentiary, a state prison, and a military stockade—a billboard quips, "How about doin' some TIME in Leavenworth?" Bud Parmer, site acquisition administrator for Florida Department of Corrections concedes, "There's a new attitude . . . small counties want a shot in the arm economically. A prison is a quick way to do it" (Glamser, 1996, p. 3A). Economically strapped towns induce jail and prison construction by offering land, cash incentives, and cut-rate deals on utilities; in return for these accommodations, locals receive jobs and spur other businesses such as department stores, fast-food chains, and motels, all of which contribute to the tax base (see Kilborn, 2001; Martin, 2000; Thies, 2001).

Whereas prisons are tightly courted on Main Street, on Wall Street the larger corrections industry has created a bull market—further evidence that crime does indeed pay. Tremendous growth in the prison population, coupled with astonishing increases in expenditures, has generated a lucrative market economy with seemingly unlimited opportunities for an array of financial players: entrepreneurs, lenders, investors, contractors, vendors, and service providers. The American Jail Association promoted its conference with advertisements reeking of crass commercialism: "Tap Into the Sixty-Five Billion Dollar Local Jails Market" (Donziger, 1996a). The World Research Group organized a 1996 convention in Dallas entitled "Private Correctional Facilities: Private Prisons, Maximize Investment Returns in This Exploding Industry." Without much hesitation, corporate America has caught the scent of new public money. The Dallas meeting included representatives from AT&T, Merrill Lynch, Price Waterhouse, and other golden logo companies (Teepen, 1996).

The prison industry also has attracted other capitalist heavyweights, including the investment houses of Goldman Sachs and Salomon Smith Barney who compete to underwrite corrections construction with tax-exempt bonds that do not require voter approval. Defense industry titans Westinghouse Electric, Alliant Techsystems, Inc., and GDE Systems, Inc. (a division of the old General Dynamics) also have entered the financial sphere of criminal justice, not to mention manufacturers of name-brand products currently cashing in on the spending frenzy in corrections. While attending the American Correctional Association's annual meeting, Rod Ryan, representing Dial Corporation, boasted, "I already sell $100,000 a year of Dial soap to the New York City jails. Just think what a state like Texas would be worth" (Elvin, 1994/1995, p. 4).

Privatizing Punishment

The operative word for describing corrections in a free-market economy is privatization. Although private financial interests have shaped the course of criminal justice throughout modern history (Spitzer & Scull, 1977a, 1977b), the recent wave of commercialization and profiteering is traced to the Reagan era of the early 1980s. At that time, the prevailing political and economic philosophies encouraged government officials to turn to the private sector to administer public services, such as sanitation, health care, security, fire protection, and education. It was believed that the application of free-market principles to public services would enable private corporations to compete against each other to provide the best service at the lowest cost. In that context, the privatization of prisons was introduced as a new and novel approach to some old correctional problems, most notably, overcrowding and mounting costs. Judith Greene, a policy analyst, summarizes the phenomenon:

> The private prison industry emerged in the U.S. amid a rising tide of neo-liberal free market economic ideas and neo-conservative zeal for moralistic discipline that propelled the country's criminal justice through a series of campaigns to 'get tough on crime.' Reagan administration officials' ardor for mandatory prison sentences and zero-tolerance approaches to crime control and drug enforcement launched a national crusade to 'take back' criminal justice policies and practices from the hands of the supposedly liberal elite of criminologists and a defense-oriented legal establishment. The rapid embrace of their ideas by the public sent prison population levels shooting through the roof. (2003a, p. 56; see also Sinden, 2003)

Modern-day privatization has brought profits to Wall Street. Beginning in the early 1980s, the privatization movement spread swiftly nationwide. By 2000, a total of 31 states, the District of Columbia, and the federal prison system reported that more than 87,000 of their prisoners were being held in private facilities. Those private correctional facilities held 5.8% of all state prisoners and 10.7% of federal inmates. Texas (with 13,985 prisoners housed in private facilities) and Oklahoma (with 6,931) relied more on private corrections than any other states. In addition, five states had at least 20% of their correctional population in private facilities: New Mexico (40%), Alaska (33%), Montana (32%), Oklahoma (30%), Hawaii (24%), and Wisconsin (21%) (Beck & Harrison, 2001). In juvenile corrections and halfway houses, privatization has an even greater presence. Privatization also has extended to maximum-, medium-, and minimum-security units; local and county jails; women's institutions; and detention centers for the Bureau of Immigration and Customs Enforcement (BICE, formerly known as the Immigration and Naturalization Service [INS] detention centers).

Today, the scope of privatization is vast, reaching beyond institutions that are owned and operated by private companies. Most correctional institutions use some form of privatization in such areas as medical and mental health services, substance abuse counseling, educational programs, food services, and the management of prison industries. However, private ownership and management of correctional institutions themselves generate the most controversy. "Although the correctional system has long contracted for various private services with good results, contracting for facility ownership and management is a significant departure from traditional reliance on private support services" (Durham, 1994, p. 264; James, Bottomley, Liebling, & Clare, 1997).

Corrections-Industrial Complex

The most significant development emerging from the current wave of privatization is the corrections-industrial complex, a term reminiscent of the military-industrial complex popularized by sociologist C. Wright Mills and President Dwight D. Eisenhower. In his critically acclaimed work *The Power Elite* (1956), Mills presents evidence of an integrated collective of politicians, business leaders (i.e., defense contractors), and military officials who together determine the course of state policy. Eisenhower went further in his 1961 farewell address, commenting that government "must guard against the acquisition of unwarranted influence" by the military-industrial complex (1985, p. 748).

Nowadays, scholars are applying similar concepts to the growing corrections industry. Many penologists point to a corrections-industrial establishment that has clearly surfaced, including politicians, business leaders, and criminal justice officials (Adams, 1996; Wood, 2003). More specifically, the corrections-industrial complex is an incarnation of the iron triangle of criminal justice where subgovernment control is established.

Operating well below the radar of public visibility, key players in the corrections subgovernment strongly influence the course of policy and spending. They include (a) private corporations eager to profit from incarceration (e.g., Corrections Corporation of America, Correctional Services Corporation, Wackenhut Corrections), (b) government agencies anxious to secure their continued existence (e.g., Bureau of Justice Assistance, National Institute of Justice), and (c) professional organizations (e.g., the American Bar Association, the American Correctional Association) (Lilly & Deflem, 1996; Lilly & Knepper, 1993). The iron triangle of criminal justice draws on power from each of those sectors in a formidable alliance and, according to critics, is a daunting source of influence over government (see Austin & Irwin, 2001; Shelden & Brown, 2000).

It should be emphasized that the vast majority of economic activity in the corrections-industrial complex is restricted to purchasing of goods and services (Lilly & Deflem, 1996). "States pretty much have a monopoly in the prison industry. . . . Although private companies, backed by venture capital firms, have been trying to cash in on the prison boom, so far they have only made progress through niche marketing" (Adams, 1996, pp. 462–463). Still, there is considerable speculation that state (and federal) officials will eventually transfer a larger proportion of their inmates to private corrections.

The corrections industry operates according to a somewhat unique set of economic dynamics in that the supply–demand principle functions in reverse. "More supply brings increased demand. Industry insiders know that there are more than enough inmates to go around" (Adams, 1996, p. 463). That point is particularly significant considering the ongoing production of prisoners in American capitalist society, fueled by the war on drugs and other tough-on-crime initiatives. Thus, investors are betting that the corrections industry will continue to proliferate because its raw materials—prisoners—are relatively cheap and in constant supply. Such growth expectations of privatized corrections already have materialized on Wall Street where correctional corporations, investors, and shareholders are enjoying healthy returns, compounding capital for punitive profit.

Private Prisons, Public Problems

Financial players in private corrections claim emphatically that their motives are forthright and benevolent and insist that their investments serve not only the private sector but also the common good. Private businessman

Ted Nissen, of Behavior Systems Southwest, contends that the prison system is a disaster and that he simply wants to improve it while earning a profit (Nissen, 1985, p. 194). CCA founder Tom Beasely intones, "There are rare times when you get involved in something that is productive and profitable and humanistic. We're on the verge of a brand new industry" (Quoted in Egerton, 1984, p. 19). Proponents of privatization point out rather accurately that government has failed at establishing a correctional system that meets even its most basic objectives; compounding matters, correctional facilities continue to be plagued by overcrowding and inadequate programs and services. The strategy of private corrections corporations has remained unchanged for two decades: Persuade state officials that privatization can save tax dollars because their companies can build and operate prisons more cheaply than government.

To their advantage, businesses, unlike their government counterparts, do not have to deal with red tape, such as open bidding on contracts and job security for state employees. Advocates say that because privatization has shown promise in other spheres of public services (e.g., health care, sanitation), a similar approach can succeed in corrections. Invoking their own sense of legitimacy, defenders of privatization proclaim, "Law and tradition both make quite clear that privatization has been, and continues to be, an acceptable alternative to conventional governmental discharge of public responsibilities" (Durham, 1994, p. 274).

Supporters of private corrections also believe many of the attacks on privatization are driven by ideologies that are biased against profit motives. To those charges, critics insist that profiting from corrections is different fundamentally from other forms of privatization because it reduces the administration of justice to the accumulation of capital at the expense of programmatic and humanitarian ideals. Those critics argue forcefully that the right and power to punish are reserved for and limited to the state (Parenti, 1999; Welch, 2004a). Civil liberties groups challenge privatization on the grounds that the government should not retreat from its responsibility of safely securing the incarceration of those sentenced to prison or jail. Abdicating that authority to the lowest bidder runs counter to the fundamental principles of the administration of justice because criminal punishment is a public, not a private matter (see Shichor, 1999, 2002). In surveying the privatization of corrections, several other issues and criticisms persist: accountability and liability; questionable claims of cost savings, abuse of inmates and security lapses, and the reproduction of inequality. In examining each of those issues, there is evidence of the harmful effects of private corrections on people, communities, and society.

Accountability and Liability

For years, concerns have been raised about liability and accountability in private corrections, heightening fears that a legal limbo might exist where neither the state nor the private sector would be held answerable for infringements of the constitutional rights of its prisoners. That problem has been particularly evident in cases in which private corrections managers have failed to comply with safety codes, or, even more dramatic, when the death or serious injury of prisoners has resulted. In 1984, the terrain of legal liability was clarified when a court found both the government and the private company liable for damages in the death of one inmate and the serious injury of another (*Medina v. O'Neill*, 1984). Even more significantly, the U.S. Supreme Court, in *Richardson v. McKnight* (1997), ruled that employees of private correctional firms under contract with a state or local government are not entitled to the immunity from prisoner lawsuits that protects corrections officers who are on the public payroll. In that case, an inmate in a CCA facility sued two corrections officers for injuries caused by keeping him in unduly tight physical restraints. In his dissenting opinion, however, Justice Antonin Scalia echoed the chorus of privatization, claiming that the decision would make private corrections more expensive for taxpayers. Revealing cynicism and contempt for those behind bars, Scalia added that this case would also lead to windfalls for prisoners who bring suits and the lawyers who represent them (see Greenhouse, 1997; Verhovek, 1997).

A lack of clear lines of accountability can create surreal scenarios, such as the one in Texas where 240 sex offenders from Oregon were transferred to a private correctional facility owned and operated by CCA (which earned more than $14,000 per day). Two of those prisoners (with histories of sexual violence) escaped, assaulted a guard, and stole an automobile. When CCA managers notified Houston law enforcement officials of the escape, police wanted to know why they had not been apprised of the shipment of sex offenders to their jurisdiction. CCA responded they had no legal obligation to notify city or county officials. Susan Hart, a CCA spokeswoman, answered defensively, "We designed and built the institution. It is ours" (Bates, 1998a, p. 11). But the plot thickens: CCA expected Texas law enforcement officials to hunt down and apprehend the escaped convicts. Hart told reporters, "It's not our function to capture them" (Bates, 1998a, p. 11). The plot thickens even more: Although Texas officials had the legal authority to arrest the escapees for assault and car theft, they could not charge them with escape because in Texas it was not yet a crime to flee a private corporation. Lawmakers quickly remedied the problem by passing the appropriate legislation. Still, that scenario raises concerns about not only the legality of privatization but also the potential to jeopardize public safety and impose unnecessary burdens on other sectors of the criminal justice system (e.g., law enforcement). That problem is especially disconcerting given that private corrections companies have dubious records that include hiring poorly trained security staff. Many of these poorly trained corrections officers work at low wages, contributing to high turnover and a work environment lacking professionalism.

Questionable Claims of Cost Savings

Although the claim of cost savings is the main justification for the privatization movement, there remains little evidence of significant cost-effectiveness (Austin & Coventry, 2001; General Accounting Office, 1996; McDonald, Fournier, Russell-Einhorn, & Crawford 1998; Pratt & Maahs, 1999). In cases in which a savings was documented, the cost reduction was produced by lower labor costs; in effect, private correctional companies hired staff at considerably lower wages with fewer job benefits (Miller, 2003). As a result of hiring personnel at lower wages, private prisons assembled correctional staffs that had less experience and training than their public counterparts. Understandably, staff inexperience and poor training leave the facility vulnerable to many problems including turnover, drug misconduct, escapes, and violence (Austin, Crane, Griego, O'Brien, & Vose, 2000; Camp & Gaes, 2002; Clark, 1998; Crane, 2000).

One of the keys to lowering costs is promoting competition whereby private companies will try to outbid each other by keeping their costs to a minimum. However, if there are fewer private companies in the correctional marketplace, as is the case today, it is less likely that costs will be controlled. The two largest private correctional companies are Corrections Corporation of America (CCA) and Wackenhut Corrections Corporation (WCC). As reported in the most recent census, CCA held 37,244 prisoners in 45 facilities, accounting for 53.8% of the total number of inmates in private prisons. WCC housed 19,001 prisoners in 26 facilities, 27.4% of the total number of privately held inmates. To illustrate the relative size of those companies, CCA was the ninth largest prison system—only seven states and the federal prison system held more prisoners. WCC was the 19th largest correctional provider in the nation.

Together, CCA and WCC held 56,245 prisoners, or 81.3% of the adult inmates in private facilities (Camp & Camp, 1998).

What is good news for the leading private correctional companies in terms of a greater share of the market and increased profits is bad news for government in terms of less choice among competitors and increased costs. The General Accounting Office (1996) concluded that private corrections did not fulfill the claim that their services would generate a substantial savings; moreover, there is evidence that privatization of corrections invites political corruption, leads to poor-quality services, and exacerbates the conditions that lead to abuse and violence. While the financial figures of CCA and Wackenhut Corrections confirm high dividends, those windfalls remain in the private sector without passing a savings to taxpayers, even though the raw materials (i.e., prisoners) belong legally to the public sector (as wards of the state). Upon closer scrutiny, we see that privatizing corrections has less to do with saving tax dollars and more to do with shifting funds from the public to the private sector.

Abuse of Inmates and Security Lapses

Opponents of privatization contend that the safety of prisoners hangs in the balance when private correctional companies assume custody. Although it is difficult to determine whether inmates are abused more by officers in private facilities than by those in governmental institutions, there is evidence that improperly screened and inadequately trained corrections officers in private facilities lack skills necessary to deal with frustrated and potentially aggressive convicts. Poorly trained staff members have been known to instigate and escalate prison tension, resulting in disturbances and riots; for instance, an investigation team concluded that the riot at the INS facility in New Jersey was partially caused by guards harassing and abusing inmates (Immigration and Naturalization Services, 1995). Adding to the list of human rights violations (including sexual and physical assault) in privately operated BICE (formerly known as INS) facilities around the country, detainees are typically confined to warehouse-like dormitories for 23 hours a day, where they are denied fresh air and natural light. Detainee access to visitors, counsel, and the courts also is routinely obstructed by arbitrary rules of the staff and corporation. Idleness due to the lack of institutional programs contributes further to inmate stress, thus enhancing the risk of disorder and violence (Welch, 2002a; 2003a, 2003b).

For years, private correctional facilities have been the sites of numerous acts of violence. Two correctional officers at a CCA prison in Walensburg, Colorado, repeatedly beat a prisoner while he was handcuffed, shackled, and unable to resist ("Ex-Prison Supervisors Told They Will Be Jailed," 2000). In a CCA facility for juveniles in South Carolina, child advocates were horrified to learn that children were abused by staff, including instances in which some boys were hogtied and shackled together (Bates, 1998a). In that case, the jury awarded the victims $3 million in punitive damages, concluding that the use of force was so malicious that it was "repugnant to the conscience of mankind" (*William P. v. Corrections Corporation of America*, 2000; see also Greene, 2003b; Hecht & Habsha, 2003). Allegations of rape and assault at a privately run juvenile facility in Colorado prompted state officials to concede that the safety of children at private jails is not guaranteed (Friedman, 2003; Robbins, 1997). In 2000, Wackenhut Corrections Corporation abandoned a contract to operate a juvenile prison housing 226 inmates in Jena, Louisiana, after a judge in New Orleans and the Justice Department found that the juveniles were being beaten, physically abused, and deprived of adequate food and clothing. Director of the Juvenile Justice Project of Louisiana, David Utter, commented, "Privatization has been a failure in Louisiana and the sooner we end that experiment the better" (Butterfield, 2000, p. A21).

Abuse of women inmates in private prisons also is well documented (Amnesty International, 1999). At the Central Arizona Detention Center, a guard captain gave a marijuana cigarette to six female prisoners, then had male officers search their cells. They were told that drug possession charges could be avoided if they would perform a strip tease for the officers. When they complied, the officers became sexually aggressive. After a female inmate filed an official complaint over the incident, she was beaten by three guards (van Wormer, 2003; see also George, 2003; McNair, 2000; "$1.4 million awarded," 2001).

Under privatization there are also fiscal incentives to cut corners on security features of an institution, resulting in noncompliance with safety standards. In fact, private corrections companies are cutting corners by introducing so-called "innovations." A corrections official in Virginia, who oversees the operations of private prisons in the state, inspected a medium-security institution being constructed by CCA that did not have guard towers—an "innovation" that saved the corporation $2.5 million (Bates, 1998a). One can imagine that in the public sector, prison officials who eliminated guard towers in a prison would probably lose their jobs, but in the private sector, the focus of attention is on profit, not custodial security.

Hiring fewer guards is another sure way to reduce operating and labor costs, thereby guaranteeing greater profits for private corrections corporations. For security purposes, however, that personnel tactic runs counter to conventional wisdom of maintaining an appropriate ratio of guards to inmates. CCA claims that the use of pods, whereby one guard in a control room can supervise 250 prisoners, does not jeopardize security. Corrections and security experts argue that prisons of that size require many more staff to ensure safety (Bates, 1998a; Greene, 2003a, 2003b).

Allegations of inadequate medical services for prisoners continue to surface, especially in light of the escalating costs of health care (Alexander, 2003; refer to Chapter 5). A shift supervisor in a CCA facility testified that an inmate who died from an undiagnosed complication during pregnancy suffered in agony for more than 12 hours before CCA officials permitted her to be transported to a hospital. It has been reported that private corrections companies ensure profits by "picking jackets," selecting only the healthiest inmates from the state prison population to minimize medical expenditures. Once prisoners become ill, private corrections officials ship them back to state facilities, where taxpayers underwrite the inmates' health care (Bates, 1998b). It should be noted that the increased incarceration of nonviolent offenders is welcomed by private corrections companies interested in "picking jackets" for docile inmates.

Reproducing Inequality

As noted throughout this chapter, the rising correctional population has generated financial opportunities for investors in privatized corrections, reinforcing a vicious circle of incarceration and dividends. Moreover, prisoners serve as commodities for a corrections industry operating on expectations of growth, thereby widening the net of coercive social control. Those developments have direct implications for the reproduction of inequality. Individuals most vulnerable to becoming commodified by social control are the poor and people of color, given their overrepresentation in the criminal justice system (see Morris, 2003). Indeed, the prevailing trend in imprisonment portends grave consequences for racial minorities in the United States. A key irony is that the impoverished and racial minorities who have been marginalized and devalued in the mainstream economy have considerable value in the corrections industry, ranging from $25,000 to $74,000 per year (Welch, 2003e, 2004a).

Marc Mauer of the Sentencing Project reminds us that privatization threatens to erode any humanistic approaches to crime. "Apparently, we need no longer worry about either harm suffered by victims of crime or the dismal state of our prison system as long as investors are getting good returns. This may prove to be the most lasting impact of the movement to translate societal problems into profit-making opportunities" (Mauer, 1998, p. 2). Likewise, debts accrued in building a corrections empire are paid at the expense of vital social services: education, health care, and housing. California, Connecticut, New York, Ohio, Pennsylvania, and other states have cut millions from their public education and social service budgets while increasing their spending on corrections (Butterfield, 1995; Cass, 1996). In Idaho, where crime is low, the government "locks up people for crimes that most states do not even consider felonies [e.g., simple drug possession, writing a bad check, drunken driving, and driving without a valid license]. Among the states, its rate of incarceration is growing faster than all but two. Its prisons are filling so quickly that Idaho has to fly people out of state to find cells for them" (Egan, 1998, p. A-1). Idaho is one of the poorest states in the union. It is near the bottom in spending for children and at the top in reported child abuse (Egan, 1998). Those developments serve as a reminder that social services have functioned traditionally as noncoercive measures of crime control (see Smith, 2003).

Those regressive social policies are made possible by not only the pull of private capital but also the push of political rhetoric that panders to fears about crime. By playing on citizens' fear of crime, politicians not only weaken the bonds of communities, producing alienation, but also fail to protect people because imprisonment does little to deter street crime. A keen observer noted a broader paradox: "The tremendous profits accruing to the prison-industrial complex demonstrate that the free market works best when people aren't free" (Pranis, 1998, p. 3).

Economic Ironies and Rural Prisons

The expansion of rural prisons in the 1990s was dramatic. In that period, 245 prisons were built in or near small towns nationwide, a trend that produced a new prison every 15 days. Overall, approximately 235,000 prisoners were housed in those prisons employing a total of 75,000 workers (Beale, 2001). With the demise of farming, mining, and timbering in those areas, corrections has emerged as a leading source of revenue. Many proponents of rural prisons tell their constituents that corrections work is stable, nonpolluting, and withstands seasonal fluctuations. Eager to cash in, county governments offer financial concessions, such as donating land, so as to improve their bidding for state and federal prisons.

While the potential for rural prisons to serve as economic engines has been highly touted, there have been few comprehensive evaluations offering a reality check. Recently, however, public policy analyst Tracy Huling (2002) took a hard look at the claims that rural prisons offer small towns financial salvation. Huling's work, much of which is embodied in her documentary *Yes, in My Backyard* (1999), shows that rural prisons seldom remedy economic problems for struggling communities, and worse, building correctional facilities in those towns tends to have a corrosive effect. "Despite the prevailing wisdom regarding prisons as economic panaceas, evidence suggests that prison boosters in rural America should be careful what they wish for (Huling, 2002, p. 201; Kilborn, 2003).

Rural prisons are fraught with multiple ironies. While those facilities are hailed for much-needed job growth, the majority of correctional work does not go to people living in the community. Positions in high-paying management and security slots have educational requirements rarely found among small-town residents. Union rules uphold seniority; hence, many of the corrections officers in new prisons are veterans from other state institutions. The competition for the remaining job openings is fierce. Local residents not only must compete against each other but also with desperate people traveling long distances with the hope of landing a job (Conover, 2000; Gilmore, 2002). In Malone, New York, a new state prison was accompanied by 750 jobs. Due to seniority rules and competition from outsiders, local townspeople were left with few prospects. The village's director of the Office of Community Development could barely conceal his contempt when he learned that his community would not be awarded the majority of new prison jobs: "Did we get seven hundred fifty jobs? We didn't get a hundred" (McCarthy, 2000). Although private prisons offer local residents more job opportunities than state institutions, wages are considerably lower; as a result, they suffer from low morale and a turnover rate that is three times higher than that of state prisons (Huling, 2002; see Austin et al., 2000; Camp & Gaes, 2002).

Economists, such as Thomas Johnson at the University of Missouri, conclude that prisons have weak economic linkages. Automobile manufacturers, by contrast, attract other industries such as delivery services, radio assemblers, and electronics companies, producing a vibrant economic environment (Raher, 2001). Making matters worse, prisons tend to stigmatize small towns, discouraging other growing industries, such as software companies, from moving in. Realizing their inability to draw other industries, small towns across the nation have pushed for the construction of more prisons in their backyard. That clustering of correctional facilities has produced a number of rural penal colonies where prisons dominate the community's economic, social, political, and cultural landscape (Huling, 2002; Thies, 2001).

Even so, local political leaders who battle for new prisons insist that correctional work spawns other economic sources such as restaurants, motels, and stores. But economists warn of a replacement effect in which national chains, such as McDonald's and Wal-Mart, drive out local merchants while failing to offer good-paying jobs. Compounding matters, revenue generated by national chains is not reinvested in the community, thereby reducing the local circulation of dollars. Even new housing developments, built on speculation that prison workers would buy homes, have gone under because many employees stay put, opting to commute. Local officials continue to promote the idea that prisons are good for the community by pointing to work projects that assign inmates chores such as repairing and painting government buildings, hospitals, and churches. For their work, prisoners are commonly paid a rate of less than 50 cents an hour. While the municipality saves on labor costs, in the long run that strategy contributes to the displacement of local workers who must depend on low-paying jobs for their financial survival (Gilmore, 2002).

The rural prison movement contributes to socioeconomic disparities that reach beyond small towns. Taking advantage of the revised census formula, inmates are counted in the populations where the prison is located. Consequently, rural communities siphon tax dollars from the low-income urban neighborhoods where prisoners, mostly African-American or Latino, lived until incarcerated. There is a similar political fallout as well. Considering that prisoners (in 48 states) have lost the right to vote, they cannot participate politically either in the region where they are imprisoned or in their home residence. Being disenfranchised, prisoners are not only personally marginalized; their own communities are as well (Perl, 2003).

Despite clear and convincing evidence that prisons do not provide economic security for rural regions, the drumbeat for additional prison construction persists. Local political leaders, concerned with placating voters, rally to win bids for new correctional facilities. As Gilmore (2002) and Huling (2002) reveal, small towns are giving more than receiving. While sacrificing their self-esteem by becoming a "prison town," those communities are allocating funds to prisons that could be better spent on programs that benefit their residents. As one lawmaker from North Dakota points out, "For every dollar that you're spending on corrections, you're not spending that on primary and secondary education, you're not spending it on the colleges or tourism. It's just money down a rat hole, basically" (Clement, 2002, p. 1; see also Parenti, 2003b).

Student Activism Takes Aim at Prison Profiteering

As discussed previously in this chapter, the prison industry borrows heavily from the principles of privatization, an economic tactic that shifts public funds into the hands of corporate interests. Such profiteering is not confined to American corporations. Given the forces of globalization, prison expansion has become a worldwide phenomenon, as multinational corporations exact their influence on correctional policy. Consider the arrival of Sodexho Alliance, a catering company based in Paris. Realizing the potential to diversify beyond the feeding of inmates, Sodexho entered into a major stock agreement with the world's largest private prison outfit, Corrections Corporation of America (CCA). For years to follow, Sodexho not only would become CCA's leading shareholder, but it embarked on joint ventures with CCA that produced the expansion of private prisons around the globe. "The companies also had mutual membership in, and financial sponsorship of, the American Legislative Exchange Council—a right-wing state lobby group that pushes prison privatization and 'tough-on-crime' legislation along, with a host of other conservative causes" (Pranis, 2003, pp. 156–157; see also Chevigny, 2000; Greene, 2002).

While prison corporations, like other capital projects, must contend with the flux of a market economy, rarely do they expect to deal seriously with other social forces, such as public opinion and student activism. In large part, that insulation explains why Sodexho was caught off guard when a national network of students, called "Not With Our Money!" launched a major campaign to bring prison profiteers to their knees. So that we may connect the dots here, scores of universities contract to Sodexho Marriott to provide campus meals for students. That alliance between colleges and corporations served as an opportunity for student activists committed to consciousness-raising campaigns linking prison issues to campus democracy and workers' rights. The dreaded dining hall, where all students had experienced exploitation, became the focal point of protest. Soon the "Dump Sodexho" campaign was born, a form of activism that took cues from other recently successful student movements.

Most notably, Dump Sodexho was inspired by the anti-sweatshop committees that forced universities to face the moral dilemma of making money from merchandise manufactured by cheap labor overseas. Dump Sodexho hit 60 college campuses in less than one year; seven universities responded by canceling their contracting with Sodexho. At Buffalo State College, students joined forces with a member of the City Council, a prison guard, and a former inmate, all condemning private prisons and related industries that profit from the incarceration apparatus. Their protests became too much for administrators to ignore. Eventually, Sedexho Vice President Hal D. Payne, allowed himself to be grilled by 35 students. "How," an African American student asks Payne, "can an African American administrator of a public college, which is itself being drained of resources by prison expansion, defend doing business with a company connected to punishment for profit?" (Pranis, 2003 p. 158).

The goal of Dump Sodexho went beyond having universities cut their ties with the catering giant. The campaign pushed further, pressuring Sodexho to divorce itself from CCA by dumping its stock. While boycotts have proven effective in other protests, that tactic was dismissed by Dump Sodexho because the company would profit by preparing less food while drawing revenue from the student meal plans that are sold on a semester basis. Therefore, activists turned toward direct action that challenged "business as usual" on campus. Kevin Pranis, campaign organizer for Not With Our Money!, a grassroots project to end U.S. universities' financial alliances with prison industries, summarizes the approach.

> As students discovered in the course of the campaign, campus food service is basically a scam in which one company is given a monopoly contract to serve in exchange for keeping the administration worry free. The company often accomplishes this by providing the school with no-interest 'loans' for capital improvements that are then repaid through the 'contract'—that is, the money students pay for their (often mandatory) meal plans. In fact, students discovered an eerie parallel between the outsourcing of food service and the privatization of prisons—in both cases, companies have little incentive to provide good service, because those most affected have little or no voice in contracting. (2003, p. 160)

Dump Sodexho escalated to larger protests and direct actions at Ithaca College, Arizona State University, Oberlin College, American University, Xavier University, University of Texas, and DePaul University. Those protests generated considerable press coverage nationwide, creating the kind of negative public attention that corporations often go to great lengths to avoid. Amid the controversy, CCA felt secure in keeping Sodexho on board. Susan Hart, CCA's spokeswoman, characterized the students' actions as ineffective. Evidently, Hart spoke too soon. On May 22, 2001, Sodexho announced that it would sell its CCA stockholdings and its executive would resign from the CCA board of directors (Pranis, 2003; see also Welch & Turner, 2004).

While organizations battling private prisons hail the achievements of Dump Sodexho, they realize that there is much more work to be done. Although Sodexho and CCA suffered an embarrassing defeat by American student activists, together they continue to pursue contracts in the United Kingdom and Australia, where privatized prisons are gaining ground (see Gaylord, 2001; Nathan, 2003a, 2003b). Setting the stage for another round of conflict, Not With Our Money! is working with allies in Australia, France, and the United Kingdom in an effort to force Sodexho out of the private prison business for good. Human rights considerations are increasingly evident in such activism in Europe, especially since governments are turning to private prisons to detain asylum seekers and refugees (Molenaar & Neufeld, 2003; Schuster, 2003). To head off the debilitating effects of global private prisons, activists are organizing in ways that unite concerned people across borders (Berg, 2003; Moore, Burton, & Hannah-Moffat, 2003). Their objective is straightforward: to neutralize corporate influence in the sphere of correctional policy, thereby taking the profit out of punishment.

Conclusion

While critics question the tortured logic of increasing expenditures in criminal justice that have failed to improve public safety, the corrections industry continues to generate ideological and financial windfalls for politicians, corporations, and a growing cast of opportunists. Through various forms of lobbying, political and economic elites promote the idea that prison expansion serves positive functions for private and public sectors (Welch, Fenwick, & Roberts, 1997, 1998). The prevailing version of the corrections enterprise is evidence that history is written by the winners. Still, keeping privatization in a favorable light requires the reproduction of several interlocking myths.

The first myth is that street crime is rising. Over the past 20 years, in fact, property and violent crime have remained relatively constant or dropped. The second myth involves the popular belief that American government is soft on crime. To the contrary, the United States deals more harshly with lawbreaking than any comparable industrial nation, especially in the realm of coercive drug control and its mandatory minimum sentences. As a result of continued prison expansion, there are more cells than violent offenders to fill them. So rather than being supervised in the community, many nonviolent offenders are imprisoned for the purpose of occupying expensive correctional space, including drug addicts who need treatment more than mere punishment. Finally, the claim that prisons save money is also a persistent myth. Whereas it is prudent to incapacitate violent offenders, imposing lengthy sentences on nonviolent lawbreakers forces government to waste funds on imprisonment that would otherwise be spent on social services and programs that offer crime-control dividends. With those contradictions in clear view, Donziger adds, "If more prisons paid off in less crime, the results would be obvious by now" (1996a, p. 24).

This chapter contributes to critical penology by challenging the uncritical acceptance of a crime-punishment nexus while scrutinizing market forces shaping social control. The economic-punishment nexus produces ironies realized at societal and individual levels. Numerous accounts confirm that a prison enterprise geared toward accumulating capital does so by slashing operating costs, most notably labor (i.e., professional, well-trained staff) and much-needed programs and services (e.g., education, medical care, substance abuse treatment). The end results are neglect, abuse, and violence. At the societal level, the prevailing reliance on incarceration, for purposes of social control, generating profits, or both, threatens democracy by shifting even greater power to the state and corporations. In its wake, citizens, especially the impoverished and racial minorities, are left vulnerable to an overzealous, over financed criminal justice machine.[1]

Note

1. Another important aspect of the economic-punishment nexus is the current misuse of prison labor in the United States (see Burton-Rose, 1998; Parenti, 1999; Welch, 2004a).

End-of-Chapter Questions

1. How has the war on drugs contributed to the production of raw materials for the corrections industry?

2. What is meant by the "bait and switch" tactic in criminal justice?

3. What are some of the problems facing private prisons?

4. How does the privatization of prisons contribute to social inequality?

10

Confronting Corrections

Karen Shook, a 44-year old single mother of three, was sentenced to prison for 20 to 40 years. She was convicted of conspiring to sell two and a half ounces of cocaine, her first offense. Naturally, she feels that her sentence is unduly harsh, especially considering that she operated only as an intermediary and that the main player in the drug transaction was assigned a 3-year prison term. "I got longer than most people get for violent crimes" (Butterfield, 2003a). After serving 10 years, however, Shook was released after Michigan lawmakers embarked on sweeping changes that altered the state's mandatory minimum sentences for drug violations, known as the toughest in the nation. Legislative rewriting of its drug laws did not mark a shift in correctional philosophy; rather, it was a response to the emergent fiscal pressures to spend less on prisons. As a result, the reform was expected to save Michigan $41 million in 2003. "In the end, the impossible happened. I had appeal after appeal turned down by the courts, then it was the Legislature that wrote the law the other way that got me out," explained Shook (Butterfield, 2003a).

Ranked highly on the list of ironic features of imprisonment is wasteful spending on prisons. Such fiscal mismanagement not only fails to enhance public safety, it also transfers to corrections the funds that should be allocated to social services such as education, health care, and housing. Indeed, together those social services improve communities and, in return, reduce street crime. In California, where lawmakers grapple with the state's massive budget deficit, it has been disclosed that the government continues to spend $1 billion a year on a failed system of sending back to prison huge numbers of parolees charged with minor violations (Butterfield, 2003b). The research group commissioned to study the parole system found that 67% of those sent to prison in California were parolees returned for violating a technical condition of their release, nearly twice the national average of 35%. Such technical violations (e.g., missing an appointment with a parole officer, failing a drug test) are not considered criminal offenses. California spends $900 million per year imprisoning parole violators and $465 million on supervising them; most of those funds go to parole agents who spend much of their time completing paperwork to send violators back to prison. According to Nancy Lyons, deputy executive director of the commission, "This means that California's parole system is a billion dollar failure"(Butterfield, 2003b). In 1980, one in four parolees in California ended up back in prison, compared with the two of three being returned in 2002.

The commission insists that resources could be better allocated for drug treatment, job training, and education for prisoners before release. More than three-quarters of the 160,000 prisoners report drug or alcohol problems, but only 6% receive treatment, and only one-third participate in job or education programs. While other states are exploring ways to reduce correctional spending, California—with the nation's largest and most expensive prison system—remains on the prison treadmill. The corrections industry figures prominently in the battle over the budget. In particular, the prison guard lobby imposes its heavy influence by pressuring legislators to defeat measures designed to curtail spending, thus protecting its high-paying jobs (Parenti, 1999; Welch, 2004a).

This concluding chapter confronts the ironies of imprisonment in a manner that sharpens the lens of critical penology. While reiterating some of the chief themes that echo throughout the book, special attention is turned to how popular images of crime are perpetuated by the media and the political establishment. As we shall discuss, turbulent and exaggerated notions of crime—evidence of moral panic—are contoured along lines of race, class, and gender. By relying on racially inspired criminal stereotypes, politicians and their constituents sound the alarm for greater reliance on incarceration, producing measures such as 3-strikes laws that have proven expensive and self-defeating. Those developments, however, ought not to be attributed merely to the swinging pendulum of political opinion that alternates between liberal and conservative moods.

Nowadays, criminologists attend to an emergent culture of control in which tough-on-crime initiatives are situated.

Critical Penology and the Culture of Control

In a recent trend, criminologists have begun exploring in depth the significance of crime, punishment, and social control in the context of culture. In *The Culture of Control: Crime and Social Order in Contemporary Society,* David Garland (2001) sets out to interpret how the United States—a nation committed to individual freedoms and civil liberties—has become the world's leader in incarceration (see also Chivigny, 2003; Useem, Liedka, & Piehl, 2003). Since the 1970s, the United States (and the United Kingdom) has undergone considerable social transformations that have had an effect on the way people view and experience crime; in turn, those cultural shifts have led to changes in the criminal justice system. While the rehabilitative ideal was losing currency, greater emphasis on punitive sanctions became consistent with a society that was growing increasingly conservative. Penal sanctions, such as renewed enthusiasm for the death penalty, chain gangs, and correctional bootcamps, became hallmarks of expressive punishments symbolizing public outrage over crime.

Criminal victimization, revealed in the slogan "we are all victims," has become a collective experience stoked by the media and politicians realizing that they have tapped into a public psyche consumed with undifferentiated anxiety over economic insecurity, racial tension, and a host of other social problems (Bottoms, 1995; Chambliss, 1999; Stetson & Sullivan, 2000). That cultural development produced punishments imbued with emotion as citizens—mad as hell—overwhelmingly supported tough-on-crime sanctions such as 3-strikes legislation and mandatory minimum drug sentences. With few exceptions, politicians wrestled away from criminal justice policy experts the decision making that would ultimately create the largest prison population in the nation's history. It is telling that the prison—an institution condemned by conservatives as a failure—would emerge as a key symbol for a culture committed to control and order (see Bottoms & Preston, 1983; Sparks, Bottoms, & Hay, 1996).

The use of prisons for the expressed purpose of retribution, no matter what the social and financial costs, reflects a shift in criminological thinking that has gained popularity over the past several decades (see

Young, 2003a, 2003b). Chief among those changes was an emphasis on the consequences of crime rather than the causes.

Preoccupation with the consequences of crime has led to an emergent *criminology of the other,* in which lawbreakers are characterized as menacing strangers who threaten not only individual safety but also the entire social order. That way of thinking about crime draws on popular fears and resentments in ways that support harsher penal sanctions. While the older social democratic criminology has not vanished completely, it tends to be drowned out by the shrill emotionalism that has captured the crime issue. The *criminology of the other,* according to Garland (2001) is antimodern in nature insofar as it rejects modern concepts of crime and progressive methods of dealing with social problems, such as confronting racial and socioeconomic inequality. Conforming to the precepts of moral panic, the *criminology of the other* re-dramatizes crime, reinforces a disaster mentality, and retreats into intolerance and authoritarianism. In doing so, it clings to criminal stereotypes resonating with racism and classism, and that sense of "otherness" perpetuates an "us versus them" worldview (see Young, 1999). The *criminology of the other* is "deeply illiberal in its assumption that certain criminals are 'simply wicked' and in this respect intrinsically different from the rest of us" (Garland, 2001, p. 184).[1] That view of crime is deeply imbedded in the culture of control, producing moral panic. Two examples of moral panic worth exploring are juvenile *superpredators* and *wilding,* both of which illuminate the social construction of crime and the problems it creates.

Juvenile Superpredators

As a conceptual framework, moral panic has improved our understanding of the social construction of crime, particularly those forms of lawlessness perceived as being *new*: for example, mugging (Hall, Critcher, Jefferson, Clarke, & Roberts, 1978), crack babies (Humphries, 1999), crank (i.e., methamphetamines or "speed") (Jenkins, 1994b), and freeway violence (Best, 1999). According to Stanley Cohen, moral panic has occurred when

> A condition, episode, person or group of persons emerges to become defined as a threat to societal values and interest; its nature is presented in a stylized and stereotypical fashion by the mass media; the moral barricades are manned by editors, bishops, politicians, and other right-thinking people. (Cohen, 1972, p. 9)

Cohen (1972, 2002) encountered moral panic while studying societal reaction to unconventional youths in England. In his ground-breaking treatise, *Folk Devils and Moral Panics*, Cohen explored the roles of the media, politicians, and criminal justice officials in fueling anxiety over British youth culture in 1964, when Mods and Rockers were depicted as new threats to public safety. Together, the media and members of the political establishment publicized exaggerated claims of dangers posed by unconventional youth; in turn, inflammatory rhetoric was used to justify enhanced police powers and greater investment in the traditional criminal justice apparatus.

Over the past decade, there has been renewed concern over youth crime. However, rather than exploring the problem objectively (by way of social science), politicians, law enforcement officials, and even some university professors have participated in moral panic, a turbulent, excited, or exaggerated response to a social problem (Welch, Fenwick, & Roberts 1997, 1998). Consider the following alarmist and sensationalistic statements about youth crime:

> These are not the Cleaver kids soaping up some windows. These are middle school kids conspiring to hurt their teacher, teenagers shooting people and committing rapes, young thugs running gangs and terrorizing neighborhoods and showing no remorse when they get caught. (Zell Miller, Georgia governor, as quoted in "Prisons Getting Tougher," 1994)

> Our streets are being stained with the blood of our children, and it's going to stop. Damn it. It has got to stop. (Pete Wilson, California governor, as quoted in "Growing Anxiety Over Crime," 1994)

> Unless we act now, while our children are still young and impression-able, we may indeed have a bloodbath of teen violence by the year 2005. (James Alan Fox, Dean of the College of Criminal Justice at Northeastern University in Boston, as quoted in "Youth Violence Raising Concern," 1995)

Perhaps the most memorable example of moral panic over youth violence was the claim by Professsor John J. DiIulio of Princeton University that American society was facing a new breed of *superpredators*. The notion of superpredators fueled the media's distortion of youth crime while enabling law-and-order enthusiasts to commit further to more penalties, police, and prisons. DiIulio's remark even made its way into legislation. In 1996, Congress introduced the Violent Youth Predator

Act. Although the bill was later renamed, congressional hearings on the subject were loaded with DiIulio's claim of superpredators. James Wooten, president of the Safe Streets Coalition, testified to lawmakers,

> They live in an aimless and violent present, have no sense of the past and no hope for the future; and act, often ruthlessly, to gratify whatever urges or desires drive them at the moment. They commit unspeakable brutal crimes against other people, and their lack of remorse is shocking. They are what Professor DiIulio and others call urban 'superpredators.' They are the ultimate nightmare, and their numbers are growing. (Federal Document Clearing House, 1997; see also Schiraldi & Keppelhoff, 1997)

In classic moral panic fashion, the term superpredator took on a life of its own. Not only were superpredators believed to be the new menace of society, but their numbers were also perceived as growing. According to DiIulio, the "swelling legion of Godless, Fatherless, valueless kids" will result in an additional 270,000 superpredators roaming the streets by the year 2010. Without offering data to support his claim, DiIulio stated that 6% of all newly born children would become superpredators. However, Professor Franklin Zimring at the University of California at Berkeley took exception to the theory of superpredators. "Congress and professors and others can make catastrophic errors in statistical projections. Not little ones. Whoppers" (Mills, 1999, p. 3). "If DiIulio were correct in his estimation, we would already have 1.9 million of these superpredators on the streets, enough to make the whole country look like one of Quentin Tarantino's nightmares. We do not" (Kappeler, Blumberg, & Potter, 2000, p. 184; see also Bernard, 1999; Glassner, 1999).

Alarmist reactions to crime offered by politicians, law enforcement officials, and some professors contribute substantially to moral panic because their messages are delivered by seemingly credible authorities who add a heightened sense of anxiety and urgency. In turn, moral panic over youth crime demands greater expenditure in the criminal justice apparatus aimed at street crime. Unquestionably, youth crime is indeed a social problem, producing social and personal harms (see Barak, 2003b). The concept of moral panic does not mean that "there's nothing there," but rather that the state-sponsored strategies designed to deal with such problems are "fundamentally inappropriate" (Cohen, 1972, p. 204). While the following statements clearly address the problem of serious juvenile offenses, they also endorse a state-sponsored intervention that many criminologists find inappropriate.

The laws were written when kids were committing juvenile crimes, but now they're committing adult crimes like rape and murder. The laws are anachronistic and need to be changed. (Andrew J. Stein, Chairman of the New York City Commission on Juvenile Offenders, as quoted in "Charging Youth Offenders as Adults," 1994)

Punishment has to be swift and certain. When children commit adult crimes, they should be prosecuted as adults. We can't coddle criminals because they are young. We're not just talking about gang members. What we are seeing is total disregard for pain and human life among the young. It's scary, and I predict it will only get worse. (Jeanine Ferris Pirro, Westchester [NY] County District Attorney, as quoted in "Prosecutor Takes Aim on Violence," 1994)

Critics of harsher penalties for youthful offenders insist that moral panics contribute to the escalating *vocabulary of punitive motives.* Moreover, those punitive motives are used to justify flawed strategies of dealing with crime, especially those neglecting the root causes of crime and violence, including social, political, and economic inequality (Melossi, 1985; Welch, Fenwick, & Roberts, 1997, 1998).

Wilding: *Manufacturing Menace in the Media*

In an effort to discover *new* types of menace, the media tends to publicize exaggerated claims of dangers posed by adolescents. With that phenomenon in mind, a study set out to examine moral panic emerging in New York City in 1989 after a young woman, while jogging in Central Park, was attacked and raped by seven youths. The tragic event popularly became known as *wilding,* a stylized term describing sexual violence committed by a group of urban teenagers. As a newly discovered menace to public safety, *wilding* consumed the media and also caught the attention of politicians and members of the local criminal justice establishment who campaigned for tougher measures in dealing with youth violence (Welch, Price, & Yankey, 2002, 2004).

Whereas a common view of moral panic suggests that pseudo-disasters quickly burst into formation but then dissipate, Welch, Price, and Yankey (2002, 2004) stress their lingering effects. In particular, moral panic over wilding reinforces racial biases prevalent in criminal stereotypes, particularly the popular perception that young black (and Latino) males constitute a dangerous class. Compounded by sensationalistic news coverage on *wilding,* along with *carjacking, gang banging,* and other stylized forms of lawlessness associated with urban teens, minority youth remains a lightning rod for public fear, anger, and anxiety over impending social disorder, all of which contributes to additional law-and-order campaigns. It is important to note that moral panic often touches on bona fide social ills. Still, rather than enlightening the public toward an informed understanding of the problem—in this case, youth violence—the media and politicians pander to popular fear, resulting in renewed hostility toward a group of people who serve as easy targets for scapegoating, namely young black and Latino males.

As is typically the case in moral panic, the source of immediate threat is discovered by the media in its search for an original twist to a news story. Customarily, the media conveys the newness of a breaking story in the form of an expression, word, or phrase; indeed, *wilding* captured the public's imagination about crime, producing an amplified fear of sexual violence. Three days after the April 19, 1989, attack on the Central Park jogger, the *New York Times* reported,

> The youths who raped and savagely beat a young investment banker in Central Park on Wednesday night were part of a loosely organized gang of 32 schoolboys whose random, motiveless assaults terrorized at least eight other people over nearly two hours, senior police investigators said yesterday.
>
> Chief of Detectives Robert Colangelo, who said the attacks appeared unrelated to money, race, drugs or alcohol, said that some of the 20 youths brought into questioning had told investigators that the crime spree was the product of a pastime called "wilding." (Pitt, 1989, p. 1)

As if details of the brutal attack were not sufficient to drive the story, the media relied on the word *wilding* for purposes of news sensationalism; conveniently, legal terminology (i.e., rape, assault, and attempted murder) was replaced by inflammatory language imbued with moral panic. Conforming to the classic genesis of moral panic, law enforcement officials also participated in the initial reification of the term. The chief of detectives not only described *wilding* as a "pastime" for the suspects, but contributed to its invention by suggesting that the activity was a new form of menace: "'It's not a term that we in the police had heard before,' the chief said, noting that the police were unaware of any similar incidents in the park recently" (Pitt, 1989, p. 1).

As a storytelling institution, the media relied on the dramatic style of infotainment in its coverage of the Central Park jogger attack. Moreover, repetition of the story reinforced popular notions of violence, victimization, and criminal stereotypes, all of which fueled moral panic. Consider the following features of the criminal event. The attack occurred in New York City's Central Park, a city and a public space that have been mythologized with a notorious reputation for predatory violence. The victim was a white female whose physical attributes, social status, and personal biography were injected into virtually every media account. She was described as young, beautiful, and educated, as well as being a Manhattan investment banker (Barth, 1989, p. 8). Perhaps adding to the story's enduring level of interest, the victim's identity was withheld.

Seven youths were charged as adults with rape, assault, and attempted murder. Eventually, charges against one suspect were dropped; another youth turned state witness and as part of a plea bargain, he pleaded guilty to one count of robbery (for an earlier incident, not in connection with the rape incident) and all other charges against him were dropped (Wolff, 1989). Although acquitted of attempted murder, three youths were convicted of first-degree rape and first-degree assault and sentenced to maximum juvenile prison terms of 5 to 10 years (Sachar, 1990). A sixth youth was convicted of attempted murder and rape; although 14 years old at the time of the crime, he was sentenced to a maximum 5- to 10-year prison term as a juvenile. Finally, the seventh defendant was acquitted of attempted murder and rape but convicted of assault, riot, and sexual abuse and sentenced to 8-1/2 to 26 years in prison (Phillips, Nolan, & Pearl, 1990).

The trial may have put to rest the legal concerns of the crime, but in the public consciousness, a new form of menace had been discovered. *Wilding* had been added to a growing roster of crimes associated with urban culture, along with mugging, looting, gang banging, drive-by shootings, and carjacking. Curiously, though, the term *wilding* has its roots in contemporary music and urban culture, specifically Tone-Loc's rap remake of the 1960s pop tune "Wild Thing." It is commonly believed that *wilding* is an abbreviated pronunciation of "Wild Thing." Still, music critic Dave Marsh doubts the suspects ever used the term to describe the attack on the Central Park jogger: "In fact, it's a fantasy, dreamed up in a reporter's shack or a precinct house. Nobody has ever heard kids use anything like that phrase; you can be sure you won't hear it in any of the taped confessions in the trial" (Marsh, 1990, p. 50). Marsh contends that the term *wilding* was invented as a conservative reaction to anti-hip-hop hysteria. "'Wilding' retains its forceful currency because here in New York, cradle of rap and hip hop though it is, the powers-that-be don't approve of that culture" (1990, p. 50). Marsh joins many social commentators who condemn the use of the word *wilding* to describe the attack on the Central Park jogger because it trivializes the brutal nature of the offense and contributes to racial tension (Gates, 1990).

The popular use of buzz words such as *wilding*, mugging, looting, gang banging, drive-by shootings, and carjacking, generally are racially biased because they are used to describe black (and Latino) lawbreakers more often than white offenders. Eventually, the term *wilding* made a further impact on society and culture by becoming another synonym for youth violence, contributing to fear of crime and moral panic. Not only does youth violence have a new name, *wilding*, it also has a face, typically that of young black (and Latino) males residing in urban centers. As a complex phenomenon, the invention of the term *wilding* feeds moral panic by drawing on racial criminal stereotypes. While much of the pioneering work on moral panic emphasized its implications for the political economy, nowadays that facet of the paradigm tends to be neglected in contemporary scholarship. Returning to that earlier theme, Welch et al. (2002, 2004) demonstrate that moral panic over youth violence symbolizes not only a threat to society at large but also to a prevailing political economy that thrives on racial and economic inequality.

In 2002, 13 years after the trial, a Manhattan judge threw out the convictions of the five young men sentenced to prison for the attack of the Central Park Jogger. Following an unusual sequence of events, the Judge Charles T. Tejada granted recent motions made by defense attorneys and the Manhattan district attorney, to vacate all convictions in light of new evidence identifying another man, Matias Reyes, as the lone attacker. Reyes, a convicted murderer and rapist serving time for another offense, stepped forward in January 2002, claiming that he, and he alone, violently raped the Central Park jogger. Reyes's testimony was corroborated by matching DNA evidence. The decision to vacate the convictions of the young men, who had completed their prison sentences and are now in their mid-twenties, raises grave questions about their confessions and police interrogation tactics (Saulny, 2003). In 2003, three of the men who served time after being falsely convicted filed federal civil rights lawsuit against New York City, the Police Department, and prosecutors, claiming that their convictions were based on "racial animus and a wide conspiracy among law enforcement officials" (Saulny, 2003, p. B3).

Consequences of the *criminology of the other* are evident in expressive punishments that Garland characterizes as acting out.

[Acting out] is a mode that is concerned not so much with controlling crime as with expressing the anger and outrage that crime provokes. It is this predicament and the authorities' deeply ambivalent reactions to it—rather than any coherent programme or singular strategy—that have shaped crime control and criminal justice in the late modern period. (2001, p. 110)

With those cultural transformations in clear view, it is understandable how expressive punishments receive tireless public support. The lack of foresight in criminal justice planning creates problems for both the short and long term. Among the most flawed criminal justice legislation in recent memory is California's 3-strikes law.

Three Strikes, You're Out

Sentencing laws designed to control habitual offenders have been in existence since the 1920s, but their popularity re-emerged in the 1990s, commonly called "Three Strikes and You're Out." Those laws require judges to sentence "repeat offenders" with three convictions to longer prison terms. The rationale of three-strikes laws is simple, resting on the basic assumptions of deterrence: "If the cost of a behavior greatly exceeds its benefits, the behavior is less likely to be chosen. If the behavior continues in spite of the cost the cost must be increased" (Mentor, 2002, p. 813). Half the states in the United States have a version of the three-strikes law, but it is the 1994 California statute that has become controversial, in large part because it imposes a penalty of 25 years to life. Compounding matters, California's three-strikes law is the only one of its kind to treat a misdemeanor as the third strike; conversely, the typical three-strikes law applies only to felonies, and in some cases only violent felonies. Opponents of California's "three strikes" law argue that treating a misdemeanor as a felony violates the principle of penal proportionality (Greenberg, 2002). In other words, the punishment does not fit the crime. In fact, some legal scholars go as far as to argue that such sentencing violates the Eighth Amendment's ban on cruel and unusual punishment (Zimring, Hawkins, & Kamin, 2001; Zeigler & del Carmen, 2001).

More recently, the U.S. Supreme Court decided to review whether sentences of 25 years to life in prison imposed under California's three-strikes law are unconstitutionally cruel when the third strike is a minor property offense. Specifically, the High Court examined two cases. One defendant,

Gary A. Ewing, who had previous convictions for robbery and burglary, received a 25-years-to-life sentence for theft of three golf clubs. In the other case, Leandro Andrade, who had earlier convictions for burglary, received 50 years to life for shoplifting videotapes valued at $153.54 from two K-Mart department stores. The U.S. Court of Appeals for the Ninth Circuit ruled that the sentence was so disproportionate to the crime as to violate the Eight Amendment's prohibition against cruel and unusual punishment. In 2003, the U.S. Supreme Court upheld California's "three-strikes" law, rejecting constitutional challenges to the sentences of Ewing and Andrade. Justice Sandra Day O'Connor added that any criticism of the law "is appropriately directed at the Legislature" (Greenhouse, 2002; see *Ewing v. California*, 2002; *Lockyer v. Andrade*, 2003).

By 2002, the third strike for more than half of the 7,000 prisoners sentenced under California law was a nonviolent offense. Of those, 340 were sentenced for a crime of petty theft with a prior conviction (Greenhouse, 2002). It is important to keep in mind that three-strikes laws are fraught with contradictions. Such legislation marks a major development in the politicization of crime in which politicians issue unsubstantiated claims that judges are soft on crime. Moreover, three-strikes laws were passed by legislatures at a time when there was a general impression that violent crime was increasing, even though the overall crime rate was dropping (Greenberg, 2002; Tyler & Boeckmann, 1997). Three-strikes laws also were formulated according to the notion that rehabilitation was no longer a viable option in controlling crime.

Still, key events in California mobilized the three-strikes movement, in particular, the murders of Kimber Reynolds and Polly Klaas, whose parents embarked on a widely publicized campaign to pass the referendum known as Proposition 184. In 1994, California voters approved the three-strikes law by a 72 to 28% margin. However, even as the legislation was being written, a study indicated that although there would be a reduction in crime, the new law would lead to a 120% increase in California's prison budget due to the enormous growth in its correctional population (Zimring et al., 2001).

Other evaluations of three-strikes laws demonstrate that such measures have not reduced violent crime (Shichor & Sechrest, 1996) and more recently, Kovandzic, Sloan, and Vieraitis (2002) found that jurisdictions with three-strikes laws experienced short-term and long-term increases in homicide (see Marvell & Moody, 2001). Similarly, the National Institute of Justice (NIJ) found that even though three-strikes laws were intended to target serious offenders, more than 70% of defendants charged under such statutes were nonviolent offenders. That NIJ report also revealed that three-strikes laws significantly reduced plea bargaining from 90% of criminal cases to 14%, leading to greater jail overcrowding (Flynn, 1995). Finally, three-strike laws have contributed to racial disparities in the prison population, since minorities have been disproportionately prosecuted and sentenced under such laws (Austin 1999; Austin & Irwin, 2001). Three-strikes laws, especially in California, will eventually have an enormous impact on a growing elderly prison population that is more costly to house due to the rocketing cost of medical and heath care (Auerhahn, 2002; Mauer, 2002).

A Final Look at Prisonomics

Facing greater costs and budget deficits, political leaders committed to prison expansion have been forced to pay homage to a monster of their own creation. Lately there have been signs that the spending frenzy on corrections is losing its zeal. State legislatures, realizing the long-term fiscal damage caused by allocating too many dollars into corrections, are reversing their commitment to expensive incarceration. In 2003, a total of 25 states passed laws restricting lengthy mandatory minimum sentences, reinstating parole and early release, and substituting incarceration with drug treatment. Suggesting a new approach to crime control, lawmakers say that, "Instead of being tough on crime, it is more effective to be smart about crime" (Butterfield, 2003a, p. A1).

Consider, for instance, Washington State, the first to implement a three-strikes law. There, legislators are rolling back many of the more punitive features of that statute while introducing drug treatment and early-release initiatives. Those recent changes do not represent a shift in crime control philosophy, but rather a fiscal acknowledgement that spending habits in the past were wasteful. "You have to look at the people behind these laws. They are not all advocates of the liberal philosophy," says Joseph Lehman, secretary of the Washington Department of Corrections (Butterfield, 2003a, p. A15). Interestingly, the state's new drug policy earned overwhelming support by the same Republicans who in the 1980s sponsored laws that doubled prison terms for drug violations. Lawmakers in Washington are quick to tally the fiscal benefits of their new approach to crime, boasting a savings of $45 million annually. Political insider Dan Satterberg commented on the recent turnaround on correctional funding: "It is a recognition that you can't incarcerate your way out of this problem"

(Butterfield, 2003a, p. A15). Likewise in Oklahoma where a similar movement has taken shape, state senate President Cal Hobson conceded, "Oklahoma has always prided itself on being a law-and-order-state. Now we have more law and order than we can afford" (Butterfield, 2002, p. A30).

With corrections becoming the fastest growing item on their budgets, many states are assertively downsizing costs attached to prisons, even laying off corrections officers in Iowa and shutting down prisons in Ohio and Illinois (Butterfield, 2002). In Kentucky, Governor Paul E. Patton ordered a mass commutation of 567 nonviolent prisoners in an effort to close a huge $500 million budget gap. A recent Kansas law mandating treatment rather than incarceration for first-time offenders is expected to divert to drug treatment 1,400 offenders per year, saving taxpayers the extra burden of maintaining a prison system that offers little in return. Responding to similar financial forces, Michigan, a state that boasts of having the toughest antidrug penalties in the nation, has rolled back many of its mandatory minimum sentences. "Truth in sentencing" laws that require prisoners to serve a longer proportion of their term in order to be eligible for parole have been relaxed in Iowa, Missouri, and Wisconsin. In Colorado, lawmakers have imposed limits on prison time served by parolees who have committed technical violations, such as failing a urine test. Parole, once considered dead, has been reinvigorated by states as a way to deal with the twin pressures of limited funds and a surging prison population. Without attracting too much public attention, the state assembly in New York has quietly created a mechanism for early release that bypasses the parole board (Butterfield, 2003a). Similar loopholes have been discovered by legislators in Arkansas, Kentucky, Montana, and Texas, allowing more convicts to serve their sentences in the community. Lawmakers in Georgia, Idaho, Nebraska, and Utah also are scrambling to reduce reliance on prisons in order to save tax dollars.

In an effort to trim budgets further, many correctional systems are reducing spending on food for prisoners. In Arizona, Iowa, Minnesota, North Carolina, Texas, and Virginia, some new food plans involve cutting the number of calories per day while others propose eliminating a meal on weekends and holidays. Critics insist that such cuts will save little money since prison food represents a very small portion of operating costs; the lion's share of the budget is devoted to salaries for corrections officers. "This kind of stuff never gets you very much money," explains Michael Jacobson, criminology professor at John Jay College of Criminal Justice and former commissioner of corrections for New York City (Butterfield, 2003c, p. A18). Texas chairman of the House Corrections

Committee, Ray Allen, justifies reductions in food plans, arguing, "Since we can't cut a single corrections officer, and their salaries are 80 percent of prison costs, there isn't much else left to cut" (Butterfield, 2003c, p. A18). Experts claim that reductions in prison diets contribute to health problems, particularly in light of fewer fresh vegetables and fruits and more processed meats, starches, and powdered milk.

Recent reductions in criminal justice budgets go beyond spending on prisons, affecting prosecution as well. Flying in the face of the victims' rights movement, Virginia Commonwealth Attorney, Harvey L. Bryant III, announced that cutbacks in his office mean that he will no longer prosecute the 2,200 misdemeanor domestic violence cases he received each year. Bryant conceded, "I deeply regret that the victims of domestic violence will no longer have a prosecutor on their side. But something had to go. I'm two assistant attorneys short" (Butterfield, 2002, p. A30).

Although recent developments in prisonomics might be seen as encouraging signs that lawmakers are realizing the importance of reducing the government's reliance on imprisonment, the federal criminal justice apparatus continues to move in the direction of the control culture. In 2003, John Ashcroft, the tough-on-crime attorney general, ordered federal prosecutors to all but eliminate plea bargaining and reach for the most serious charges they can prove, most notably capital crimes punishable by death (Glaberson, 2003; New York Times, "John Ashcroft's Death Penalty Edicts," 2003). Those polarities reveal stark contradictions in the national criminal justice agenda. Frank Bowman, a former federal prosecutor and current professor at the Indiana University School of Law, notes,

> The states and the federal government are moving in quite different directions. At the Justice Department, you have a group of people in control who really are true believers in incarceration. They have almost a religious zeal to see that people get sentenced to prison for a long time. At the same time, in dozens of states with the toughest laws on nonviolent crime, including New York, Texas, and California, people are scratching their heads and saying, you know, incarcerating people for a long time doesn't work. (von Zielbauer, 2003, p. 41)

Clearly while federal authorities continue to adopt ideological approaches to crime control, state governments are becoming more responsive to budgetary restrictions, forcing them to spend criminal justice dollars more wisely. Moreover, there are important structural differences insofar as most state governments are required by law to balance their annual budgets while the federal government is not. Michael

Jacobson adds, "As long as Ashcroft does not feel particularly financially constrained, then he's not going to feel a lot of pressure and the politics of this will still work at the federal level" (von Zielbauer, 2003, p. 42).

Conclusion

This book set out to explore the ironies of imprisonment embodied in numerous correctional policies and practices. Its aim is to reveal the inconsistencies and contradictions of American prisons while advancing further a critical penology. The book began by taking into account socio-historical knowledge that allows us to comprehend the not-so-linear development of institutional punishment. In the development of the penitentiary, we see the importance that social forces such as politics, economics, religion, and technology have had on shaping penal sanctions.

Behind the facade of crime control, corrections serve the larger function of social control, among other things, by regulating surplus labor amid crucial economic downturns. During periods when there is less demand for labor, offenders are more likely to be sentenced to prison (Rusche & Kirchheimer, 1939/1968; Sutton, 2000; Weiss, 2001).

While a critical penology distinguishes itself from other mainstream perspectives on punishment by remaining attentive to socio-historical development, it also discerns key facets of the political economy that determine the pattern of penal sanctions. Specifically, there is symmetry between the correctional apparatus and the structural components of capitalism, together reinforcing inequality and repressive mechanisms of social control. Indeed, race and class weigh heavily in this critical analysis. It has been suggested that political and economic institutions stoke racial tensions, realizing that a society divided by race is easier to control than one divided by class. Racism among workers is evidence of a false consciousness blinding their ability to identify major sources of economic inequality, particularly in a polarized economy in which the rich get richer, the poor get poorer, and the middle classes take on greater amounts of debt to conceal their lack of real prosperity.

Certainly the war on drugs offers one of most obvious examples of sentencing disparities adversely affecting the poor and people of color. If white, middle-income, suburban youth were sentenced to prison at the same rate as their minority counterparts for comparable drug violations, it is easy to speculate that there would be enormous public anger over that use of incarceration. Politicians and criminal justice officials avoid such wrath by frequently making treatment and alternative sentences available for white and middle-income drug offenders, while subjecting the impoverished and racial minorities to the harshest of sanctions. The hypocrisy is that many whites and middle class people fail to see the injustice of mandatory minimum sentences unless it affects them directly (see Cole, 1999). Adopting a public health model to the drug problem in lieu of the militarization and criminalization approaches promises to undermine sanctimonious politics that perpetuate racial and socioeconomic biases.[2]

The war on drugs also creates problems for correctional health care, especially in light of prisoners suffering from HIV/AIDS. Moreover, the lengthy sentences that have become the hallmark of America's tough-on-drugs campaign are putting more drug violators behind bars for longer stretches of time. Ironically, correctional facilities also are now being forced to serve as infirmaries and retirement homes for aging inmates. Once again, we see in plain view the foolishness of resorting to expensive forms of incarceration for a population that poses relatively little risk to public safety.

Violence behind bars is indicative of other ironies of imprisonment. Through escalation, nonenforcement, and covert facilitation, we understand more fully the role of authorities in situating and perpetuating violence. In examining the two most prevalent types of violence (i.e., inmate-versus-inmate violence and staff-versus-inmate violence), special consideration is given to chief contributing factors, such as the lack of expertise in preventing and managing aggression. In addition, institutional violence is fueled by the creation of self-fulfilling prophecies coupled with secondary gains in which aggression has its own rewards.

The death penalty is riddled with similar contradictions. Research on brutalization theory offers evidence that well-publicized executions tend to promote lethal violence rather than deter it (Bailey, 1998; Cochran, Chamlin, & Seth, 1994). Capital punishment sets the United States apart from other Western democracies that regard executions as unjust, inhumane, and inconsistent with progressive ideals in crime control. Racial disparities along with the execution of capital offenders who are mentally ill, mentally retarded, or who were minors at the moment of the crime remind us of the profound ethical issues regarding death sentences.

The war on terror, especially since the events of September 11th, 2001, has become a central concern for the American criminal justice system. Controversies over racial/ethnic profiling, compounded by indefinite detention shrouded by secrecy, will continue to fuel public debate over whether such tactics are fair, just, and in the end, effective. Thus far, there is considerable evidence that authorities are overreaching. Abuses against immigrants, foreign nationals, and others held by the U.S. government point to grave threats to civil liberties and human rights (Cole, 2003b; Parenti, 2003b; Welch, 2002a).

Campaigns against terrorism also contribute to the expansion of the corrections-industrial complex, producing a form of punitive profit in which prisoners, jail inmates, immigration detainees, and those swept up in post-September 11th dragnets, serve as its raw materials. That form of social control is not confined to the United States, but is gliding in the path of globalization (Barak, 2000). Commercial interests in imprisonment are fast becoming influential in policy making in Australia and Western Europe (Schuster, 2003; Welch & Schuster, 2003).

Returning to the subject of culture, it is fitting that the book close with some thoughts on the sociology of denial. Cohen (2001, 2002) reminds us that investigations into social problems ought to confront both polarities of societal reaction. Moral panic represents one extreme, namely overreaction. Still, we must not neglect underreaction at the other end of the spectrum. American prison expansion over the past few decades contributes to problems at both extremes. By fueling overreaction in the form of moral panic over crime and drugs, a large segment of the poor and people of color are cast as threats to the social order. Moreover, since the wars on crime and drugs rest on well-publicized enforcement campaigns designed to place politicians and the criminal justice establishment in a favorable light, they tend to deflect critical attention from the harsh reality of imprisonment.

Mandatory minimum drug sentences, three-strikes penalties, and similar forms of punishment generate significant collateral damage. Individual offenders along with their families and communities suffer the consequences of the government's fetish for incarceration. By ignoring the harms generated by the prison apparatus, underreaction perpetuates the reliance on prisons that in turn reproduces racial and socioeconomic injustice. That way of thinking—or not thinking—contributes to what Cohen (2001) calls a culture of disbelief. In that respect, problems created by mass incarceration are denied, becoming part of a larger collective consciousness that fails to reconcile the ironies of imprisonment.

Notes

1. Garland (2001) also examines critically the emergence of the *criminology of the self* that includes the *criminologies of everyday life* (e.g., routine activity theory, crime as opportunity, lifestyle analysis, situational crime

prevention, and some versions of rational choice theories) and the impact they have had on current criminal justice strategies.

2. A recent study on the use of juvenile waivers in New Jersey reveals an interesting irony in the realm of drug use. Morrell (2003, p. 177) finds that a "youthful offender who has some 'Use or Serious Drug Use,' as measured by past record, crime, or substance abuse, faces increased risk of being waived to Adult Court relative to those cases with no drug use. This appears to be a strong indicator to the court that the offender is not a good risk for rehabilitation." That finding seems to demonstrate the influence of the emerging culture of control (Garland, 2001) insofar as the criminal justice apparatus continues to become more punitive. Only in a culture of control can the need for treatment as evidenced by "Use or Serious Drug Use" be used to justify punishment rather than rehabilitation. The American culture of control is so blinded by the fetish of establishing risk that it fails to recognize even the most fundamental need for drug treatment.

End-of-Chapter Questions

1. Describe the culture of control.

2. What is moral panic and how does it contribute to the construction of juvenile superpredators?

3. Describe the controversy surrounding the so-called *wilding* incident in Central Park.

4. Why has California's three-strikes law proven to be so disastrous?

Cases

Adams v. Poag, 61 F.3d 1537, 11th Cir. (1995).

Al Jundi v. Mancusi, F.2d 2287 (1991).

Atkins v. Virginia, 00-8452, 536 US 304 (2002).

Doe v. Meachum, 126 F.D.R. 444 (D. Conn., 1989).

Dunn v. White, 800 F.2d 1188, 10th Cir. (1989).

Edwards v. U.S., 96–8732, S.Ct. (1996).

Ewing v. California, No. 01–6978 (2002).

Farmer v. Brennan, 114, S.Ct. 1970 (1994).

Farmer v. Moritsugu, 742 F.Supp. 525, WD Wisc. (1990).

Ford v. Wainwright, 477 U.S. 699 (1986).

Gregg v. Georgia, 428 U.S. 153 (1976).

Harris v. Thigpen, 941 F.2d 1495, 11th Cir. (1991).

Herrera v. Collins, 91-7328, 506 US 390 (1993).

Hudson v. McMillian, 60 U.S. Law Week 4151 (Feb. 25, 1992).

Inmates of Attica v. Rockefeller, 453 F.2d 12, 18, 22, 2d Cir. (1971).

Lockyer v. Andrade, No. 01–1127 (2003).

McClesky v. Kemp, 41 CrL 4107 (1987).

Medina v. O'Neill, 589 F. Supp. 1028 (1984).

Miranda v. Arizona, 384 U.S. 436 (1966).

New Jersey v. Smith, NJ Super.Ct., App. Div., No. A-636389-T4 (1993).

Nolley v. County of Erie, 776 F.Supp. 715 W.D. NY (1991).

Penry v. Lynaugh, 57 U.S.L.W. 4958 (1989).

Proctor v. Alameda County, Calif. Super.Ct., Alameda Cnty., No. 693983–8 (1992).

Richardson v. McKnight, 96–318 (1997).

Roe et al. v. Fauver et al., D.NJ No.88–1225-AET (1992).

Ruiz v. Estelle, 74–329. E.D. Tex. (Dec. 19, 1980).

U.S. v. Armstrong, 21 F 3rd 1431, 9th Cir. (1995).

Weeks v. Texas, Texas Ct. Crim.App., No. 92–1154 (1992).

Whitney v. California, 274 US 357 (1927).

William P. v. Corrections Corporation of America, C/A No.: 3:98–290–17 ("Verdict Phase I" document, filed on December 14, 2000).

Bibliography

Abbott, J. H. (1981). *In the belly of the beast: Letters from prison.* New York: Vintage.

Abbott, K. (1998, April 2). Parolee with tuberculosis sues county jail, state prison. *Rocky Mountain News,* p. A31.

Abramsky, S. (2002, July 1). The shame of prison health: Just-released inmates with infectious diseases need continuous treatment. *The Nation,* pp. 28–34.

The abusive detention of Sept. 11. (2003, June 3). *New York Times,* p. A30.

Adams, K. (1996). The bull market in corrections. *Prison Journal, 76,* 461–467.

Adams, R. (1998). *Abuses of punishment.* New York: St. Martin's Press.

Adamson, C. (1984). Toward a marxian theory of penology: Captive criminal populations as economic threats and resources. *Social Problems, 31,* 435-458.

Aguirre, A., Jr., & Baker, D. (2000a). Special issue on Latinos and the criminal justice system. *Justice Professional, 13* (1).

Aguirre, A., Jr., & Baker, D. (2000b). Latinos and the United States criminal justice system: Introduction. *Justice Professional, 13*(1), 3–6.

Ainlay, J. (1975). Book review: The new criminology and critical criminology. *Telos, 26,* 213–225.

Akers, R. (1979). Theory and ideology in Marxist criminology. *Criminology, 16,* 527–544.

Akerstrom, M. (1986). Outcasts in prison: The cases of informers and sex offenders. *Deviant Behavior, 7,* 1–12.

Alexander, E. (2003). Private prisons and health care: The HMO from hell. In A. Coyle, A. Campbell, and R. Neufeld (Eds.), *Capitalist punishment: Prison privatization & human rights,* pp. 67–74. Atlanta: Clarity.

American Civil Liberties Union. (2001). Know your rights: What to do if you're stopped by the police, the FBI, the INS, or the customs service. Retrieved December 20, 2003, from www.aclu.org

American Medical Association. (1992). *Code of medical ethics.* Chicago: Author.

Amnesty International. (1999). *'Not part of my sentence': Violations of human rights of women in custody.* New York: Author.

Amnesty International. (2003). *Annual report.* New York: Author.

Anno, B. J., Faiver, K., & Harness, J. (1996). A preliminary model for determining limits for correctional care services. *Journal of Correctional Health Care, 3,* 67–84.

Applebome, P. (1993, March 3). Alabama releases man held on death row for six years. *New York Times,* pp. A-1, B-11.

Aronowitz, S., & DiFazio, W. (1994). *The jobless future: Sci-tech and the dogma of work.* Minneapolis: University of Minnesota Press.

Arrigo, B. A. (1995). The peripheral core of law and criminology: on postmodern social theory and conceptual integration. *Justice Quarterly, 12*(3), 447–472.

Arrigo, B. A. (2003). Psychology and the law: The critical agenda for citizen justice and radical social change. *Justice Quarterly, 20*(2), 399–444.

Arvanites, T., & Asher, M. (1995). The direct and indirect effects of socioeconomic variables on state imprisonment rates. *Criminal Justice Policy Review, 7*(1), 27–53.

Ashcroft, J. (2003, December 6). Testimony of attorney general John Ashcroft before a hearing of the senate judiciary committee on DOJ oversight: Preserving our freedoms while defending against terrorism. Washington, DC: U.S. Government Printing Office.

Auerhahn, K. (2002). Selective incapacitation, three strikes, and the problem of aging prison populations: Using simulation modeling to see the future. *Criminology and Public Policy, 1,* 3: 353–388.

Austin, J. (1999). The impact of three strikes and you're out. *Punishment and Society, 1,* 131–162.

Austin, J., & Coventry, G. (2001). *Emerging issues on privatized prisons.* Washington, DC: Bureau of Justice Assistance.

Austin, J., Crane, R., Griego, B., O'Brien, J., & Vose, G. A. (2000). *The consultants' report on prison operations in New Mexico correctional institutions.* Middletown, CT: Criminal Justice Solutions.

Austin, J., & Irwin, J. (2001). *It's about time: America's imprisonment binge* (3rd ed.). Belmont, CA: Wadsworth.

Austin, J., Marino, A., Bruce, L., Carroll, P., McCall, L., & Richards, S. C. (2003). The use of incarceration in the United States. *Critical Criminology 10*(1), 17–41.

Bailey, W. C. (1983). Disaggregation in deterrence and death penalty research: The case of murder in Chicago. *Journal of Criminal Law and Criminology, 74,* 827–859.

Bailey, W. C. (1998). Deterrence and brutalization, and the death penalty. *Criminology, 36,* 711–734.

Bailey, W. C., & Peterson, R. D. (1987). Police killings and capital punishment: The post-Furman period. *Criminology, 25,* 1–26.

Baldus, D. (1998). Racial discrimination and the death penalty. *Cornell Law Review, 83,* 1638–1770.

Baldus, D., Pulaski, C., & Woodworth, G. (1983). Comparative review of death sentences: An empirical study of the Georgia experience. *Journal of Criminal Law and Criminology, 74,* 661–753.

Baldus, D., Woodworth, G., & Pulaski, C. (1990). *Equal justice and the death penalty: A legal and empirical analysis.* Boston: Northeastern University Press.

Baldus, D., Woodworth, G., & Pulaski, C. (1994). Reflections on the 'inevitability' of racial discrimination in capital sentencing and the 'impossibility' of its prevention, detection, and correction. *Washington and Lee Law Review, 51,* 359–430.

Barak, G. (1982). Punishment and corrections. *Crime and Social Justice, 18,* 108-117.

Barak, G. (2000). *Crime and crime control: A global view.* Westport, CT: Greenwood.

Barak, G. (2003a). Revisionist history, visionary criminology, and needs-based justice. *Contemporary Justice Review, 6*(3), 217–225.

Barak, G. (2003b). *Violence and nonviolence: Pathways to understanding.* Thousand Oaks, CA: Sage.

Barlow, M., Barlow, D. E., & Chiricos, T. G. (1995a). Economic conditions and ideologies of crime in the media: A content analysis of crime news. *Crime & Delinquency, 41*(1), 3–19.

Barlow, M., Barlow, D. E., & Chiricos, T. G. (1995b). Mobilizing support for social control in a declining economy: Exploring ideologies of crime within crime news. *Crime & Delinquency, 41*(2), 191–204.

Barnes, H. (1972). *The evolution of penology in Pennsylvania.* Montclair, NJ: Patterson Smith. (Original work published 1968)

Barnes, H., & Teeters, N. (1946). *New horizons in criminology* (3rd ed.). New York: Prentice Hall.

Barnett, R., & Cavanaugh, J. (1994). *Global dreams: Imperial corporations and the new world order.* New York: Touchstone.

Barth, I. (1989, April 30). "Punch-out": Brutal fun for Brownsville teens. *New York Newsday,* p. 8.

Bates, E. (1998a, January 5). Private prisons. *The Nation,* pp. 11–18.

Bates, E. (1998b, May 4). Private prisons, cont. *The Nation,* p. 5.

Baudrillard, J. (1983). *Simulations.* New York: Semiotext.

Baum, D. (1996). *Smoke and mirrors: The war on drugs and the politics of failure.* Boston: Little, Brown.

Bayer, R. (1984). Lethal injection and capital punishment. *Journal of Prison and Jail Health, 4,* 7–15.

Bayer, R., & Kirp, D. (1992). The United States at the center of the storm (pp. 7–47). In D. Kirp & R. Bayer (Eds.), *AIDS in the industrialized democracies: Passions, politics, and policies.* New Brunswick, NJ: Rutgers University Press.

Beale, C. (2001, August 18). *Cellular rural development: New prisons in rural and small town areas in the 1990s.* Paper presented at the annual meeting of the Rural Sociological Society, Albuquerque, NM.

Beck, A., & Harrison, P. (2001). *Prisoners in 2000.* Washington, DC: U.S. Department of Justice, Bureau of Justice Statistics.

Becker, H. S. (1963). *Outsiders: Studies in the sociology of deviance.* New York: Free Press.

Becker, H. S. (1967). Whose Side Are We On? *Social Problems, 14,* 239–247.

Bedau, H. A., & Radelet, M. L. (1987). Miscarriages of justice in potentially capital cases. *Stanford Law Review, 40,* 21–179.

Berg, J. (2003). Prison privatization developments in South Africa. In A. Coyle, A. Campbell, & R. Neufeld (Eds.), *Capitalist punishment: Prison privatization & human rights,* pp. 179–188. Atlanta: Clarity.

Bernard, T. (1981). The distinction between conflict and radical criminology. *Journal of Criminal Law and Criminology, 72,* 362–379.

Bernard, T. J. (1999). Juvenile crime and the transformation of juvenile justice: Is there a juvenile crime wave? *Justice Quarterly, 16*(2): 337–356.

Berry, B. (2000). Exclusion, inclusion, and violence: Immigrants and criminal justice. In Criminal Justice Collective of Northern Arizona (Ed.), *Investigating differences: Human and cultural relations in criminal justice,* pp. 59–70.

Bessler, J. D. (2003). *Kiss of death: America's love affair with the death penalty.* Boston: Northeastern University Press.

Best, J. (1999). *Random violence: How we talk about new crimes and new victims.* Berkeley: University of California Press.

Birbeck, C. (1999). Latin American and Latina and Latino experiences with prisons and police. *International Criminal Justice Review, 9,* 88–95.

Blomberg, T., & Cohen, S. (2003). *Punishment and social control* (2nd ed.), pp. 19–44. New York: de Gruyter.

Blomberg, T., & Lucken, K. (2000). *American penology: A history of control.* New York: de Gruyter.

Blume, J. (1998). Post-McClesky racial discrimination claims in capital cases. *Cornell Law Review, 83,* 1771–1810.

Blumer, H. (1969). *Symbolic interactionism: Perspective and method.* Englewood Cliffs, NJ: Prentice Hall.

Bohm, R. (1982). Radical criminology: An explication. *Criminology, 19,* 565–589.

Bohm, R. (1999). *Deathquest: An introduction to the theory and practice of capital punishment in the United States.* Cincinnati, OH: Anderson.

Bonczar, T., & Snell, T. (2003). *Capital punishment 2002.* Washington, DC: U.S. Department of Justice, Bureau of Justice Statistics.

Bonger, W. A. (1916). *Criminology and economic conditions.* Boston: Little, Brown.

Bosworth, M. (1998). The imprisoned subject: Agency and identity in prison. *Social Pathology, 4*(1), 48–54.

Bottoms, A. (1995). The philosophy and politics of punishment and sentencing. In C. Clarkson & R. Morgan (Eds.), *The politics of sentencing reform.* Oxford: Clarendon Press.

Bottoms, A. (1999). Interpersonal violence and social order in prisons. In M. Tonry & J. Petersilia (Eds.), *Crime and Justice: A Review of Research, 26*, 205–281.

Bottoms, A., & Preston, R. (1983). *The coming penal crisis.* Edinburgh, Scotland: Scottish Academic Press.

Bottoms, A., & Tonry, M. (2002). *Ideology, crime and criminal justice: A symposium in honour of Sir Leon Radzinowicz.* Cambridge, UK: University of Cambridge, Institute of Criminology.

Bove, L., & Kaplan, L. (1995). *From the eye of the storm.* Atlanta: Rodopi.

Bowers, W. J. (1980). The pervasiveness of arbitrariness and discrimination under post-Furman statutes. *Journal of Criminal Law and Criminology, 74*, 1067-1100.

Bowers, W. J. (1984). *Legal homicide: Death as punishment in America, 1864–1982.* Boston: Northeastern University Press.

Bowers, W. J. (1988). The effect of execution is brutalization, not deterrence. In K. Hass & J. Inciardi (Eds.), *Challenging capital punishment: Legal and social science approaches* (pp. 49–90). Newbury Park, CA: Sage.

Bowers, W. J. (1993). Capital punishment and contemporary values: People's misgivings and the court's misperceptions. *Law and Society Review, 27*, 157–175.

Bowers, W. J., & Pierce, G. (1975). The illusion of deterrence in Isaac Ehrlich's research on capital punishment. *Yale Law Journal, 85*, 187–208.

Bowers, W. J., & Pierce, G. (1980a). Arbitrariness and discrimination under post-Furman capital statutes. *Crime and Delinquency, 74*, 1067–1100.

Bowers, W. J., & Pierce, G. (1980b). Deterrence or brutalization: What is the effect of executions. *Crime and Delinquency, 26*, 453–484.

Box, S., & Hale, C. (1982). Economic crisis and the rising prisoner population in England and Wales. *Crime and Social Justice, 18*, 33–44.

Bragg, R. (1995, May 13). A killer racked by delusions dies in Alabama's electric chair. *New York Times*, p. 7.

Bright, S. B. (1997). Legalized lynching: Race, the death penalty and the United States courts. In W. Shabas (Ed.), *The international sourcebook on capital punishment* (pp. 3–29). Boston: Northeastern University Press.

Bright, S. B. (2002). Discrimination, death, and denial: Race and the death penalty. In D. Dow & M. Dow (Eds.), *Machinery of death: The reality of America's death penalty of regime* (pp. 45–78). New York: Routledge.

Brock, D. E., Sorensen, J., & Marquart, J. W. (1999). Racial disparities after Penry. *Justice Professional, 12*(2), 159-172.

Brooke, J. (1997, November 2). Prisons: A growth industry. *New York Times*, p. 20.

Brundage, W. (1993). *Lynching in the new South: Georgia and Virginia, 1880–1930.* Urbana-Champaign: University of Illinois Press.

Bureau of Justice Statistics. (1995). *Drugs and crime facts, 1994.* Washington, DC: U.S. Department of Justice.

Bureau of Justice Statistics. (1998). *Prisoners in 1997*. Washington, DC: U.S. Department of Justice.

Bureau of Justice Statistics. (2002). *Corrections statistics*. Retrieved December 12, 2003, from www.ojp.usdoj.gov/bjs/correct

Bureau of Justice Statistics (2003). *Capital punishment statistics*. Retrieved December 26, 2003, from www.ojp.usdoj.gov/bjs/

Burton-Rose, D. (1998). *The celling of America: An inside look at the U.S. prison industry*. Boston: Common Courage.

Burton-Rose, D. (2003). Our sisters' keepers. In T. Herivel & P. Wright (Eds.), *Prison nation: The warehousing of America's poor* (pp. 258–269). New York: Routledge.

Butler, J. (1990). *Gender trouble: Feminism and the subversion of identity*. New York: Routledge.

Butterfield, F. (1995, April 12). New prisons cast shadow over higher education. *New York Times*, p. A21.

Butterfield, F. (1998, June 7). New study adds to evidence of bias in death sentences. *New York Times*, p. 20.

Butterfield, F. (2000, April 27). Company to stop operating troubled prison. *New York Times*, p. A21.

Butterfield, F. (2001, September 29). New drug-offender program draws unexpected clients. *New York Times*, p. A6.

Butterfield, F. (2002, June 3). Study shows building prisons did not prevent repeat crimes. *New York Times*, p. 11.

Butterfield, F. (2003a, November 11). With cash tight, states reassess long jail terms. *New York Times*, pp. A1, A15.

Butterfield, F. (2003b, November 14). Study calls California parole system a $1 billion failure. *New York Times*, p. A24.

Butterfield, F. (2003c, September 30). States putting inmates on diets to trim budgets. *New York Times*, p. A18.

Cady, D. L., & Werner, R. (1991). *Just war, nonviolence, and nuclear deterrence: Philosophers on war and peace*. Wakefield, NH: Longfield Academic.

Camp, C. G., & Camp, G. M. (1998). *The corrections yearbook, 1997*. South Salem, NY: The Criminal Justice Institute.

Camp, S. D., & Gaes, G. (2002). Growth and quality of U.S. private prisons: Evidence from a national survey. *Criminology and Public Policy, 1,* 3, 427–449.

Camp, S., Gaes, G., Langan, N., & Saylor, W. (2003). The influence of prisons on inmate misconduct: A multilevel investigation. *Justice Quarterly, 20,* 3, 501–533.

Canedy, D. (2003, April 4). Florida urged to withdraw AIDS leaflet invoking Jesus. *New York Times*, p. A12.

Cardwell, D. (2003, June 13). Muslims face deportation, but say U.S. is their home. *New York Times*, p. A22.

Cass, J. (1996, May 20). As public fears swell, so do Pa. prisons: Other budget items face cuts to fund cells. *Philadelphia Inquirer,* pp. A1, A8.

Castelle, G., & Loftus, E. (2001). Misinformation, and wrongful convictions. In S. Westervelt & J. Humphrey (Eds.), *Wrongly convicted: Perspectives on failed justice.* New Brunswick, NJ: Rutgers University Press.

Centers for Disease Control and Prevention. (1997). Transmission of HIV possibly associated with exposure of mucous membrane to contaminated blood. *Morbidity and Mortality Weekly Report, 46,* 27: 620.

Chambliss, W. J. (1975). Toward a political economy of crime. *Theory and Society, 2,* 2: 149–170.

Chambliss, W. J. (1995). Another lost war: The costs and consequences of drug prohibition. *Social Justice, 22*(2), 101–124.

Chambliss, W. J. (1999). *Power, politics, and crime.* Boulder, CO: Westview.

Charging youth offenders as adults. (1994, June 25). *New York Times,* p. 27.

Chen, D. W. (2000, January 5). $8 million offered to end Attica inmates' suit. *New York Times,* pp. A1, B5.

Chesney-Lind, M. (2002). Imprisoning women: The unintended victims of mass imprisonment. In M. Mauer & M. Chesney-Lind (Eds.), Invisible punishment: *The collateral consequences of mass imprisonment,* pp. 79–94. New York: The Free Press.

Chevigny, B. G. (2000, July 24/31). Prison activists come of age: In California, resistance to prison expansion builds on the past. *The Nation,* pp. 27–30.

Chiricos, T. G., & Bales, W. D. (1991). Unemployment and punishment: An empirical assessment. *Criminology, 29,* 701–724.

Chiricos, T, G., & DeLone, M.A. (1992). Labor surplus and punishment: A review and assessment of theory and evidence. *Social Problems, 39,* 421–446.

Chivigny, P. (2003). The populism of fear: Politics of crime in the Americas. *Punishment & Society, 5*(1), 77–96.

Chomsky, N. (2003). Drug policy as social control. In T. Herivel & P. Wright (Eds.), *Prison nation: The warehousing of America's poor,* pp. 57–59. New York: Routledge.

Christie, N. (1994). *Crime control as industry.* Oslo: Universite-flag.

Clark, J. (1998). *Report to the attorney general: Inspection and review of the northeast Ohio correctional center.* Washington, DC: Office of the Corrections Trustee for the District of Columbia.

Clear, T. (1994). *Harm in American penology: Offenders, victims, and their communities.* Albany: State University of New York Press.

Clear, T., & Frost, N. (2002). Private prisons. *Criminology and Public Policy, 1,* 3, 425–426.

Clement, D. (2002). Big house on the prairie. *Fedgazette, Federal Reserve Bank of Minneapolis, (14)*1.

Clemetson, L. (2003, September 27). More Americans in poverty in 2002, census study says: Household income falls. *New York Times,* pp. A1, A10.

Cochran, J. K., Chamlin, M., & Seth, M. (1994). Deterrence or brutalization? An impact assessment of Oklahoma's return to capital punishment. *Criminology, 32,* 107–134.

Cohen, L. P. (2001, November 1). Denied access to attorneys some INS detainees are jailed without charges. *Wall Street Journal,* pp. EV1–3.

Cohen, S. (1972). *Folk devils and moral panics.* London: Macgibbon and Kee.

Cohen, S. (1979). The punitive city: Notes on the dispersal of social control. *Contemporary Crisis, 3,* 339–363.

Cohen, S. (1985). *Visions of social control.* Cambridge, UK: Polity Press.

Cohen, S. (2001) *States of denial: Knowing about atrocities and suffering.* Cambridge, UK: Polity.

Cohen, S. (2002). *Folk devils and moral panics: The creation of the mods and rockers* (3rd ed.). London: Routledge.

Cole, D. (1999). *No equal justice: Race and class in the American criminal justice system.* New York. The New Press.

Cole, D. (2003a, June 8). Guantanamo gulag. *The Nation,* p. 5.

Cole, D. (2003b, January 13/20). Blind sweeps return. *The Nation,* p. 5.

Cole, D. (2003c). Enemy aliens: Double standards and constitutional freedoms in the war on terrorism. New York: The New Press.

Cole, D., & Dempsey, J. X. (2002). *Terrorism and the constitution: Sacrificing civil liberties in the name of national security.* New York: The New Press.

Colvin, M. (1982). The New Mexico prison riot. *Social Problems, 29,* 449–463.

Colvin, M. (1992). *The penitentiary in crisis: From accommodation to riot in New Mexico.* Albany: State University of New York Press.

Committee on Armed Services. (1988). *The role of the military in drug interdiction.* Washington, DC: U.S. Government Printing Office.

Common Sense for Drug Policy. (2002). Annual causes of death in the United States. Retrieved December 15, 2003, from www.drugwarfacts.org/causes

Concerns rise of civil rights being ignored. (2001, October 17). *Chicago Tribune,* pp. EV1–3.

Conover, T. (2000). *New jack: Guarding at Sing Sing.* New York: Random House.

Contemporary Justice Review. (2003). *Radical criminology: Whatever happened to it?* Special Issue, 6, 3.

Cooper, M. (2000, January 5). Nassau guard admits role in jail beating: Says he was lookout for 2 guards inside cell. *New York Times,* pp. B1, B5.

Courtenay, W., & Sabo, D. (2001). Preventative health strategies for men in prison. In D. Sabo, T. Kupers, & W. London (Eds.), *Prison masculinities* (pp. 157–172). Philadelphia: Temple University Press.

Covington, J. (1995). Racial classification in criminology: The reproduction of racialized crime. *Sociological Forum, 10,* 4, 547–568.

Covington, J. (1997). The social construction of the minority drug problem. *Social Justice. 24*(4), 117–147.

Coyle, A., Campbell, A., & Neufeld, R. (2003). *Capitalist punishment: Prison privatization & human rights.* Atlanta: Clarity.

Coyle, M., Strasser, F., & Lavelle, M. (1990). Fatal trial and error in the nation's Death Belt. *National Law Journal, 12*(40), 30–44.

Crane, R. (2000). Monitoring of Guadalupe and Lea County correctional facilities. In J. Austin, R. Crane, B. Griego, J. O'Brien, & F. Vose (Eds.), *The consultants' report on prison operations in New Mexico correctional institutions.* Middletown, CT: Criminal Justice Solutions.

Crawford, C., Chiricos, T., & Kleck, G. (1998). Race, racial threat, and sentencing of habitual offenders. *Criminology, 36*(3): 481–512.

Crews, G., & Montgomery, R. (2002). Prison violence. In D. Levinson (Ed.), *Encyclopedia of crime and punishment,* pp. 1240–1244. Thousand Oaks, CA: Sage.

Cullen, F. (1995). Assessing the penal harm movement. *Journal of Research in Crime and Delinquency, 32,* 338–358.

Cullen, F., & Wozniak, J. (1982, Winter). Fighting the appeal of repression. *Crime and Social Justice, 18,* 23–32.

Currie, E. (1985). *Confronting crime: An American challenge.* New York: Pantheon.

Currie, E. (1993). *Reckoning: Drugs, the cities, and the American future.* New York: Hill & Wang.

Currie, E. (2003). Of punishment and crime rates: Some theoretical and methodological consequences of mass incarceration. In T. Blomberg & S. Cohen (Eds.), *Punishment and social control* (2nd ed.), pp. 483–494. New York: de Gruyter.

Cusac, A. (2003). The judge gave me ten years. He didn't sentence me to death. In T. Herivel & P. Wright (Eds.), *Prison nation: The warehousing of America's poor,* pp. 195–203. New York: Routledge.

Dabney, D. A., & Vaughn, M. S. (2000). Incompetent jail and prison doctors. *Prison Journal, 80*(2), 151–183.

D'Allessio, S. J., & Stolzenberg, L. (2002). A multilevel analysis of the relationship between labor surplus and pretrial incarceration. *Social Problems, 49,* 178–193.

Danner, M., Michalowski, R., & Lynch, M. (1994). What does "critical" mean? *Critical Criminologist, 6*(2), 2.

Davey, M. (2003, June 17). Texas frees 12 on bond after drug sweep inquiry. *New York Times,* p. A16.

Davis, M. (1995). The state's Dr. Death: What's unethical about physicians helping at executions. *Social Theory and Practice, 21*(1), 31–60.

De Beaumont, G., & De Tocqueville, A. (1833). *On the penitentiary system in the United States, and its application to France.* Philadelphia: Carey, Lea, & Blanchard.

Decker, S., & Kohfeld, C. (1990). The deterrent effect of capital punishment in the five most active execution states: A time series analysis. *Criminal Justice Review, 15,* 173–191.

Declaration on the protection of all persons from enforced disappearances. (1992, December 18). General Assembly res. 47/133, 47 U.N. GAOR Supp. (No. 49) at 207, U.N. Doc. A/47/49. Adopted by General Assembly resolution 47/133. Retrieved March 15, 2004, from http://www1.umn.edu/humanrts/instree/h4dpaped.htm

DeJesus-Torres, M. (2000). Microaggressions in the criminal justice system at discretionary stages of its impact on Latino(a) Hispanics. *Justice Professional, 13*(1), pp. 69–90.

Derrida, J. (1976). *Of grammatology* (G. C. Spivak, Trans.). Baltimore: Johns Hopkins University Press.

Deutsch, M., Cunningham, D., & Fink, E. (1991). Twenty years later: Attica civil rights case finally cleared for trial. *Social Justice, 18*(3), 13–25.

Dewan, S. K., & Rashbaum, W. K. (2003, December 14). Arrests jolt the police, but some see a pattern. *New York Times,* p. 53.

Diaz-Cotto, J. (1998). *Gender, ethnicity, and the state: Latina and Lationo prison politics.* Albany: State University of New York Press.

Diaz-Cotto, J. (2000). The criminal justice system and its impact on Latinas(os) in the United States. *Justice Professional, 13*(1), pp. 49–68.

Dieter, R. (1997). *Innocence and the death penalty: The increasing danger of executing the innocent.* Washington, DC: Death Penalty Information Center.

The disgrace of juvenile executions. (2002, October 24). *New York Times,* p. A34.

Donaldson, S. D. (2001). A million jockers, punks, and queens. In D. Sabo, T. Kupers, & W. London (Eds.), *Prison masculinities,* pp. 118–126. Philadelphia: Temple University Press.

Donohue, B. (2001, October 30). Rights groups prodding feds for information on detainees. *Star-Ledger* (NJ), pp. EV1–2.

Donziger, S. (1996a, March 17). The prison-industrial complex: What's really driving the rush to lock 'em up. *The Washington Post,* p. 24.

Donziger, S. (1996b). *The real war on crime: The report of the National Criminal Justice Commission.* New York: HarperPerennial.

Donziger, S. (1998, March 16). Profits from prisons. *The Nation,* pp. 2, 24.

Dougherty, L. (1998, July 11). 9 guards indicted in beating. *St. Petersburg Times,* p. 1.

Dow, D. R., & Dow, M. (2002). *Machinery of death: The reality of America's death penalty of regime.* New York: Routledge.

Dow, M. (2001, November 11). We know what INS is hiding. *Miami Herald,* pp. EV1-3.

Dray, P. (2002). *At the hands of persons unknown: The lynching of black America.* New York: Random House.

Dreyfus, H. L., & Rabinow, P. (1983). *Michel Foucault: Beyond structuralism and hermeneutics*. Chicago: University of Chicago Press.

Drummond, T. (1999, June 21). Cellblock seniors: They have grown old and frail in prison. Must they still be locked up? *Time*, p. 60.

Dunaway, R. G., Cullen, F. T., Burton, Jr., V. S., & Evans, T. D. (2000). The myth of social class and crime revisited: An examination of class and adult criminality. *Criminology, 38*(2), 589–632.

Dunlop, D. (1995, June 26). Personalizing Nazis' homosexual victims. *New York Times*, pp. A1, B4.

Durham, A. M. (1994). *Crisis and reform: Current issues in American punishment*. Boston: Little, Brown

Durham, A. M. (1989). Newgate of Connecticut: Origins and early days of an early American prison. *Justice Quarterly, 6*, 89–116.

Dwight, L. (1826). *First annual report*. Boston: Boston Prison Discipline Society.

Dyer, J. (2000). *The perpetual prisoner machine*. Boulder, CO: Westview Press.

Eckholm, E. (1995, February 25). Studies find death penalty tied to race of the victims. *New York Times*, pp. B1, B2.

Edelman, M. (1988). *Constructing the political spectacle*. Chicago: University of Chicago Press.

Egan, T. (1998, April 16). As Idaho booms, prisons fill and spending on poor lags. *New York Times*, pp. A1, A16.

Egan, T. (1999, February 28). War on crack retreats, still taking prisoners. *The New York Times*, pp. A1, 22.

Egerton, J. (1984, September). The Tennessee walls. *The Progressive*, p. 19.

Egler, D. (1986, June 5). Canton, Mt. Sterling win prison prize. *Chicago Tribune*, p. 2.

Ehrenfeld, R. (1990). *Narco terrorism: How governments around the world have used the drug trade to finance and further terrorist activities*. New York: Basic Books.

Ehrenreich, B. (2001). *Nickel and dimed: On (not) getting by in America*. New York: Metropolitan.

Ehrlich, I. (1975). The deterrent effect of capital punishment: A question of life and death. *American Economic Review, 65*, 397–417.

Eigenberg, H. (1994). Rape in male prisons: Examining the relationship between correctional officers' attitudes toward male rape and their willingness to respond to acts of rape. In M. Braswell, R. Montgomery, & L. Lombardo (Eds.), *Prison violence in America* (pp. 145–166). Cincinnati, OH: Anderson.

Eisenhower, D. D. (1985). Farewell radio and television address to the American people. In A. Mason & G. Baker (Eds.), *Free government in the making* (pp. 747–749). New York: Oxford University Press.

Election-year posturing on drugs. (1996, August 19). *New York Times*, p. A12.

Elliot, A. (2003, June 7). In Brooklyn, 9/11 damage continues. *New York Times*, p. A9.

Elvin, J. (1992). A rare win for man behind bars. *Civil Liberties, 376,* 6.

Elvin, J. (1994/1995). 'Corrections-industrial complex' expands in U.S. *National Prison Project Journal, 10,* 1–4.

Engels, F. (1973). *The conditions of the working class in England.* Moscow: SU Progress. (Originally published in 1845)

Everett, R. S., & Nienstedt, B. C. (1999). Race, remorse, and sentencing reduction: Is saying you're sorry enough? *Justice Quarterly, 16*(1): 99–122.

Ex-prison supervisors told they will be jailed for beating prisoner. (2000, October 27). *Associated Press,* p. 1.

Farber, M. (1944). Suffering and time perspective in the prisoner. In K. Lewin (Ed.), *Authority and frustration* (pp. 155–213). Iowa City: Iowa University Press.

Farmer, P. (2002). The house of the dead: Tuberculosis and incarceration. In M. Mauer & M. Chesney-Lind (Eds.), *Invisible punishment: The collateral consequences of mass imprisonment,* pp. 237–257. New York: The Free Press.

Federal Document Clearing House. (1997, April 16). *Remarks made by James Wooten before the subcommittee on youth violence of the senate committee on the judiciary.* Washington, DC: U.S. Government Printing Office.

Ferrell, J. (1996). *Crimes of style: Urban graffiti and the politics of criminality.* Boston: Northeastern University Press.

Ferrell, J. (1997). Against the law: Anarchist criminology. In B. MacLean & D. Milovanovic (Eds.), *Thinking critically about crime,* pp. 146–154. Vancouver, BC, Canada: Collective Press.

Ferrell, J. (1998). Stumbling toward a critical criminology: And into the anarchy and imagery of postmodernism, In J. Ross (Ed.), *Cutting the edge: Current perspectives in critical criminology.* Westport, CT: Praeger.

Fine, R. (1980). The birth of the bourgeois punishment. *Crime and Social Justice, 13,* 19–26.

Flanagan, T. (1996). Reform or punish: Americans' views of the correctional system. In T. Flanagan & D. Longmire (Eds.), *Americans view crime and justice* (pp. 75–92). Thousand Oaks, CA: Sage.

Flavin, J. (1998). Police and HIV/AIDS: The risk, the reality, the response. *American Journal of Criminal Justice, 23,* 1, 33–58.

Flavin, J. (2002). HIV/AIDS and the criminal justice system. In D. Levinson (Ed.), *Encyclopedia of crime and punishment,* pp. 831–837. Thousand Oaks, CA: Sage.

Fleisher, M. (1989). *Warehousing violence.* Newbury Park, CA: Sage.

Flynn, E. (1995). Three-strikes legislation: Prevalence and definitions. In *Critical criminal justice issues* (158837), pp. 122–133. Washington, DC: National Institute of Justice.

Foley, L., & Powell, R. (1982). The discretion of prosecutors, judges, and jurists in capital cases. *Criminal Justice Review, 7,* 16–22.

Forst, B. (1983). Capital punishment and deterrence: Conflicting evidence? *Journal of Criminal Law and Criminology, 74,* 927–942.

Foucault, M. (1979). *Discipline and punish: The birth of the prison.* New York: Vintage.

4 cleared in massacre. (1991, November 23). *New York Newsday,* p. 8.

Fox, B. (2001, October 4). Attacks probed in closed courts. *Associated Press,* pp. EV1–3.

Frankford, E., & Snitow, A. (1972, July/August). The trap of domesticity: Notes on the family. *Socialist Revolution, 9,* 83–94.

Friedman, A. (2003). Juvenile crime pays—But at what cost? In T. Herivel & P. Wright (Eds.), *Prison nation: The warehousing of America's poor,* pp. 174–180. New York: Routledge.

Friedman, M. (1992). Cruel and unusual punishment in the provision of prison medical care: Challenging the deliberate indifference standard. *Vanderbilt Law Review, 45,* 921–949.

Friedrichs, D. (1996). *Trusted criminals.* Belmont, CA: Wadsworth.

Gans, H. (1995). *The war against the poor.* New York: Basic Books.

Garfinkel, H. (1956). Conditions of successful degradation ceremonies. *American Journal of Sociology, 61,* 420–424.

Garland, D. (1990). *Punishment in modern society: A study in social theory.* Chicago: University of Chicago Press.

Garland, D. (2001). *The culture of control: Crime and social order in contemporary society.* Chicago: University of Chicago Press.

Garland, D. (2002). *Mass imprisonment: Social causes and consequences.* London: Sage.

Garvey, S. P. (2000). The emotional economy of capital sentencing. *New York University Law Review, 75,* 26–73.

Gates, H. L. (1990, July 15). The case of 2 Live Crew tells much about the American psyche. *New York Times,* Section 4, p. 18.

Gaylord, B. (2001, December 2). Australia migrants, many children, land at troubled camp. *New York Times,* p. A4.

General Accounting Office. (1990). *Death penalty sentencing: Research indicates pattern of racial disparities.* Washington, DC: Government Printing Office.

General Accounting Office. (1996). *Private prisons and cost savings.* Washington, DC: Government Printing Office.

General Accounting Office. (2003). *Better management oversight and internal controls needed to ensure accuracy of terrorism-related statistics.* Washington, DC: General Accounting Office.

George, A. (2003). Women prisoners as customers: Counting the costs of the privately managed Metropolitan Women's Correctional Center: Australia. In A. Coyle, A. Campbell, & R. Neufeld (Eds.), *Capitalist punishment: Prison privatization & human rights,* pp. 202–210. Atlanta: Clarity.

Giddens, A. (1982). *Profiles and critiques in social theory*. Berkeley: University of California Press.

Gil, D. (1996). Preventing violence in a structurally violent society: Mission impossible. *American Journal of Orthopsychiatry, 66*, 77–84.

Gilmore, R. W. (2002). *Golden gulag*. Berkeley, CA: University of California Press.

Glaberson, W. (2003, December 24). Judge Denounces Attorney General's Death-Penalty Push. *New York Times*, p. B2.

Glamser, D. (1996, March 13). Towns now welcoming prisons. *USA Today*, p. 3A.

Glasser, I. (2003, June 8). Arrests after 9/11: Are we safer? *New York Times*, p. WK12.

Glassner, B. (1999). *The culture of fear: Why Americans are afraid of the wrong things*. New York: Basic Books.

Glyn, A. (1990). Contradictions of capitalism. In J. Eatwell, M. Milgate, & P. Newman (Eds.), *The new Pelgrave: Marxian economics* (pp. 104–109). New York: Norton.

Goffman, E. (1961). *Asylums: Essays on the social situation of mental patients and other inmates*. Garden City, NY: Anchor.

Goffman, E. (1963). *Stigma: Notes on the management of spoiled identity*. Englewood Cliffs, NJ: Prentice Hall.

Gordon, D. (1994a). Drugspeak and the Clinton administration: A lost opportunity for drug policy reform. *Social Justice, 21*(3), 30–36.

Gordon, D. (1994b). *The return of the dangerous classes: Drug prohibition and policy politics*. New York: Norton.

Gostin, L. O. (1995). The resurgent tuberculosis epidemic in the era of AIDS: Reflections on public health, law, and society. *Maryland Law Review 54*, 1–131.

Gourevitch, A. (2003, January). Detention disorder: Ashcroft's clumsy round-up of foreigners lurches forward. *The American Prospect*, pp. EV1–7.

Gowdy, V. (2001). Should we privatize our prisons? The pros and cons. In E. Latessa, A. Holsinger, J. Marquart, and J. Sorensen (Eds.), *Correctional contexts: Contemporary and classical readings*, pp. 198–207. Los Angeles: Roxbury.

Grapendaal, M., Leuw, E., & Nelen, H. (1992). Drugs and crime in an accommodating social context: The situation in Amsterdam. *Contemporary Drug Problems, 19*, 303–326.

Gray, J. P. (2001). *Why our drug laws have failed and what we can do about it*. Philadelphia: Temple University Press.

Greenberg, D. F. (1977). The dynamics of oscillatory punishment process. *Journal of Criminal Law and Criminology, 68*, 643–651.

Greenberg, D. F. (1981). *Crime and capitalism*. Palo Alto, CA: Mayfield.

Greenberg, D. F. (2002). Striking out in democracy. *Punishment & Society, 4*, 2. pp. 237–252.

Greene, J. (2002). Entrepreneurial corrections: Incarceration as a business opportunity. In M. Mauer & M. Chesney-Lind (Eds.), *Invisible punishment: The collateral consequences of mass imprisonment*, pp. 95–114. New York: The Free Press.

Greene, J. (2003a). Lack of correctional services. In A. Coyle, A. Campbell, & R. Neufeld (Eds.), *Capitalist punishment: Prison privatization & human rights*, pp. 39–47. Atlanta: Clarity.

Greene, J. (2003b). Bailing out private jails. In T. Herivel & P. Wright (Eds.), *Prison nation: The warehousing of America's poor*, pp. 138–147. New York: Routledge.

Greenfeld, L. A., & Snell, T. L. (2000). *Women offenders*. Washington, DC: U.S. Department of Justice, Bureau of Justice Statistics.

Greenhouse, L. (1997, June 24). Immunity from suits is withheld for guards in privately run jails. *New York Times*, p. B10.

Greenhouse, L. (2002, April 2). Supreme court taps cases to decide 3-strikes issue: Heft given to third strike is central. *New York Times*, p. A16.

Greifinger, R., Heywood, N., & Glaser, J. (1993). Tuberculosis in prison: Balancing justice and public health. *Journal of Law, Medicine, and Ethics, 21*, 3/4: 332–341.

Gross, B. (1982). Some anticrime proposals for progressives. *Crime and Social Justice, 18*, 45–56.

Gross, J. (1993, January 25). California inmates win better prison AIDS care. *New York Times*, p. A12.

Groves, B., & Sampson, R. (1986, Spring). Critical theory and criminology. *Social Problems, 33*, S58-S80.

Growing anxiety over crime. (1994, January 24). *New York Times*, p. A14.

Guerin, D. (1970). *Anarchism*. New York: Monthly Review Press.

Hall, B. (1829). Travels in North America: The years 1927–1828. Edinburgh, Scotland: Scottish Academic Press.

Hall, S., Critcher, C., Jefferson, T., Clarke, J., & Roberts, B. (1978). *Policing the crisis: Mugging, the state and law and order*. New York: Holmes and Meiser.

Hallsworth, S. (2002). The case for a postmodern penality. *Theoretical Criminology, 6*, 2, pp. 145–163.

Hammett, T., Harmon, P., & Maruschak, L. (1999). *1996–1997 update: HIV/AIDS, STDs, and TB in correctional facilities*. Washington, D.C.: National Institute of Justice.

Harding, T. (1987). Health in prisons. *Council of Europe Prison Information Bulletin, 10*, 9–11.

Harlow, E., Matas, D., & Rocamora, J. (1995). *The machinery of death: A shocking indictment of capital punishment in the United States*. New York: Amnesty International.

Harrison, P. M., & Karberg, J. (2003). *Prison and jail inmates at midyear 2002*. Washington, DC: U.S. Department of Justice, Bureau of Justice Statistics.

Hassel, J., & Misseck, R. E. (1996, January 31). 6 more union county officers arrested in probe of alleged abuse of detainees. *The Star Ledger*, pp. 1, 10.

Hatsukami, D., & Fischman, M. (1996). Crack cocaine and cocaine hydrochloride: Are the differences myth or reality? *Journal of the American Medical Association, 276*, 1580–1588.

Hawkins, R., & Tiedeman, G. (1975). *The creation of deviance*. Columbus, OH: C. Merrill.

Hawthorne, N. (1962). *The scarlet letter*. Columbus: Ohio State University Press. (Original work published 1850)

Healey, Joseph. (1995). *Race, ethnicity, gender, and class*. Thousand Oaks, CA: Pine Forge Press.

Hecht, M. E., & Habsha, D. (2003). International law and the privatization of juvenile justice. In A. Coyle, A. Campbell, and R. Neufeld (Eds.), *Capitalist punishment: Prison privatization & human rights*, pp. 75–86. Atlanta: Clarity.

Heger, H. (1972). *The men with the pink triangle*. New York: Alyson.

Heidegger, M. (1949). *Existence and being*. Chicago: Henry Regnery.

Hentoff, N. (1995, February 21). Executing the retarded in our name. *Village Voice*, pp. 30–31.

Herbert, B. (2002, August 5). Tulia's shattered lives. *New York Times*, p. A15.

Herivel, T. (2003). Wreaking medical mayhem on women prisoners in Washington state. In T. Herivel & P. Wright (Eds.), *Prison nation: The warehousing of America's poor*, pp. 174–180. New York: Routledge.

Herivel, T., & Wright, P. (2003). *Prison nation: The warehousing of America's poor*. New York: Routledge.

Hirsch, A. J. (1992). *The rise of the penitentiary: Prisons and punishment in early America*. New Haven, CT: Yale University Press.

Hirschi, T. (1969). *Causes of delinquency*. Berkeley: University of California Press.

Hirst, P. Q. (1975). Radical deviancy theory and Marxism: A reply to Taylor and Walton. In I. Taylor, P. Walton, & J. Young (Eds.), *Critical criminology* (pp. 233–237). Boston: Routledge & Kegan Paul.

Hoffman, J. (1998, March 29). Police tactics chipping away suspects' rights. *New York Times*, pp. A-1, A-40.

Holmes, S. A. (1994, November 6). The boom in jails is locking up lots of loot. *New York Times*, p. E3.

Hoy, D. C. (1979). Taking history seriously: Foucault, Gadamer, Habermas. *Union Seminary Quarterly Review, 34*(2), 85–95.

Huber, J., & Schneider, B. (1992). *The social contexts of AIDS*. Thousand Oaks, CA: Sage.

Huff, C. R. (2002). Wrongful conviction and public policy. *Criminology, 40*, 1, 1–18.

Huff, C. R., Rattner, A., & Sagarin, E. (1996). *Convicted but innocent: Wrongful conviction and public policy*. Thousand Oaks, CA: Sage.

Huggins, M. (1998a). United States foreign police in Latin America: An international protections racket. *Contemporary Justice Review, 1*, 467–494.

Huggins, M. (1998b). *Political policing: The United States in Latin America.* Durham, NC: Duke University Press.

Huling, T. (Writer/Producer) (1999). Yes, in my backyard [Documentary film]. Galloping Girls Production and WSKG Public Broadcasting.

Huling, T. (2002). Building a prison economy in rural America. In M. Mauer & M. Chesney-Lind (Eds.), *Invisible punishment: The collateral consequences of mass imprisonment,* pp. 197–213. New York: The Free Press.

Human Rights Watch. (1996). *All too familiar: Sexual abuse of women in U.S. prisons.* New York: Author.

Human Rights Watch. (1998). *Locked away: Immigration detainees in jails in the U.S.* New York: Author.

Human Rights Watch. (2001). *Beyond reason: The death penalty and offenders with mental retardation.* New York: Author.

Human Rights Watch. (2002). *Presumption of guilt: Human rights abuses of post-September 11th detainees.* New York: Author.

Human Rights Watch. (2003). *World report 2003: Events of 2002.* New York: Author.

Humphries, D. (1999). *Crack mothers: Pregnancy, drugs, and the media.* Columbus: Ohio State University.

Humphries, D., & Greenberg, D. (1981). The dialectics of crime control. In D. Greenberg (Ed.), *Crime and capitalism.* Palo Alto: CA: Mayfield.

Husak, D. (2000). Liberal neutrality, autonomy, and drug prohibitions. *Philosophy and Public Affairs, 29,* 1, 43–80.

Husak, D. (2002). *Legalize this! The case for decriminalizing drugs.* New York: Verso.

Husserl, E. (1962*). Ideas.* New York: Collier.

Ignatieff, M. (1978). *A just measure of pain: The penitentiary in the Industrial Revolution 1750–1850.* New York: Columbia University Press.

Immigration and Naturalization Services (INS). (1995). *Interim report, executive summary: The Elizabeth, New Jersey, contract detention facility operated by ESMOR Inc.* Washington, DC: Author.

Inciardi, J. A. (2002). *The war on drugs III: The continuing saga of the mysteries and miseries of intoxication, addiction, crime, and public policy.* Boston: Allyn & Bacon.

International Covenant on Civil and Political Rights (1966, December 16) Adopted by General Assembly resolution 2200A (XXI). Retrieved March 15, 2004, from http://www.unhchr.ch/html/menu3/b/a_ccpr.htm

Irwin, J. (1985). *The jail: Managing the underclass in American society.* Berkeley: University of California Press.

Irwin, J., Schiraldi, V., & Ziedenberg, J. (2000). America's one million nonviolent prisoners. *Social Justice, 27*(2), 135–147.

Jackson, B. (1992). The Indians of Attica: A taste of white man's justice. In B. Jackson (Ed.), *Disorderly conduct* (pp. 122–128). Urbana-Champaign: University of Illinois Press.

Jackson, G. (1970). *Soledad brother.* New York: Bantam.

Jackson, J. (1996). *Legal lynching: Racism, injustice, and the death penalty.* New York: Marlowe.

Jackson, J. L., Sr., & Jackson, J. L., Jr. (2001). *Legal lynching: The death penalty and America's future.* New York: Free Press.

James, A., Bottomley, A., Liebling, A., & Clare, E. (1997). *Private prisons: Rhetoric and reality.* Thousand Oaks, CA: Sage.

Jankovic, I. (1982). Labor market and imprisonment. In A. Platt & P. Takagi (Eds.), *Punishment and penal discipline* (pp. 105–112). San Francisco: Crime and Justice Associates.

Janofsky, M. (2003, May 29). Utah officials preparing for another firing squad, to be used as soon as next month. *New York Times,* p. A16.

Jenkins, P. (1994b). The 'ice age': The social construction of a drug panic. *Justice Quarterly, 11,* 1. p. 7–31.

Jilani, H. (2002). Antiterrorism strategies and protecting human rights. *Amnesty Now, 27,* 2, 1. p. 15–17.

John Ashcroft's death penalty edicts (Editorial). (2003, February 7). *New York Times,* p. A24.

Johns, C. (1991). The war on drugs: Why the administration continues to pursue a policy of criminalization and enforcement, *Social Justice, 18,* 147–165.

Johns, C. (1996). *Operation just cause: The war on drugs and the invasion of Panama.* New York: Praeger.

Johnson, R. (1998). *Deathwatch: A study of the modern execution process.* Belmont: CA: West/Wadsworth.

Johnson, R., & Toch, H. (1982). *The pains of imprisonment.* Prospect Heights, IL: Waveland.

Jones, C. (1995, October 28). Crack and punishment: Is race the issue? *The New YorkTimes,* pp. A1, A10.

Jurik, N. (1999). Socialist feminism, criminology, and social justice. In B. Arrigo (Ed.), *Social justice, criminal justice* (pp. 31–50). Belmont, CA: Wadsworth.

Kalinich, D. B. (1980). *Power, stability and contraband: The inmate economy.* Prospect Heights, IL: Waveland.

Kalinich, D. B., & Stojkovic, S. (1985). Contraband: The basis for legitimate power in a prison social system. *Crime and Behavior: An International Journal, 12,* 435–451.

Kalinich, D. B., & Stojkovic, S. (1987). Prison contraband systems: Implications for prison management. *Journal of Crime and Justice, 10*(1), 1–21.

Kappeler, V. E., Blumberg, M., & Potter, G. (2000). *The mythology of crime and criminal justice* (3rd ed.). Prospect Heights, IL: Waveland.

Kappeler, V. E., Vaughn, M., & del Carmen, R. (1991). Death in detention: An analysis of police liability for negligent failure to prevent suicide. *Journal of Criminal Justice, 19,* 381–393.

Katz, J. (1988). *Seductions of crime: Moral and sensual attraction in doing evil.* New York: Basic Books.

Katz, S. R. (1997). Presumed guilty: How schools criminalize Latino youth. *Social Justice, 24*(4), 77–117.

Kautt, P., & Spohn, C. (2002). Crack-ing down on the black drug offenders? Testing for interactions among offenders' race, drug type, and sentencing in federal drug sentences. *Justice Quarterly, 19,* 1, 1–35.

Keil, T., & Vito, G. (1989). Race, homicide severity, and application of the death penalty: A consideration of the Barnett Scale. *Criminology, 27,* 511–536.

Keyes, D., Edwards, W. & Perske, R. (2002, June). People with mental retardation are dying—legally. *Journal of Mental Retardation, 22,* 44–61.

Kilborn, P. T. (2001, August 1). Rural towns turn to prisons to reignite their economies. *New York Times,* pp. A1, A12.

Kilborn, P. T. (2003, October 13). A small town loses its prisoners and livelihood. *New York Times,* p. A9.

Kilborn, P. T., & Clemetson, L. (2002, June 2). Gains of 90's did not lift all, census shows. *New York Times,* pp. A1, A24.

The killing ground. (1980, February 18). *Newsweek,* pp. 66–76.

King, D. (1978). The brutalization effect: Execution publicity and the incidence of homicide in South Carolina. *Social Forces, 57,* 683–687.

Kirk, R. (1991, July). Sowing violence in Peru: War on drugs. *The Progressive, 55,* pp. 30–32.

Kitsuse, J. (1962). Societal reactions to deviant behavior: Problems of theory and method. *Social Problems, 9,* 247–256.

Klein, D., & Kress, J. (1976). Any woman's blues: A critical overview of women, crime, and the criminal justice system. *Crime and Social Justice, 5,* 34–49.

Klein, L., Forst, B., & Filatov, V. (1978). The deterrent effect of capital punishment: An assessment of the estimates. In A. Blumstein, J. Cohen, & D. Nagin (Eds.), *Deterrence and incapacitation: Estimating the effects of criminal sanctions on crime rates.* Washington, DC: National Academy of Sciences.

Klein, P. (1920). *Prison methods in New York State.* New York: Columbia University Press.

Klockars, C. B. (1979). The contemporary crisis of Marxist criminology. *Criminology, 16,* 477–515.

Kocieniewski, D. (1997, January 5). New York pays a high price for police lies. *New York Times,* p. A1.

Kolarik, G. (1996, January). DNA, changed testimony, gain acquittal. *American Bar Association Journal,* pp. 34–35.

Kovandzic, T., Sloan J., & Vieraitis, L. (2002). Unintended consequences of politically popular sentencing policy: The homicide promoting effects of 'Three Strikes' in U.S. cities. *Criminology and Public Policy, 1*(3), 399–425.

Kowalski, D. (2003, December 19). Detention Nation. *The Texas Observer,* pp. 28–29.

Kraska, P. (1993a). *Altered states of mind: Critical observations of the drug war.* New York: Garland.

Kraska, P. (1993b). Militarizing the drug war: A sign of the times. In P. Kraska (Ed.), *Altered states of mind: Critical observations of the drug war* (pp. 159–206). New York: Garland.

Kraska, P. (1996). Enjoying militarism: Political/personal dilemmas in studying U.S. police paramilitary units. *Justice Quarterly, 13,* 405–430.

Kraska, P. (1997). The military as drug police: Exercising the ideology of war. In L. Gaines & P. Kraska (Eds.), *Drugs, crime and justice: Contemporary perspectives* (pp. 297–320). Prospect Heights, IL: Waveland.

Kraska, P., & Kappeler, V. (1997). Militarizing American police: The rise and normalization of paramilitary units. *Social Problems, 44,* 1–18.

Krauss, C. (1996, November 27). 2 ex-officers of 30th are sentenced for drug deals. *New York Times,* p. B2.

Kropotkin, P. (1975). *The essential Kropotkin* (E. Capouya & K. Tompkins, Eds.). New York: Liveright.

Kunkel, J., & Taylor, B. (1995). George Bush and the Gulf War: Measuring values. In L. Bove & L. Kaplan (Eds.), *From the eye of the storm* (pp. 45–61). Atlanta: Rodopi.

Kuntz, T. (1997, January 12). Banality, nausea, triple execution: Guards on inmates' final hours. *New York Times,* p. E-7.

Kupers, T. (2001). Rape and the prison code. In D. Sabo, T. Kupers, & W. London (Eds.), *Prison masculinities,* pp. 111–117. Philadelphia: Temple University Press.

Lamb-Mechanick, D., & Nelson, J. (2000). *Prison health care survey: An analysis of factors influencing per capita costs.* Washington, DC: American Correctional Association.

Langan, P., & Levin, D. (2002). *Recidivism of prisoners released in 1994.* Washington, DC: U.S. Department of Justice, Bureau of Justice Statistics. (http://www.ojp.usdoj.gov/bjs/pub/pdf/rpr94.pdf)

Lanza-Kaduce, L., Parker, K., & Thomas, C. (1999). A comparative recidivism analysis of releases from private and public prisons. *Crime & Delinquency, 45,* 28–47.

Lawyers Committee for Human Rights. (2003). *Imbalance of powers: How changes to U.S. law & policy since 9/11 erode human rights and civil liberties.* New York: Author.

Lea, J. (2002). *Crime and modernity: Continuities in left realist criminology.* London: Sage.

Lee, H. (1960). *To kill a mockingbird.* New York: HarperCollins.

Lemert, E. (1972). *Human deviance, social problems and social control.* Englewood Cliffs, NJ: Prentice Hall.

Leo, R. A. (2001). False confessions: Causes, consequences, and solutions. In S. Westervelt & J. Humphrey (Eds.), *Wrongly convicted: Perspectives on failed justice.* New Brunswick, NJ: Rutgers University Press.

Leone, M. C. (2002). Prisoners, elderly. In D. Levinson (Ed.) *Encyclopedia of crime and punishment,* pp. 1250–1131. Thousand Oaks, CA: Sage.

Lesieur, H., & Welch, M. (1991). Public disorder and social control. In J. Sheley (Ed.), *Criminology: A contemporary handbook* (pp. 175–198). Belmont, CA: Wadsworth.

Lesieur, H., & Welch, M. (1995). Vice crimes: Individual choices and social controls. In J. Sheley (Ed.), *Criminology: A contemporary handbook* (2nd ed., pp. 201–269). Belmont, CA: Wadsworth.

Lesieur, H., & Welch, M. (2000). Vice crimes: Personal autonomy versus societal dictates. In J. Sheley (Ed.), *Criminology: A contemporary handbook* (3rd ed., pp. 233–285). Belmont, CA: Wadsworth.

Levy, R., & Zander, H. (1994). Introduction. In G. Rusche and O. Kirchheimer, *Peine et structure sociale* (pp. 9–82). Paris: Les Editions du Curf.

Lewin, T. (2001, November 16). Inmate education is found to lower risk of new arrest. *New York Times,* p. A22.

Lewis, N. (2002, March 20). Justice department opposes lower jail terms for crack: Aides cite small disparity against powder. *New York Times,* p. A24.

Lewis, N. (2003, June 19). Secrecy is backed on 9/11 detainees: Appeals court, 2–1, says U.S. can withhold their names. *New York Times,* p. A1, A16.

Lewis, P. (1978). Life on death row: A post-Furman profile of Florida's condemned. In P. W. Lewis & K. D. Peoples (Eds.), *The Supreme Court and the criminal process: Cases and comments.* Philadelphia: W. B. Saunders.

Lichtblau, E. (2003a, June 19). Bush issues racial profiling ban but exempts security inquiries: Use of race and ethnicity in 'narrow' instances. *New York Times,* pp. A1, A16.

Lichtblau, E. (2003b, June 3). U.S. report faults the roundup of illegal immigrants after 9/11: Many with no ties to terror languished in jail. *New York Times,* pp. A1, A18.

Lichtblau, E. (2003c, February 14). Terror cases rise, but most are small-scale, study says. *New York Times,* p. A16.

Liebman, J., Fagan, J., West, V. & Lloyd, J. (2000). Capital attrition: Error rates in capital cases, 1973–1999. *Texas Law Review, 78,* 1839–1865.

Lilly, J. R., & Deflem, M. (1996). Profit and penality: An analysis of the corrections-commercial complex. *Crime & Delinquency, 42*(1), 3–20.

Lilly, J. R., & Knepper, P. (1993). The corrections-commercial complex. *Crime & Delinquency, 39*(2),150–166.

Liptak, A. (2002, August 30). 3 justices call for reviewing death sentences for juveniles. *New York Times,* pp. A1, A15.

Liptak, A. (2003, October 7). Critics say execution drug may hide suffering. *New York Times,* pp. A1, A18.

Liptak, A. (2003a, June 9). The pursuit of immigrants in America after Sept. 11. *New York Times* (late edition—final), sec. 4, p. 14.

Liptak, A. (2003b, June 3). For jailed immigrants a presumption of guilt. *New York Times,* p. A18.

Liptak, A., & Rimer, S. (2002, June 21). With little guidance, states face hard debate on who is retarded. *New York Times,* pp. A1, A14.

Lockwood, D. (1980). *Prison sexual violence.* New York: Elsevier.

Lockwood, D. (1982). The contribution of sexual harassment to stress and coping in confinement. In N. Parisi (Ed.), *Coping with imprisonment* (pp. 45–64). Beverly Hills, CA: Sage.

Lowman, J., & MacLean, B. (1991). Prisons and protests in Canada. *Social Justice, 18*(3), 130–154.

Lynch, M. J. (1988). The poverty of historical analysis in criminology. *Social Justice, 15,* 173–185.

Lynch, M. J. (1998). *Beating a dead horse: Is there any basic empirical evidence for the deterrent effect of imprisonment?* Unpublished manuscript, University of South Florida, Tampa.

Lynch, M. J., & Groves, W. B. (1989a). *A primer in radical criminology* (2nd ed.). New York: Harrow & Heston.

Lynch, M. J., & Groves, W. B. (1989b, March). *Radical criminology, radical policy?* Paper presented at the annual meeting of the Criminal Justice Sciences, Washington, DC.

Lynch, M. J., Michalowski, R., & Groves, W. B. (2000). *The new primer in radical criminology: critical perspectives on crime, power, and identity.* New York: Criminal Justice Press.

Lynch, M., J., & Stretesky, P. (1999). Marxism and Social Justice. In B. Arrigo (Ed.), *Social justice/criminal justice: The maturation of critical theory in law, and deviance* (pp. 13–29). Belmont, CA: West/Wadsworth.

MacLean, B., & Milovanovic, D. (1997). *Thinking critically about crime.* Vancouver, BC, Canada: Collective Press.

Maeve, M. K., & Vaughn, M. (2001). Nursing with prisoners: The practice of caring, forensic nursing or penal harm. *Advances in Nursing Science, 24,* 2, 47–64.

Maguire, B. (1988). The applied dimension of radical criminology: A survey of prominent radical criminologists. *Sociological Spectrum, 8,* 133–151.

Mahan, S. (1994). An "orgy of brutality" at Attica and the "killing ground" at Sante Fe. In M. Braswell, S. Dillingham, & R. Montgomery (Eds.), *Prison violence in America* (2nd ed., pp. 253–264). Cincinnati, OH: Anderson.

Malcolm, A. (1988, December 24). Prisons seen facing surge of the elderly. *New York Times,* p. A1.

Mann, M. (1984). *The international encyclopedia of sociology.* New York: Continuum.

Marable, M. (2003). 9/11: Racism in a time of terror. In S. Aronowitz & H. Gautney (Eds.), *Implicating empire: Globalization & resistance in the 21st century world order* (pp. 3–14). New York: Basic Books.

Mariner, J. (2003). Deliberate indifference: State authorities' response to prisoner-on-prisoner sexual abuse. In T. Herivel & P. Wright (Eds.), *Prison nation: The warehousing of America's poor* (pp. 231–244). New York: Routledge.

Marquart, J. W. (1986). Prison guards and the use of physical coercion as a mechanism of prisoner control. *Criminology, 24,* 347–366.

Marquart, J. W., & Crouch, B. M. (1985). Judicial reform and prisoner control: The impact of *Ruiz v. Estelle* on a Texas penitentiary. *Law and Society Review, 19,* 557–586.

Marquart, J., Ekland-Olson, S., & Sorensen, J. (1994). *The rope, the chair, and the needle: Capital punishment in Texas, 1923–1990.* Austin: University of Texas Press.

Marquart, J., Merianos, E., Cuvelier, S., & Carroll, L. (1996). Thinking about the relationship between health dynamics in the free community and the prison. *Crime and Delinquency, 42,* 331–360.

Marsh, D. (1990, June 19). New York forum: Hip hop gets a bad rap. *New York Newsday,* pp. 50, 52.

Marshall, I. H. (1997). *Minorities, migrants, and crime.* Thousand Oaks, CA: Sage.

Martin, R. (2000). Community perceptions about prison construction: Why not in my backyard? *Prison Journal, 80*(3): 265–294.

Martin, S. J., & Ekland-Olson, S. (1987). *Texas prisons: The walls came tumbling down.* Austin: Texas Monthly Press.

Maruschak, L. M. (2001). *HIV in prisons and jails, 1999.* Washington, DC: Bureau of Justice Statitistics.

Maruschak, L., & Beck, A. (2001). *Medical problems of inmates, 1997.* Washington, DC: Bureau of Justice Statistics.

Marvell, T., & Moody, C. (2001). The lethal effects of three-strikes laws. *Journal of Legal Studies, 30,* pp. 89–97.

Marx, G. (1981). Ironies of social control: Authorities as contributors to deviance through escalation, nonenforcement, and covert facilitation. *Social Problems, 28,* 221–233.

Marx, K. (1906). *Capital, Volume 1* (S. Moore & E. Aveling, Trans.; F. Engels, Ed.). New York: International.

Marx, K. (1967). *Capital, Volume 1.* New York: International. (Originally published 1867)

Marx, K. (1981). Crime and accumulation. In D. Greenberg (Ed.), *Crime and capitalism.* Palo Alto, CA: Mayfield.

Masters, W., & Johnson, V. (1988). *Crisis: Heterosexual behavior in the age of AIDS.* New York: Grove.

Mata, A., & Herrerias, C. (2002). Immigrant bashing and nativist political movements. In R. Mann & M. Zatz (Eds.), *Images of color, images of crime* (pp. 137–152). Los Angeles: Roxbury.

Matthews, R. (1999). *Doing time: An introduction to the sociology of punishment.* Houndmills, Hampshire, UK: Macmillan Press.

Matthews, R., & Young, J. (1986). *Confronting crime.* London: Sage.

Matza, D., & Morgan, P. (2003). Controlling drug use: The great prohibition. In T. Blomberg & S. Cohen (Eds.), *Punishment and social control* (2nd ed., pp. 133–148). New York: de Gruyter.

Mauer, M. (1998, March 16). Letter to the editor. *The Nation,* p. 2.

Mauer, M. (1999). *Race to incarcerate.* New York: New Press.

Mauer, M. (2002). Analyzing and responding to the driving forces of prison population growth. *Criminology and Public Policy, 1*(3), 389–392.

Mauer, M., & Chesney-Lind, M (2002). *Invisible punishment: The collateral consequences of mass imprisonment.* New York: The Free Press.

Mauer, M., & Huling, T. (1995). *Young black Americans and the criminal justice system: Five years later.* Washington, DC: Sentencing Project.

Mauro, T. (1999, December 9). Texas executes inmate who tried suicide day earlier. *USA Today,* p. 3A.

May, J. P. (2000). *Building violence: How America's rush to incarcerate creates more violence.* Thousand Oaks, CA: Sage.

McAdams, J. C. (1998). Racial disparity and the death penalty. *Law and Contemporary Problems, 61,* 168–191.

McArthur, J. C. (1987). Neurological manifestations of AIDS. *Medicine, 66,* 407–437.

McCarthy, B. (1995). Patterns in prison corruption. In D. Close & N. Meier (Eds.), *Morality in criminal justice: An introduction to ethics.* Belmont, CA: Wadsworth.

McCarthy, S. (2000, April 15). Malone got a lock on prisons, then . . . *Albany Times Union,* p. 1.

McCloskey, J. C. (2001). One man's view. In L. Nelson & B. Foster (Eds.), *Death watch: A death penalty anthology* (pp. 261–275). Upper Saddle River, New Jersey: Prentice Hall.

McDonald, D. (1999). Medical care in prisons. In M. Tonry & J. Petersilia (Eds.), *Prisons, crime and justice: Annual review of research.* Chicago: University of Chicago.

McDonald, D., Fournier, E., Russell-Einhorn, M. & Crawford, S. (1998). *Private prisons in the United States: An assessment of current practice.* Boston: Abt. Associates.

McNair, J. (2000, April 16). Wackenhut prisons mired in abuse scandals. *Miami Herald,* p. 1.

Medical care for the prison population. (1991). Report from the Committee on the Judiciary, U.S. House of Representatives. Washington, DC: Government Printing Office.

Meeker, J. W., Dombrink, J., & Mallett, L. K. (2000). Access to justice for the poor and moderate-income populations: Issues for California Latinos. *Justice Professional, 13*(1), pp. 91–102.

Megill, A. (1979). Foucault, structuralism, and the ends of history. *Journal of Modern History, 51,* 451–503.

Meisenhelder, T. (1985). An essay on time and the phenomenology of imprisonment. *Deviant Behavior, 6,* 39–56.

Melossi, D. (1976). The penal question in capital. *Crime and Social Justice, 5,* 26–33.

Melossi, D. (1977). Prison and labor in Europe and Italy during the formation of capitalist mode of production. In D. Melossi & M. Pavarini (Eds.), *The prison and the factory: Origins of the penitentiary system*. London: McMillan.

Melossi, D. (1985). Punishment and social action: Changing vocabularies of punitive motive within a political business cycle. *Current Perspectives in Social Theory, 6,* pp. 169–197.

Melossi, D. (2003). A new edition of punishment and social structure thirty-five years later: A timely event. *Social Justice, 30*(1), 248–263.

Melossi, D., & Pavarini, M. (1981). *The prison and the factory: Origins of the penitentiary system*. Totowa, NJ: Barnes & Noble.

Menhard, S., Mihalic, S., & Huizinga, D. (2001). Drugs and crime revisited. *Justice Quarterly, 18*(2), pp. 301–322.

Mentor, K. (2002). Habitual felony laws. In D. Levinson (Ed.), *Encyclopedia of crime and punishment* (pp. 813–816). Thousand Oaks, CA: Sage.

Michalowski, R. J. (1985). *Order, law, and crime: An introduction to criminology*. New York: Random House.

Michalowski, R. J. (1996). Critical criminology and the critique of domination: The story of an intellectual movement. *Critical Criminology 7*(1), 9–16.

Michalowski, R. J., & Bolander, M. (1976). Repression and the criminal justice system in capitalist America. *Sociological Inquiry, 46,* pp. 95–106.

Miller, J. (2003). Worker rights in private prisons. In A. Coyle, A. Campbell, & R. Neufeld (Eds.), *Capitalist punishment: Prison privatization & human rights* (pp. 140–151). Atlanta: Clarity.

Miller, K., & Radelet, M. (1993). *Executing the mentally ill: The criminal justice system and the case of Alvin Ford*. Newbury Park, CA: Sage.

Miller, M. (1980). Sinking gradually into the proletariat: The emergence of the penitentiary in the United States. *Crime and Social Justice, 13,* 37–43.

Mills, C. W. (1956). *The power elite*. New York: Oxford University Press.

Mills, S. (1999, May 2). On the record: Interview with Franklin Zimring. *Chicago Tribune*, section 2, p.3.

Misseck, R. E. (1995, October 13). 6 guards held in beatings. *The Star Ledger,* pp. 1, 15.

Molenaar, B., & Neufeld, R. (2003). The use of privatized detention centers for asylum seekers in Australia and the UK. In A. Coyle, A. Campbell, & R. Neufeld (Eds.), *Capitalist punishment: Prison privatization & human rights* (pp. 127–139). Atlanta: Clarity.

Moore, D. W. (1994, September). Majority advocate death penalty for teenage killers. *Gallup Poll Monthly,* No. 321, pp. 2–5.

Moore, D., Leclerc Burton, K., & Hannah-Moffat, K. (2003). "Get tough" efficiency: Human rights, correctional restructuring and prison privatization in Ontario, Canada. In A. Coyle, A. Campbell, & R. Neufeld (Eds.), *Capitalist punishment: Prison privatization & human rights* (pp. 162–178). Atlanta: Clarity.

Moore, J. (2000). Latino gangs: A question of change. *Justice Professional, 13*(1), 8–18.

Morrell, B. (2003). *Juvenile waiver: The elusive definition of rehabilitation.* Unpublished dissertation, School of Criminal Justice, Rutgers University, Newark, NJ.

Morris, M. (2003). Prison privatization: The arrested development of African Americans. In A. Coyle, A. Campbell, & R. Neufeld (Eds.), *Capitalist punishment: Prison privatization & human rights* (pp. 87–101). Atlanta: Clarity.

Morris, R. (1983). *The Devil's butcher shop: The New Mexico prison uprising.* New York: Franklin Watts.

Morton, J. B. (2001). Implications for corrections of an aging prison population. *Corrections Management Quarterly, 5,* 78–88.

Munoz, E. A. (2000). Latino sentencing dispositions, 1997–1991: An empirical assessment of 'gringo' justice. *Justice Professional, 13*(1), 19–48.

Musto, D. F. (1999). *The American disease: Origins of narcotic control* (3rd ed.). New York: Oxford University Press.

Nacci, P. L. (1982). *Sex and sexual aggression in federal prisons.* Unpublished manuscript, U.S. Federal Prison System, Office of Research.

Nacci, P. L., & Kane, T. R. (1984, March). Sex and sexual aggression in federal prisons: Inmate involvement and employee impact. *Federal Probation, 8,* 46–53.

Nadelmann, E. (1989). Drug prohibition in the United States: Costs, consequences, and alternatives. *Science, 245,* 939–947.

Nadelmann, E. (1991). The case for legalization. In J. Inciardi (Ed.), *The drug legalization debate* (pp. 17–43). Newbury Park, CA: Sage.

Nagourney, A. (1998, January 24). Pataki says root causes of crime is criminals, not society. *New York Times,* p. B4.

Nathan, S. (2003a). Private prisons: Emerging and transformative economies. In A. Coyle, A. Campbell, & R. Neufeld (Eds.), *Capitalist punishment: Prison privatization & human rights* (pp. 189–201). Atlanta: Clarity.

Nathan, S. (2003b). Prison privatization in the United Kingdom. In A. Coyle, A. Campbell, & R. Neufeld (Eds.), *Capitalist punishment: Prison privatization & human rights* (pp. 162–178). Atlanta: Clarity.

National Center on Addiction and Substance Abuse (NCASA). (1998). *Behind bars: Substance abuse and America's prison population.* New York: Columbia University.

Nelson, L. (2001). Killing kids. In L. Nelson & B. Foster (Eds.), *Death watch: A death penalty anthology* (pp. 59–74). Upper Saddle River, NJ: Prentice Hall.

New York's prison building fever. (1997, July 24). *New York Times,* p. A20.

New York State Special Commission on Attica. (1972). *Attica: The official report of the New York State Commission.* New York: Bantam.

Nieves, E. (1998, November 7). California examines brutal, deadly prisons. *New York Times,* p. A-7.

Nieves, E. (2002, July 12). Freed from jail despite his pleas, 92-year-old is found dead in river. *New York Times,* p. A12.

Nissen, T. (1985, September 14). Free-market prisons. *The Nation,* p. 194.

NJ inmate argues for reversal of 25-year AIDS bite jail sentence. (1992, December 22). *AIDS Litigation Reporter,* p. 1.

Nobiling, T., Spohn, C. & DeLone, M. (1998, October 12, 2003). A tale of two counties: Unemployment and sentence severity. *Justice Quarterly, 15*(3), 459–485.

Norris, R. L. (1985). *Prison reformers and penitential publicists in France, England, and the United States, 1774–1847.* Unpublished dissertation, American University, Washington, DC.

Nossiter, A. (1996, August 17). Mollen commission report is quoted in civil rights. *New York Times,* p. 23.

O'Farrell, N., Tovey, S., & Morgan-Capner, P. (1992). Transmission of HIV-1 infection after a fight. *Lancet, 339,* 246–252.

Office of National Drug Control Policy. (2003). *National drug control strategy.* Washington, DC: Government Printing Office.

Ogle, R. S. (1999). Prison privatization: An environmental catch 22. *Justice Quarterly, 16*(3), 579–600.

$1.4 million awarded to raped Alaska women prisoners. (2001, July). *Prison Legal News,* p. 21.

Oswald, R. B. (1972). *Attica: My story.* New York: Doubleday.

Packer, H. (1968). *The limits of the criminal sanction.* Stanford, CA: Stanford University Press.

Page, J. (2002). Violence and incarceration: A personal observation. In L. Fiftal & P. Cromwell (Eds.), *Correctional perspectives: Views from academics, practitioners, and prisoners* (pp. 147–149). Los Angeles: Roxbury.

Parenti, C. (1999). *Lockdown America: Police and prisons in the age of crisis.* New York: Verso.

Parenti, C. (2003a). Guarding their silence: Corcoran guards acquitted of rape. In T. Herivel & P. Wright (Eds.), Prison nation: The warehousing of America's poor (pp. 252–257). New York: Routledge.

Parenti, C. (2003b). Privatized problems: For-profit incarceration. In A. Coyle, A. Campbell, & R. Neufeld (Eds.), *Capitalist punishment: Prison privatization & human rights* (pp. 30–38). Atlanta: Clarity.

Parenti, C. (2003c). *The soft cage: Surveillance in America, from slave passes to the war on terror.* New York: Basic Books.

Passell, P. (1975). The deterrent effect of the death penalty: A statistical test. *Stanford Law Review, 28,* 61–80.

Paternoster, R. (1983). Race of the victim and location of crime: The decision to seek the death penalty in South Carolina. *Journal of Criminal Law and Criminology, 74,* 754–785.

Paternoster, R. (1991). *Capital punishment in America*. New York: Lexington.

Peet, J., & Schwab, D. (1995, October 22). Critics praise INS for "candid" report. *The Star Ledger*, p. 8.

Pepinsky, H. E. (1978). Communist anarchism as an alternative to the rule of criminal law. *Contemporary Crisis, 2*, 315–327.

Pepinsky, H. E., & Jesilow, P. (1985). *Myths that cause crime* (2nd ed.). Cabin John, MD: Seven Locks Press.

Perez, H. (1996, Summer). Incarcerated populations: Have they been forgotten? *Active Voice*, pp. 7–8.

Perl, R. (2003, November 24). The last disenfranchised class. *The Nation*, pp. 11–14.

Petersilia, J. (1985). *Probation and felony offenders*. Washington, DC: National Institute of Justice.

Petersilia, J. (1986). *Prison versus probation in California: Implications for crime and offender recidivism*. Santa Monica, CA: Rand.

Peterson, M. (1997, August 10). Before an election, prisons are good. The bills come later. *New York Times*, p. NJ-6.

Peterson, R., & Bailey, W. (1991). Felony murder and capital punishment: An examination of the deterrence question. *Criminology, 29*, 367–398.

Phillips, D. D. (1980). The deterrent effect of capital punishment: Evidence of an old controversy. *American Journal of Sociology, 86*, 139–148.

Phillips, K. (1990). *Politics of the rich and poor*. New York: Random House.

Phillips, K., Nolan, J., & Pearl, M. (1990, December 12). Jogger trial rage. *The New York Post*, pp. 9, 34.

Pink bracelets for homosexuals in Florida jail are challenged. (1989, December 3). *New York Times*, p. 35.

Pisciotta, A. (1994). *Benevolent repression: Social control and the American reformatory-prison movement*. New York: New York University Press.

Pitt, D. (1989, April 22). Jogger's attackers terrorized at least 9 in 2 hours. *New York Times*, pp. 1, 30.

Piven, F. F., & Cloward, R. A. (1971). *Regulating the poor: The functions of public welfare*. New York: Vintage.

Plant, R. (1986). *The pink triangle: The Nazi war on homosexuals*. New York: Henry Holt.

Plant, R. (1989, November 7). Nazis' forgotten victims: Gays. *New York Times*, p. A23.

Platt, T. (1982). Crime and punishment in the United States: Immediate and long-term reforms from a Marxist perspective. *Crime and Social Justice, 18*, 38–45.

Platt, T. (1985). Criminology in the 1980s: Progressive alternatives to "law and order." *Crime and Social Justice, 21/22*, 191–199.

Platt, T., & Takagi, P. (1974). *Punishment and penal discipline*. San Francisco, CA: Crime and Social Justice Associates.

Polych, C., & Sabo, D. (2001). Sentence—Death by lethal injection: IV-drug use and infectious disease transmission in North American prisons. In D. Sabo,

T. Kupers, & W. London (Eds.), *Prison masculinities* (pp. 173-183). Philadelphia: Temple University Press.

Porporino, F. J. (1986). Managing violent individuals in correctional settings. *Journal of Interpersonal Violence, 1,* 213–237.

Portillos, E. (2002). Latinos, gangs, and drugs. In R. Mann & M. Zatz (Eds.), *Images of color, images of crime* (pp. 192–200). Los Angeles: Roxbury.

Powers, G. (1826). *A brief account of the construction, management and discipline of the New York State Prison at Auburn.* Auburn, NY: Henry Hall.

Pranis, K. (1998, March 16). Letter to the editor. *The Nation,* pp. 2–3.

Pranis, K. (2003). Campus activism defeats multinational's prison profiteering. In T. Herivel & P. Wright (Eds.), *Prison nation: The warehousing of America's poor* (pp. 156–163). New York: Routledge.

Pratt, T., & Maahs, J. (1999). Are private prisons more cost-effective than public prisons? A meta-analysis of evaluation research studies. *Crime and Delinquency, 45,* 358–371.

Press, A. (1986, October 6). Inside America's toughest prison. *Newsweek,* pp. 46, 61.

Prison terms for officers in beatings of immigrants. (1998, May 2). *New York Times,* p. B6.

Prisons getting tougher. (1994, January 24). *New York Times,* p. A12.

Prosecutor takes aim on violence. (1994, January 30). *New York Times,* p. 15.

Purdy, M. (1997, May 26). As AIDS increases behind bars, costs dim promise of new drugs. *New York Times,* pp. 1, 28.

Purdy, M. (2000, April 16). For a paralyzed inmate, rigid drug laws are the crueler trap. *New York Times,* p. 35.

Purdy, M. (2002, May 8). It takes a tough law to hold her. *New York Times,* p. B1.

Quinney, R. (1970). *The social reality of crime.* Boston: Little, Brown.

Quinney, R. (1980). *Class, state, and crime.* New York: Longman.

Radelet, M., Bedau, H., & Putnam, C. (1992). *In spite of innocence: Erroneous convictions in capital cases.* Boston: Northeastern University Press.

Radelet, M., & Pierce, G. (1985). Race and prosecutorial discretion in homicide cases. *Law and Society Review, 19,* 587–621.

Raher, S. (2001, August 8). Things to consider when looking at a correctional facility. *Brush News-Tribune,* p. 2.

Rashbaum, W. E. (2003, May 17). Woman dies after police mistakenly raid her apartment. *New York Times,* pp. B1, B3.

Ratner, M. (2003). Making us less free: War on terrorism or war on liberty? In S. Aronowitz & H. Gautney (Eds.), *Implicating empire: Globalization & resistance in the 21st century world order,* pp. 31–46. New York: Basic Books.

Red tags for gays scrapped. (1990, Spring). *Civil Liberties, 369,* p. 7.

Reed, E. (1993). *The Penry penalty: Capital punishment and offenders with mental retardation.* Landam, MD: University Press of America.

Reiman, J. (1995). *The rich get richer and the poor get prison: Ideology, class, and criminal justice* (4th ed.). Boston: Allyn & Bacon.

Reiman, J. (2004) *The Rich get richer and the poor get prison: Ideology, class and criminal justice* (7th ed.). Boston: Allyn & Bacon.

Reinarman, C., & Levine, H. (1997). *Crack in America: Demon drugs and social justice.* Berkeley: University of California Press.

Reiss, A. (1951). Delinquency as the failure of personal and social control. *American Sociological Review, 16,* 196–207.

Report finds U.S. misstated terror verdicts. (2003, February 22). *New York Times,* p. A10.

Residents of dying California town see future in a prison. (1994, May 8). *New York Times,* p. 8.

Revived from overdose, inmate is executed. (1995, August 12). *New York Times,* p. 6.

Reyes, H., & Coninx, R. 1997. Pitfalls in tuberculosis programmes in prison. *British Medical Journal, 315,* 1447–1450.

Richards, J. (1995). George Bush, justified war morality, and the Gulf War. In L. Bove & L. Kaplan (Eds.), *From the eye of the storm* (pp. 113–128). Atlanta: Rodopi.

Richie, B. E. (2002). The social impact of mass incarceration. In M. Mauer & M. Chesney-Lind (Eds.), *Invisible punishment: The collateral consequences of mass imprisonment* (pp. 136–149). New York: The Free Press.

Richman, K., & Richman, L. (1993). The potential for transmission of human immunodeficiency virus through human bites. *Journal of Acquired Immune Deficiency Syndromes, 6,* 402–406.

Ridgeway, J. (1994, October 11). Slaughterhouse justice: Race, poverty, and politics: The essential ingredients for a death penalty conviction. *Village Voice,* pp. 23–24.

Ridgeway, J. (2002, April 9). This is your prison on drugs. *Village Voice,* p. 26.

Riedel, M. (1976). Discrimination in the imposition of the death penalty: A comparison of the characteristics of offenders, sentenced pre-*Furman* and post-*Furman. Temple Law Quarterly, 49,* 261–283.

Riley, K. J. (1996). *Snow job? The war against international cocaine trafficking.* New Brunswick, NJ: Transaction.

Robbins, I. (1997, January 5). The problems with prisons for profit. *The Washington Post,* p. 27.

Robertson, J. E. (1994). 'Catchall' prison rules and the courts: A study of judicial review of prison justice. *Saint Louis University Public Law Review, 24,* 153–173.

Robertson, J. E. (1995). 'Fight or F . . .' and constitutional liberty: An inmate's right to self defense when targeted by aggressors. *Indiana Law Review, 29*(2), 339–363.

Robertson, J. E. (1999). Cruel and unusual punishment in United Stated prisons: Sexual harassment among male inmates. *American Criminal Law Review, 36,* 1–51.

Robertson, J. E. (2000). Sexual harassment of male inmates: The case for new constitutional tort. *Correctional Law Reporter, 11*(6), 83–84, 96.

Robin, C. (2003). Fear, American style: Civil liberty after 9/11. In S. Aronowitz & H. Gautney (Eds.), *Implicating empire: Globalization & resistance in the 21st century world order* (pp. 47–64). New York: Basic Books.

Rodriguez, L. (2002). The color of the skin is the color of the crime. In R. Mann & M. Zatz (Eds.), *Images of color, images of crime* (pp. 33–36). Los Angeles: Roxbury.

Rolland, M. (1997). *Descent into madness: An inmate's experience of the New Mexico State Prison riot.* Cincinnati, OH: Anderson.

Rolland, M. (2002). Realities of fear. In L. Fiftal & P. Cromwell (Eds.), *Correctional perspectives: Views from academics, practitioners, and prisoners* (pp. 150–156). Los Angeles: Roxbury

Rose, D., & Clear, T. (1998). Incarceration, social capital, and crime: Implications for social disorganization theory. *Criminology, 36,* 441–480.

Rosenbaum, R. (1990, May). Travels with Dr. Death. *Vanity Fair,* pp. 141–166.

Ross, J. I. (1998). *Cutting the edge: Current perspectives in radical/critical criminology and criminal justice.* Westport, CT: Praeger.

Ross, J. I., & Richards, S. (2002). *Behind bars: Surviving prison.* New York: Alpha Books.

Ross, J. I., & Richards, S. (2003). *Convict criminology.* Belmont, CA: Thomson/Wadsorth.

Rothman, D. J. (1971). *The discovery of the asylum: Social order and disorder in the new republic.* Boston: Little, Brown.

Rothman, D. J. (1980). *Conscience and Convenience.* Boston: Little, Brown.

Rothman, D. J. (1990). *The discovery of the asylum: Social order and disorder in the New Republic* (2nd edition). Boston: Little, Brown.

Rubinstein, G., & Mukamal, D. (2002). Welfare and housing-denial of benefits to drug offenders. In M. Mauer & M. Chesney-Lind (Eds.), *Invisible punishment: The collateral consequences of mass imprisonment* (pp. 37–49). New York: The Free Press.

Rusche, G. (1982). Labor market and penal sanctions: Thoughts on the sociology of criminal justice. In T. Platt & P. Takagi (Ed.), *Punishment and penal discipline (pp. 10–16).* San Francisco: Crime and Social Justice Associates.

Rusche, G., & Kirchheimer, O. (1968). *Punishment and social structure.* New York: Russell & Russell. (Original work published 1939)

Russell, K. (1998). *The color of crime: Racial hoaxes, white fear, black protectionism, police aggression and other macroaggressions.* New York: New York University Press.

Russell, S. (2003). The continuing relevance of Marxism to critical criminology. *Critical Criminology, 11(2),* 113–135.

Ryan, K., & Ferrell, J. (1986). Knowledge, power, and the process of justice. *Crime and Social Justice, 25,* 178–195.

Sachar, E. (1990, August 19). Of rape and assault. *New York Newsday,* pp. 3, 36.

Saenz, A. (1986). *Politics of a riot.* Washington, DC: American Correctional Association.

Saewitz. Mike. (2002, October 17). An advocacy center alleges women's health needs are ignored and cells are overcrowded. *Sarasota Herald Tribune,* pp. EV1–2.

Sampson, R., & Lauritsen, J. (1997). Racial and ethnic disparities in crime and criminal justice in the United States. In M. Tonry (Ed.), *Ethnicity, crime, and immigration: Comparative and cross-national perspectives, Vol. 21.* Chicago: University of Chicago Press.

Sartre, J. P. (1966). *Being and nothingness.* New York: Washington Square.

Saulny, S. (2003, December 9). 3 of 5 in jogger case sue city, charging wide conspiracy. *New York Times,* p. B3.

Scheck, B., Neufeld, P., & Dwyer, J. (2000). *Actual innocence.* New York: Doubleday.

Scheff, T. (1966). *Being mentally ill: A sociological theory.* Chicago: Aldine.

Schemo, D. J. (2001, March 3). Students find drug law has big price: College aid, critics say '98 rule is biased against the poor. *New York Times,* p. A12.

Shichor, D. (1999). Privatizing correctional institutions: An organizing perspective. *The Prison Journal, 79(2),* 226–249.

Shichor, D. (2002). Issues concerning private prisons. In L. Fiftal & P. Cromwell (Eds.), *Correctional perspectives: Views from academics, practitioners, and prisoners,* (pp. 223–232). Los Angeles: Roxbury.

Schichor, D., & Sechrest, D. (1996). *Three strikes and you're out: Vengeance as public policy.* Thousand Oaks, CA: Sage.

Schiraldi, V., & Keppelhoff, M. (1997, June 5). As juvenile crime drops, experts back-pedal and public policy pays the price. *Star Tribune,* p. 24A.

Schneider, L. (1975). Ironic perspective and sociological thought. In L. Coser (Ed.), *The idea of social structure* (pp. 323–339). New York: Harcourt Brace Jovanovich.

Schur, E. (1971). *Labeling deviant behavior: Its sociological implications.* New York: Harper & Row.

Schuster, L. (2003). *The use and abuse of political asylum in Britain and Germany.* London: Frank Cass.

Schutz, A., & Luckmann, T. (1973). *The structures of the lifeworld.* Evanston, IL: Northwestern University Press.

Schwartz, H. (2002, March 31). Out of jail and out of food. *New York Times,* p. A27.

Schwartz, M. D., & Friedrichs, D. O. (1994). Postmodern thought and criminological discontent: New metaphors for understanding violence. *Criminology, 32,* 221–246.

Schwendinger, H., & Schwendinger, J. (1977). Social class and the definition of crime. *Crime and Social Justice, 7,* 4–13.

Schwendinger, H., & Schwendinger, J. (1981). The standards of living in penal institutions. In D. Greenberg (Ed.), *Crime and capitalism*. Palo Alto, CA: Mayfield.

Secombe, W. (1973, January/February). The housewife and her labour under capitalism. *New Left Review, 82*, 3–24.

Seelye, K. (1996, August 26). Dole calls for military role in the fight against drugs. *New York Times*, p. A13.

Selke, W., Corsaro, N., & Selke, H. (2002). A working class critique of criminological theory. *Critical Criminology 11*(2), 93–112.

Sengupta, S. (2001a, November 5). Ill fated path to America jail and death. *New York Times*, pp. EV1–4.

Sengupta, S. (2001b, September 13). Arabs and Muslims steer through an unsettling scrutiny. *New York Times*, pp. EV1–3.

Sentencing Project. (2002). *Life sentences: Denying welfare benefits to women convicted of drug offenses*. Washington, DC: Author.

Sforza, D. (1998a, June 2). Jails prefer education, not condoms, to curtail HIV. *The Record* [Bergen County, NJ], p. A-12.

Sforza, D. (1998b, June 2). Terms of treatment: Prisons tested by costs, burdens of HIV. *The Record* [Bergen County, NJ], pp. A-1, A-12.

Shapiro, A. (1995, May 11). An insane execution. *New York Times*, p. A29.

Shapiro, B. (2002, July 22–29). Rethinking the death penalty. *The Nation*, pp. 14–19.

Sharp, S. (2003). Mothers in prison: Issues in parent-child contact. In S. Sharp (Ed.), *The incarcerated woman: Rehabilitative programming in women's prisoners* (pp. 151–165). Upper Saddle River, NJ: Prentice Hall.

Shelden, R. G., & Brown, W. (2000). The crime control industry and the management of the surplus population. *Critical Criminology, 9*(1–2), 39–62.

Sherrill, R. (2001, January 8–15). Death trip: The American way of execution. *The Nation*, pp. 13–34.

Sherwood, M., & Posey, B. (2003). FDOC hazardous to prisoners' health. In T. Herivel & P. Wright (Eds.), *Prison nation: The warehousing of America's poor* (pp.203–209). New York: Routledge.

Shichor, D. (1999). Privatizing correctional institutions: An organizing perspective. *The Prison Journal, 79*(2), 226–249.

Shichor, D. (2002). Issues concerning private prisons. In L. Fiftal & P. Cromwell (Eds.), Correctional perspectives: Views from academics, practitioners, and prisoners (pp. 223–232). Los Angeles, CA: Roxbury.

Shilts, R. (1987). *And the band played on: Politics, people and the AIDS epidemic*. New York: St. Martin's.

Siegal, N. (2002a). Stopping abuse in prison. In T. Gray (Ed.), *Exploring corrections* (pp. 134–140). Boston: Allyn & Bacon.

Siegal, N. (2002b). Lethal lottery. In T. Gray (Ed.), *Exploring corrections* (pp. 122–126). Boston: Allyn & Bacon.

Silberman, M. (1995). *A world of violence: Corrections in America*. Belmont, CA: Wadsworth.

Sinden, J. (2003). The problem of prison privatization: The US experience. In A. Coyle, A. Campbell, & R. Neufeld (Eds.), *Capitalist punishment: Prison privatization & human rights* (pp. 39–47). Atlanta: Clarity.

Sirica, J. (1988, May 19). Testimony on AIDS. *New York Newsday*, p. 14.

Skolnick, A. (1993). Some experts suggest the nation's 'war on drugs' is helping tuberculosis stage a deadly comeback. *Journal of the American Medical Association, 268*(22), 3177–3178.

Smith, F. (2003). Incarceration of Native Americans and private prisons. In A. Coyle, A. Campbell, & R. Neufeld (Eds.), *Capitalist punishment: Prison privatization & human rights* (pp. 114–126). Atlanta: Clarity.

Smothers, R. (1998, March 7). 3 prison guards guilty of abuse of immigrants. *New York Times*, pp. A-1, B-4.

Snell, T. (1997). *Capital punishment 1996*. Washington, DC: Bureau of Justice Statistics.

Snell, T. (2001). *Capital Punishment 2000*. Washington, DC: Bureau of Justice Statistics.

Sontag, S. (1980). *Illness as metaphor*. New York: Doubleday.

Sontag, S. (1989). *AIDS and its metaphors*. New York: Farrar Straus Giroux.

Sorensen, J., & Wallace, D. H. (1999). Prosecutorial discretion in seeking death: An analysis of racial disparity in the pretrial stages of case processing in a Midwestern county. *Justice Quarterly, 16*(3), 559–578.

Sparks, R. F. (1980). A critique of Marxist criminology. In N. Morris & M. Tonry (Eds.), *Crime and justice: An annual review of research* (pp. 116–128). Chicago: University of Chicago Press.

Sparks, R. F. (2003). State punishment in advanced capitalist countries. In T. Blomberg & S. Cohen (Eds.), *Punishment and social control* (2nd ed., pp. 19–44). New York: de Gruyter.

Sparks, R. F., Bottoms, A., & Hay, W. (1996). *Prisons and the problem of order*. Oxford: Clarendon Press.

Special issue on critical resistance to the prison-industrial complex. (2000). *Social Justice, 27*, 3.

Spitzer, S. (1975). Toward a Marxian theory of deviance. *Social Problems, 22*, 638-651.

Spitzer, S., & Scull, A. (1977a). Privatization and capital development: The case of privatization. *Social Problems, 25*, 18–29.

Spitzer, S., & Scull, A. (1977b). Social control in historical perspective: From private to public responses to crime. In D. Greenberg (Ed.), *Corrections and punishment* (pp. 265–286). Beverly Hills, CA: Sage.

Spohn, C., & Holleran, D. (2000). The imprisonment penalty paid by young, unemployed black and Hispanic male offenders. *Criminology, 38*(1), 281–306.

Spohn, C., Holleran, D. (2002). The effect of imprisonment on recidivism rates of felony offenders: A focus on drug offenders. *Criminology, 40*(2), 329–357.

St. Clair, J. (2003). Bill Clinton's blood trails. In T. Herivel & P. Wright (Eds.), *Prison nation: The warehousing of America's poor* (pp. 210–125). New York: Routledge.

Stack, S. (1987). Publicized executions and homicide, 1950–1980. *American Sociological Review, 52,* 532–540.

Staples, W. G. (1990). *Castles of our consciousness: Social control and the American state, 1800–1985.* New Brunswick, NJ: Rutgers University Press.

Staples, W. G. (1997). *The culture of surveillance: Discipline and social control in the United States.* New York: St. Martin's.

Stark, R. (1972). *Police riots: Collective violence and law enforcement.* Belmont, CA: Wadsworth.

State's prisons continue to bulge, overwhelming efforts at reform. (1990, May 20). *New York Times,* pp. A1, A2.

Steffensmeier, D., & Demuth, S. (2001). Ethnicity and judges' sentencing decisions: Hispanic-Black-White comparisons. *Criminology, 39*(1), 145–178.

Steffensmeier, D., Ulmer, J., & Kramer, J. (1998). the interaction of race, gender, and age in criminal sentencing: The punishment cost of being young, black, and male. *Criminology, 36*(4), 763–798.

Sterba, J. (1991). Reconciling pacifists and just war theorists. In D. Cady & R. Werner (Eds.), *Just war, nonviolence, and nuclear deterrence: Philosophers on war and peace* (pp. 35–50). Wakefield, NH: Longfield Academic.

Sterba, J. (1995). War with Iraq: Just another unjust war. In L. Bove & L. Kaplan (Eds.), *From the eye of the storm* (pp.147–154). Atlanta: Rodopi.

Stetson, K. (1999). Crime control, governmentality and sovereignty. In R. Smandych (Ed.), *Governable places: Readings on govermentality and crime control* (pp. 45–73). Aldershot: Ashgate.

Stetson, K. (2000). Reconstructing the Government of Crime. In G. Wickham & G. Pavlich (Eds.), *Rethinking law, society, and governance* (pp. 93–108). Oxford: Hart.

Stetson, K., & Sullivan, R. (2000). *Crime, risk, and justice: The politics of crime control in liberal democracies.* Devon, UK: Willan.

Stone, L. (1983, March 31). An exchange with Michel Foucault. *New York Review of Books,* pp. 42–44.

Stone, W. G. (1982). *The hate factory: The story of the New Mexico penitentiary riot.* Agoura, CA: Dell.

Sullivan, D. (1980). *The mask of love: Corrections in America—toward a mutual aid alternative.* Port Washington, NY: Kennikat Press.

Sullivan, J. (1993, February 18). Inmate with HIV who bit guard loses appeal. *New York Times,* pp. B7.

Sullivan, J. (1995a, October 13). 6 guards in New Jersey charged with beating jailed immigrants. *New York Times,* pp. A1, B5.

Sullivan, J. (1995b, February 8). Conviction thrown out, ex-inmate faces retrial. *New York Times*, p. B5.

Sullivan, R. (1992, August 26). Ex-inmate wins award in bias case. *New York Times*, p. 4.

Sutton, J. (2000). Imprisonment and social classification in five common-law democracies 1955–1985. *American Journal of Sociology, 106*, 350–386.

Swarns, R. L. (2003a, June 7). More than 13,000 may face deportation. *New York Times*, p. A9.

Swarns, R. L. (2003b, May 10). Report raises questions on success of immigration interviews. *New York Times*, p. A13.

Sykes, G. M. (1958). *The society of captives*. Princeton, NJ: Princeton University Press.

Sykes, G. M. (1974). The rise of critical criminology. *Journal of Criminal Law and Criminology, 65*, 206–213.

Talbot, M. (2003, June 29). The executioner's I.Q. test. *New York Times Magazine*, pp. 30–35, 52, 58–60.

Talvi, S. (2003a, February 17). Round up: INS 'Special Registration' ends in mass arrests. *In These Times*, p. 3.

Talvi, S. (2003b, January 15). *It takes a nation of detention facilities to hold us back: Moral panic and the disaster mentality of immigration policy*. Retrieved Feb. 2, 2003 www.lipmagazine.org p. 3.

Talvi, S. (2003c, April 9). Reefer madness, redux. *The Nation* [online version]. Retrieved December 15, 2003, from http://www.thenation.com/doc. mhtml?i=20030421&s=talvi

Talvi, S. (2003d). Hepatitis C: A "silent epidemic" strikes U.S. prisons. In T. Herivel & P. Wright (Eds.), *Prison nation: The warehousing of America's poor* (pp. 181–186). New York: Routledge.

Talvi, S. (2003e). Not part of my sentence. In T. Herivel & P. Wright (Eds.), *Prison nation: The warehousing of America's poor* (pp. 262–268). New York: Routledge.

Tarver, M., Walker, S., & Wallace, P. H. (2002). *Multicultural issues in the criminal justice system*. Boston: Allyn & Bacon.

Taylor, I. (1999). *Crime context: A critical criminology of market societies*. Cambridge: Polity.

Taylor, I., Walton, P., & Young, J. (1973). *The new criminology*. New York: Harper & Row.

Taylor, I., Walton, P., & Young, J. (1975). *Critical criminology*. London, UK: Routledge and Keegan Paul.

Teepen, T. (1996, December 10). Locking in the profits. *Atlanta Constitution*, p. 21.

'Terrorism' cases in New Jersey relate mostly to test cheating. (2003, March 3). *The Associated Press*, p. 1.

Terry, D. (1996, July 3). After 18 years in prison, 3 are cleared of murders. *New York Times*, p. A14.

Terry, D. (1998, April 12). Jury to decide if condemned man comprehends his fate. *New York Times*, p. 22.

Thies, J. (2001). The 'big house' in a small town: The economic and social impacts of a correctional facility on its host community. *The Justice Professional, 14*(2), 221–237.

Thomas, E. (1985, September 23). The new untouchables: Anxiety over AIDS is verging on hysteria in some parts of the country. *Time*, pp. 24–26.

Thomas, J., & O'Maolchatha, A. (1989). Reassessing the critical metaphor: An optimistic revisionist view. *Justice Quarterly, 6*, 143–172.

Thompson, C. (2002, March 1). Seeking a welfare rule's repeal. *The Washington Post*, p. 31.

Tifft, L. (1979). The coming redefinitions of crime: An anarchist perspective. *Social Problems, 26*, 392–402.

Tifft, L., & Sullivan, D. (1980). *The struggle to be human: Crime, criminology and anarchism*. Orkney, UK: Cienfuegos.

Toby, J. (1979). The new criminology is the old sentimentality. *Criminology, 16*, 516-526.

Toch, H. (1992*). Living in prison*. New York: The Free Press.

Tolnay, S., & Beck, E. (1992). Toward a threat model of Southern black lynchings. In A. E. Liska (Ed.), *Social threat and social control* (pp. 33–52). Albany: State University of New York Press.

Tolnay, S., & Beck, E. (1994). Lethal social control in the South: Lynchings and executions between 1880 and 1930. In G. Bridges & M. Myers (Eds.), *Inequality, crime, and social control* (pp. 176–194). Boulder, CO: Westview.

Tourigny, S. C. (2001). Some new killing trick: Welfare reform and drug markets in a U.S. ghetto. *Social Justice, 28*(4), 49–71.

TRAC (Transactional Records Access Clearinghouse) (2003). *Criminal enforcement against terrorists and spies in the year after the 9/11 attacks*. Syracuse, NY: Syracuse University.

Tracy, J. (1996). *Direct action: Radical pacifism from the Union Eight to the Chicago Seven*. Chicago: University of Chicago Press.

Trombley, S. (1992). *The execution protocol: Inside America's capital punishment industry*. New York: Crown.

Tuberculosis can spread to community. (2001, October 29). *Reuters*, p. 1.

Tulsky, J.P., White, M.C., Dawson, C., Hoynes, T.M., Goldenson, J., & Schechter, G. (1998). Screening for tuberculosis in jail and clinic followup after release. *American Journal of Public Health 88*, 223–226.

Turk, A. (1979). Analyzing official deviance: For nonpartisan conflict analysis in criminology. *Criminology, 16*, 459–476.

Tyler, T., Boeckmann, R. (1997). Three strikes and you are out, but why? The psychology of public support for punishing. *Law and Society Review, 31*(2), 237–165.

United Nations body of principles for the protection of all persons under any form of detention or imprisonment (1988, December 9). Adopted by General Assembly resolution 43/173. Retrieved March 15, 2004, from http://www.unhchr.ch/html/menu3/b/h_comp36.htm

U.S. Department of Commerce. (1995). *Statistical abstracts of the United States.* Washington, DC: Government Printing Office.

U.S. Department of Justice. (2003a, December). *Supplemental report on September 11 detainees' allegations of abuse at the metropolitan detention center in Brooklyn, New York.* Office of the Inspector General. Washington, DC: Government Printing Office.

U.S. Department of Justice. (2003b, June).*The September 11 detainees: A review of the treatment of aliens held on immigration charges in connection with the investigation of the September 11 attacks.* Office of the Inspector General. Washington, DC: Government Printing Office.

U.S. General Accounting Office. (1994). *Bureau of prisons health care.* Washington, DC: Government Printing Office.

U.S. Sentencing Commission. (1995). *Report on penalties for crack and powdered cocaine.* Washington, DC: Government Printing Office.

Useem, B. (1985). Disorganization and the New Mexico prison riot. *American Sociological Review, 50,* 677–688.

Useem, B., & Kimball, P. A. (1987). A theory of prison riots. *Theory and Society, 16,* 87–122.

Useem, B., & Kimball, P. A. (1989). *States of siege: U.S. prison riots 1971–1986.* New York: Oxford University Press.

Useem, B., Liedka, R. V., & Piehl, A. M. (2003). Popular support for the prison build-up. *Punishment & Society, 5*(1), pp. 5–32.

Useem, B., & Reisig, M. D. (1999). Collective action in prisons: Protests, disturbances, and riots. *Criminology, 37*(4), 734–760.

van den Haag, E., & Conrad, J. (1983). *The death penalty: A debate.* New York: Plenum.

Vanneste, C. (2001). *Les Chiffres des Prisons.* Paris: L'Hartmattan.

Vaughn, M. (1995). Civil liability against prison officials for inmate-on-inmate assault: Where are we and where have we been. *Prison Journal, 75,* 12–28.

Vaughn, M. S. (1999). Penal harm medicine: State tort remedies for delaying and denying health care to prisoners. *Crime, Law & Social Change, 31,* 273–302.

Vaughn, M. S., & Carroll, L. (1998). Separate and unequal: Prison versus free-world medical care. *Justice Quarterly, 15,* 3–40.

Vaughn, M. S., & Smith, L. (1999). Practicing penal harm in the United States: Prisoners' voices from jail. *Justice Quarterly, 16*(1), 175–232.

Verhovek, S. H. (1995, January 8). When justice shows its darker side. *New York Times,* p. E6.

Verhovek, S. H. (1997, June 24). Operators are not worried by ruling. *New York Times,* p. B10.

Verhovek, S. (1998a, April 26). Halt the execution? Are you crazy? *New York Times*, p. A4.

Verhovek, S. (1998b, April 18). Texas legislator proposes the death penalty for murderers as young as 11. *New York Times*, p. A7.

Vliet, H. (1990). Separation of drug markets and the normalization of drug problems in the Netherlands: An example for other countries? *Journal of Drug Issues, 20,* 436–471.

Wacquant, L. (2000). America's new 'peculiar institution': On the prison as surrogate ghetto. *Theoretical Criminology, 4*(3), 377–389.

Wacquant, L. (2001). Deadly symbiosis: When ghetto and prison meet and mesh. *Punishment & Society, 3*(1), 95–103.

Wacquant, L. (2002). The curious eclipse of prison ethnography in the age of mass incarceration. *Ethnography, 3*(4), 1466–1381.

Wakin, D. J., & Zezima, K. (2003, August 24). Abusive ex-priest is killed in prison: At center of scandal in Boston—fellow inmate is held. *New York Times*, pp. 1, 26.

Waldo, G., & Paternoster, R. (2003). Tinkering with the machinery of death: The failure of a social experiment. In T. Blomberg & S. Cohen (Eds.), *Punishment and social control* (2nd ed., pp. 311–354). New York: de Gruyter.

Walker, S. (1998). *Popular justice: A history of American criminal justice.* New York: Oxford University Press.

Walker, S. (2001). *Sense and nonsense about crime and drugs: A policy guide* (5th ed.). Belmont, CA: Wadsworth.

Walzer, M. (1977). *Just and unjust wars.* New York: Basic Books.

Weiner, D. B. (1972). The real Dr. Guillotine. *Journal of the American Medical Association, 220,* 85–89.

Weiser, B. (2002, June 29). Judge considers an inquiry on radio case confession. *New York Times*, pp. B1, B2.

Weiss, R. P. (Ed.). (1991). Attica: 1971–1991, a commemorative issue. *Social Justice, 18,* 3.

Weiss, R. P. (2001). 'Repatriating' low-wage work: The political economy of prison labor reprivatization in the postindustrial United States. *Criminology, 39*(2), 253–292.

Welch, M. (1989). Social junk, social dynamite and the rabble: Persons with AIDS in jail. *American Journal of Criminal Justice, 14,* 135–147.

Welch, M. (1991). Persons with AIDS in prison: A critical and phenomenological approach to suffering. *Dialectical Anthropology, 16,* 51–61.

Welch, M. (1994). Jail overcrowding: Social sanitation and the warehousing of the urban underclass. In A. Roberts (Ed.), *Critical issues in crime and justice* (pp. 251–276). Newbury Park, CA: Sage.

Welch, M. (1995a). Rehabilitation: Holding its ground in corrections. *Federal Probation, 59*(4), 3–8.

Welch, M. (1995b). A sociopolitical approach to the reproduction of violence in Canadian prisons. In J. I. Ross (Ed.), *Violence in Canada: Sociopolitical perspectives,* Toronto, Ontario, Canada: Oxford University Press.

Welch, M. (1996a) Anniversary essay: The impact of David J. Rothman's *The discovery of the asylum* 25 years later. *Social Pathology,* 2(1), 32–41.

Welch, M. (1996b). Critical criminology, social justice, and an alternative view of incarceration. *Critical Criminology,* 7(2), 43–58.

Welch, M. (1996c). Race and social class in the examination of punishment. In M. Lynch & E. Patterson (Eds.), *Justice with prejudice: Race and criminal justice in America* (pp. 156–169). New York: Harrow & Heston.

Welch, M. (1996d). Prison violence in America: Past, present, and future. In R. Muraskin & A. R. Roberts (Eds.), *Visions for change: Crime and justice in the twenty-first century.* Englewood Cliffs, NJ: Prentice Hall.

Welch, M. (1996e). Prisonization. In M. D. McShane & F. P. Williams (Eds.), *Encyclopedia of American prisons* (pp. 357–363). New York: Garland.

Welch, M. (1996f). The immigration crisis: Detention as an emerging mechanism of social control. *Social Justice,* 23(3), 169–184.

Welch, M. (1997a). The war on drugs and its impact on corrections: Exploring alternative strategies to America's drug crisis. *Journal of Offender Rehabilitation, 25,* 43–60.

Welch, M. (1997b). Tougher prisons? *Critical Criminologist, 8(1),* 7–11.

Welch, M. (1997c). Regulating the reproduction and morality of women: The social control of body and soul. *Women & Criminal Justice,* 9(1), 17–38.

Welch, M. (1997d). A critical interpretation of correctional bootcamps as normalizing institutions: Discipline, punishment, and the military model. *Journal of Contemporary Criminal Justice, 13,* 184–205.

Welch, M. (1997e). Questioning the utility and fairness of INS detention: Criticisms of poor institutional conditions and protracted periods of confinement for undocumented immigrants. *Journal of Contemporary Criminal Justice, 13*(1), 41–54.

Welch, M. (1998a). Critical criminology, social control, and an alternative view of corrections. In J. Ross (Ed.), *Cutting the edge: Current perspectives in radical critical criminology and criminal justice* (pp. 107–121). Westport, CT: Praeger.

Welch, M. (1998b). Problems facing immigration and naturalization service (INS) centers: Policies, procedures, and allegations of human rights violations. In T. Alleman & R. L. Gido (Eds.), *Turnstile justice: Issues in American corrections.* Englewood Cliffs, NJ: Prentice Hall.

Welch, M. (1999a). *Punishment in America: Social control and the ironies of imprisonment.* Thousand Oaks, CA: Sage.

Welch, M. (1999b). The reproduction of institutional violence in American prisons. In R. Muraskin & A. R. Roberts (Eds.), *Visions for change: Crime and justice in the twenty-first century* (2nd ed.). Englewood Cliffs, NJ: Prentice Hall.

Welch, M. (2000a). *Flag burning: Moral panic and the criminalization of protest.* New York: de Gruyter.

Welch, M. (2000b). The correctional response to prisoners with HIV/AIDS: Morality, metaphors, and myths. *Social Pathology, 6*(2) 121–142.

Welch, M. (2000c). Adultery. In N. H. Rafter (Ed.), *Encyclopedia of women and crime*, p. 5. Phoenix, AZ: The Orix Press.

Welch, M. (2000d). The role of the Immigration and Naturalization Service in the prison industrial complex. *Social Justice, 27*(3), 73–88.

Welch, M. (2002a). *Detained: Immigration laws and the expanding INS. jail complex.* Philadelphia: Temple University Press.

Welch, M. (2002b). The reproduction of violence in U.S. prisons. In L. Fiftal & P. Cromwell (Eds.), *Correctional perspectives: Views from academics, practitioners, and prisoners* (pp. 137–146). Los Angeles: Roxbury.

Welch, M. (2002c). Assembly line justice. In D. Levinson (Ed.), *Encyclopedia of crime and punishment* (pp.77–80). Thousand Oaks, CA: Sage.

Welch, M. (2002d). Detention in INS jails: Bureaucracy, brutality, and a booming business. In R. L. Gido & T. Alleman (Eds.), *Turnstile justice: Issues in American corrections* (2nd ed.). Englewood Cliffs, NJ: Prentice Hall.

Welch, M. (2003a). Immigration and Naturalization detention centers. In M. Bosworth (Ed.), *Encyclopedia of prisons.* Thousand Oaks, CA: Sage.

Welch, M. (2003b). The trampling of human rights in the war on terror: Implications to the sociology of denial. *Critical Criminology 12*(2) (in press).

Welch, M. (2003c). Immigration and Naturalization detention centers. In M. Bosworth (Ed.), *Encyclopedia of prisons.* Thousand Oaks, CA: Sage.

Welch, M. (2003d). Ironies of social control and the criminalization of immigrants. *Crime, Law & Social Change, 39,* 319–387.

Welch, M. (2003e) Force and fraud: A radically coherent criticism of corrections as industry. *Contemporary Justice Review, 6*(3), 227–240.

Welch, M. (2003f). Chain gangs. In M. Bosworth (Ed.), *Encyclopedia of prisons.* Thousand Oaks, CA: Sage.

Welch, M. (2003g). Jack Abbott. In M. Bosworth (Ed.), *Encyclopedia of prisons.* Thousand Oaks, CA: Sage.

Welch, M. (2004a). *Corrections: A critical approach* (2nd ed.). New York: McGraw-Hill.

Welch, M. (2004b) Profiling and detention in the war on terror: Human rights predicaments for the criminal justice apparatus. In R. Muraskin & A. R. Roberts (Eds.), *Visions for change: Crime and justice in the twenty-first century* (3rd ed.). Englewood Cliffs, NJ: Prentice Hall.

Welch, M. (2005). Immigration lockdown before and after 9/11: Ethnic constructions and their consequences. In M. Bosworth & S. R. Bush-Baskette (Eds.), *Race, gender and punishment: Theorizing differences.* Boston: Northeastern University Press.

Welch, M., & Bryan, J. (2000). Moral campaigns, authoritarian aesthetics, and escalation: An examination of flag desecration in the post-*Eichman* era. *Journal of Crime and Justice, 23*(1), 25–45.

Welch, M, Bryan, N., & Wolff, R. (1999). Just war theory and drug control policy: Militarization, morality, and the war on drugs. *Contemporary Justice Review, 2*(1), 49–76.

Welch, M., Fenwick, M., & Roberts, M. (1997). Primary definitions of crime and moral panic: A content analysis of experts' quotes in feature newspaper articles of crime. *Journal of Research in Crime and Delinquency, 34,* 474–494.

Welch, M., Fenwick, M., & Roberts, M. (1998). State managers, intellectuals, and the media: A content analysis of ideology in experts' quotes in featured newspaper articles on crime. *Justice Quarterly, 15,* 101–123.

Welch, M., & Gunther, D. (1997a). Jail suicide under legal scrutiny: An analysis of litigation and its implications to policy. *Criminal Justice Policy Review, 8*(1), 75–97.

Welch, M., & Gunther, D. (1997b). Jail suicide and crisis intervention: Lessons from litigation. *Crisis Intervention and Time-Limited Treatment, 3*(3), 229–244.

Welch, M., Price, E., & Yankey, N. (2002). Moral panic over youth violence: *Wilding* and the manufacture of menace in the media. *Youth & Society, 34*(1) 3–30.

Welch, M., Price, E., & Yankey, N. (2004). Youth violence and race in the media: The emergence of *wilding* as an invention of the press. *Race, Gender & Class, 11*(2) (in press).

Welch, M., Sassi, J., & McDonough, A. (2002). Advances in critical cultural criminology: An analysis of reactions to avant-garde flag art. *Critical Criminology, 11*(1), 1–20.

Welch, M., & Schuster, L. (2003). *Globalizing the war on terror and its collateral damage: Comparing adverse effects on asylum seekers and refugees in the U.S. and Europe.* Paper presented at the European Society of Criminology Annual Congress, Helsinki, Finland.

Welch, M., & Turner, F. (2004). *Globalization in the sphere of penality: Tracking the expansion of private prisons in the United States and Europe.* Paper presented at the Prisons and Penal Policy: International Perspectives conference, City University, Islington, London.

Welch, M., Weber, L., & Edwards, W. (2000). All the news that's fit to print: A content analysis of the correctional debate in the *New York Times. The Prison Journal, 80*(3), 245–264.

Welch, M., Wolff, R., & Bryan, N. (1998). Decontextualizing the war on drugs: Content analysis of NIJ publications and their neglect of race and class. *Justice Quarterly, 15,* 601–624.

West, C., & Fenstermaker, S. (1995). Doing difference. *Gender and Society, 9,* 8–37.

Western, B., & Beckett, K. (1999). How unregulated is the US labor market? The penal system as a labor market institution. *American Journal of Sociology, 104*, 1030–1060.

Westervelt, S., & Humphrey, J. (2001). *Wrongly convicted: Perspectives on failed justice*. New Brunswick, NJ: Rutgers University Press.

White, G. (1999). Crime and the decline of manufacturing, 1970–1990. *Justice Quarterly, 16*(1), 81–98.

White man pleads guilty to killing a black man. (1998, May 31). *New York Times*, p. 22.

White, R., & F. Haines. (1996). *Crime and criminology: An introduction*. South Melbourne, Australia: Oxford University Press.

Whiting, B., & Kelly, C. (1991, September 28). Suspect: Monks resisted, slaughter began when 1 fought. *Arizona Republic*, p. A1.

Who wants new prisons? In New York, all of upstate. (1989, June 9). *New York Times*, pp. B1, B2.

Wicker, T. (1975). *A time to die*. New York: Quandrangle.

Wijngaart, G. (1990). The Dutch approach: Normalization of drug problems. *Journal of Drug Issues, 20*, 667–678.

Wilgoren, J. (2003). Illinois expected to free 4 inmates. *New York Times*, January 10: A1, A10.

Wilkins, L. T. (1965). *Social deviance*. Englewood Cliffs, NJ: Prentice Hall.

Wilkins, L. T. (1991). *Punishment, crime and market forces*. Brookfield, VT: Dartmouth.

Wilkins, L. T. (1994). Don't alter your mind—It's the world that's out of joint. *Social Justice, 21*(3), 148–153.

Williams, P. J. (2001, November 26). By any means necessary. *The Nation*, p. 11.

Wilson, W. J. (1997). *When Work Disappears*. Chicago: University of Chicago Press.

Wines, F. H. (1895). Punishment and reformation. New York: Crowell.

Winter, G. (2003, May 17). Study finds no sign that testing deters students' drug use. *New York Times*, pp. A1, A14.

Wisely, W. (2003). New Bedlam. In T. Herivel & P. Wright (Eds.), *Prison nation: The warehousing of America's poor* (pp. 168–173). New York: Routledge.

Wolff, C. (1989, October 6). Youth in Central Park rampage to aid prosecutors. *New York Times*, p. 3.

Wolff, R. P. (1998). *In defense of anarchism*. Berkeley: University of California Press.

Wonders, N. A. (1996). Determinate sentencing: A feminist and postmodern story. *Justice Quarterly, 13*(4), 611–648.

Wonders, N. (1999). Postmodern feminism, criminology, and social justice. In B. Arrigo (Ed.), *Social justice, criminal justice* (pp. 111–128). Belmont, CA: Wadsworth.

Wood, P. J. (2003). The rise of the prison industrial complex in the United States. In A. Coyle, A. Campbell, & R. Neufeld (Eds.), *Capitalist punishment: Prison privatization & human rights* (pp. 16–29). Atlanta: Clarity.

Wooldredge, J., Griffin, T., & Pratt, T. (2001). Considering hierarchical models for research on inmate behavior: Predicting misconduct with multilevel data. *Justice Quarterly, 18*(1), 203–232.

Wormer, K. van (2003). Prison privatization and women. In A. Coyle, A. Campbell, & R. Neufeld (Eds.), *Capitalist punishment: Prison privatization & human rights* (pp. 102–113). Atlanta: Clarity.

Wrongful jailing to cost Philadelphia $1 million. (1996, August 17). *New York Times*, p. 20.

Yardley, J. (2002a, November 7). Court stays execution of mentally ill Texan. *New York Times*, p. A24.

Yardley, J. (2002b, November 4). Amid doubts about competency, mentally ill man faces execution. *New York Times*, pp. A1, A18.

Yeager, M. (1979). Unemployment and imprisonment. *Journal of Criminal Law and Criminology, 70*, 586–588.

Yeoman, B. (2000, May/June). Steel town: Corrections Corporation of America is trying to turn Youngstown, Ohio, into the private-prison capital of the world. *Mother Jones*, pp. 39–45.

Young, J. (1982). The role of the police as amplifiers of deviancy, negotiators of reality and translators of fantasy. In S. Cohen (Ed.), *Images of deviance* (pp. 27–61). New York: Penguin.

Young, J. (1999). *The exclusive society*. London: Sage.

Young, J. (2003a). In praise of dangerous thoughts. *Punishment & Society, 5*(1), 97–108.

Young, J. (2003b). Merton with energy, Katz with structure: The sociology of vindictiveness and the criminology of transgression. *Theoretical Criminology, 7*(3), 389–414.

Young, R. (2003). Dying for profits. In T. Herivel & P. Wright (Eds.), *Prison nation: The warehousing of America's poor* (pp. 187–194). New York: Routledge.

Young, T. R. (1983). *Social justice vs. criminal justice: An agenda for critical criminology* (Transforming Sociology Series Special Packet 352). Longmont, CO: Red Feather Institute.

Youth violence raising concern. (1995, May 23). *New York Times*, p. A14.

Yunker, J. (1976). Is the death penalty a deterrent to homicide? Some time series evidence. *Journal of Behavioral Economics, 5*, 1–32.

Zaretsky, E. (1973a, January/April). Capitalism, the family and personal life: Part 1. *Socialist Revolution, 10*, 69–126.

Zaretsky, E. (1973b, May/June). Capitalism, the family and personal life: Part 2. *Socialist Revolution, 10*, 19–70.

Zeigler, F. A., & del Carmen, R.. 2001. Constitutional issues arising from 'Three strikes and you're out' legislation. In E. Latessa, A. Holsinger, J. Marquart, & J. Sorensen (Eds.), *Correctional contexts: Contemporary and classical readings* (pp. 253–266). Los Angeles: Roxbury.

Zielbauer, P. von (2003a, December 19). Detainees' abuse is detailed. *New York Times*, p. A32.

Zielbauer, P. von (2003b, September 28). Rethinking the key thrown away: As Ashcroft cracks down, states cut prison terms. *New York Times*, pp. 41–42.

Zimring, F., Eigen, J., & O'Malley, S. (1976). Punishing homicides in Philadelphia: Perspectives on the death penalty. *University of Chicago Law Review, 43*, 227–252.

Zimring, F., & Hawkins, G. (1973). *Deterrence: The legal threat in crime control.* Chicago: University of Chicago Press.

Zimring, F. E., & Hawkins, G. (1991a). *The scale of imprisonment.* Chicago: University of Chicago Press.

Zimring, F. E., & Hawkins, G. (1991b). What kind of drug war? *Social Justice, 18*(4), 104–121.

Zimring, F. E., Hawkins, G., & Kamin, S. (2001). *Punishment and democracy: Three strikes and you're out in California.* New York: Oxford University Press.

Index